Engaging
East Asian Integration

The **Institute of Developing Economies (IDE-JETRO)** is a Japanese government-related institution, founded in 1958 to conduct basic and comprehensive studies on economic, political, and social issues of developing countries and regions. The IDE-JETRO aims to make intellectual contributions to the world as a leading center of social-science research on Asia, the Middle East, Africa, Latin America, Oceania, and Eastern Europe. The Institute accumulates locally-grounded knowledge on these areas, clarify the conditions and issues they are facing, and disseminate a better understanding of these areas both domestically and abroad. These activities provide an intellectual foundation to facilitate cooperation between Japan and the international community for addressing development issues.

The **Institute of Southeast Asian Studies (ISEAS)** was established as an autonomous organization in 1968. It is a regional centre dedicated to the study of socio-political, security and economic trends and developments in Southeast Asia and its wider geostrategic and economic environment. The Institute's research programmes are the Regional Economic Studies (RES, including ASEAN and APEC), Regional Strategic and Political Studies (RSPS), and Regional Social and Cultural Studies (RSCS).

ISEAS Publishing, an established academic press, has issued more than 2,000 books and journals. It is the largest scholarly publisher of research about Southeast Asia from within the region. ISEAS Publishing works with many other academic and trade publishers and distributors to disseminate important research and analyses from and about Southeast Asia to the rest of the world.

Engaging
East Asian Integration

States, Markets and the Movement of People

EDITED BY

TAKASHI SHIRAISHI
JIRO OKAMOTO

IDE-JETRO
INSTITUTE OF DEVELOPING ECONOMIES
JAPAN EXTERNAL TRADE ORGANIZATION

LSEAS

INSTITUTE OF SOUTHEAST ASIAN STUDIES
Singapore

First published in Singapore in 2012
by ISEAS Publishing
Institute of Southeast Asian Studies
30 Heng Mui Keng Terrace, Pasir Panjang
Singapore 119614

E-mail: publish@iseas.edu.sg
Website: http://bookshop.iseas.edu.sg

The responsibility for facts and opinions in this publication rests exclusively with the authors and their interpretations do not necessarily reflect the views or the policy of IDE-JETRO, ISEAS or their supporters.

ISEAS Library Cataloguing-in-Publication Data

Engaging East Asian integration : states, markets and the movement of people / edited by Takashi Shiraishi and Jiro Okamoto.
  Based on papers originally presented to an International Symposium on Engaging East Asian Integration: States, Markets and the Movement of People, organized by the Institute of Developing Economies-Japan External Trade Organization, Tokyo, Japan, 9 December 2008.
  1.   East Asia—Economic integration—Congresses.
  2.   East Asia—Foreign economic relations—Japan—Congresses.
  3.   Japan—Foreign economic relations—East Asia—Congresses.
  4.   East Asia—Foreign economic relations—Australia—Congresses.
  5.   Australia—Foreign economic relations—East Asia—Congresses.
  6.   Human capital—East Asia—Congresses.
  I.   Shiraishi, Takashi, 1950-
  II.   Okamoto, Jiro, 1963-
  III.   Ajia Keizai Kenkyūjo (Japan)
  IV.   International Symposium on Engaging East Asian Integration: States, Markets and the Movement of People (2008 : Tokyo, Japan)
HF1583 E57   2012

ISBN 978-981-4380-28-7 (hard cover)
ISBN 978-981-4380-29-4 (e-book, PDF)

Typeset by International Typesetters Pte Ltd
Printed in Singapore by Photoplates Pte Ltd

Contents

Foreword

The symposium on which this book is based was held in the darkest days of the U.S.-originated global financial crisis. In the wake of the collapse of Lehman Brothers, demands were frozen and economies with high export dependency experienced radical contraction. No one knew how long this would last and what the consequences would be.

In a time of crisis we tend to speculate on known unknowns. We knew that the U.S. market would not be in a position to pull the East Asian economies along from the demand side. The triangular trade system of the United States, China, and the rest of Asia that had evolved after the 1997–98 Asian economic crisis would have to undergo radical transformations. With U.S. demand frozen, China's exports to the United States declined, which, in turn, led to the contraction of China's imports of intermediate and capital goods from the rest of Asia including Japan, South Korea, Taiwan, and ASEAN countries. This is the reason economists and business people called for turning regional demands into "domestic demands", in the hope that China would emerge as the market to pull the rest of Asia as well as the world out of this crisis.

Recalling the Great Depression of the 1930s, many of us were aware that hard times would breed nasty politics. Signs were there in the form of trade protectionism, currency manipulation, the maltreatment of illegal migrants, and the rise of political parties calling for policies to protect very narrowly defined "national interests".

And yet nothing as serious as the worst-case scenario came to pass. The United States and the European Union recovered economically, and while they are a lot weaker than we hoped, we can be far more optimistic about the future now than in December 2008.

Yet two things remain. First, the transformation of East Asian triangular trade still has a long way to go. Recent IDE-JETRO research shows that China has upgraded its intermediate and capital goods production while flooding the countries in its vicinities with inexpensive final products, a move that compels Japan, South Korea, and Taiwan to upgrade their industries while posing a threat to ASEAN economies. The Indonesian Government's call for review of the ASEAN-China FTA is a sign of this increasing tension. Although some economists argue that higher wages Chinese workers are now demanding will eventually translate into expansion of China's domestic demand and increasing imports from its neighbours, this confluence has not yet happened. China's expanding domestic demand is being met by China's expanding domestic supply, with little spillover to ASEAN countries.

Second and far more seriously, the United States, European Union, and Japan have accumulated huge debts, as highlighted by the debt crises in Portugal, Italy, Greece, and Spain. But, in fact, the more worrisome case is Japan, where debt is almost 200 per cent of the GDP and clearly unsustainable. The upper house election held in July 2010 demonstrated that the Japanese public did not want its government to raise the consumption tax. But the debt issue now looms large, and if the government is unable to do the job of tackling this issue, market forces will do so — more drastically and at a higher social and political cost. A time bomb is ticking, ever more loudly, and in the future we may look back at the present and say that the U.S.-led global financial crisis triggered the Japan-led crisis.

Whether this imminent Japanese debt crisis will radically change the political and economic landscape of East Asia is a question that only ensuing events can answer.

East Asia community building has emerged as a common agenda in the region because it promises a better arena for nurturing the politics of economic growth, which holds that the purpose of politics is to deliver economic growth, leading to the creation of employment, the rise of living standards, reduction of poverty, and the promise of a better future. Community building is also an instrument by which states in China's vicinities can productively and constructively engage China.

The transformation of the East Asian regional system has been marked at each turn by a series of momentous events. War and the collapse of the British, Japanese, and other colonial empires in the 1940s; American defeat in Indochina in the 1970s; the Plaza Accord in the 1980s; the Asian financial crisis in the late 1990s — each of these events provoked crises that led to regional transformation. To take an example, the Plaza Accord and resulting appreciation of the Japanese yen, and then the Korean won and Taiwan dollar, led to the transnational expansion of production networks and the *de facto* integration of East Asian economies. Just as the Asian financial crisis in the late 1990s marked the end of a Japan-led flying geese pattern of regional economic development, the recent American-led global financial crisis may perhaps mark the end of the U.S.-China-rest of East Asia (including Japan and Southeast Asia) triangular trade system.

And yet, despite the transformation of the regional trade system, the regional security system has remained basically unchanged since the ascendance of the United States as regional hegemon in the 1950s. This peculiar dynamic of an unchanged U.S.-led security order that excludes China, Vietnam, and other former socialist states, on the one hand, and a rapidly transforming and expanding trade system that has integrated not only the former "Free Asia" countries under the Cold War, but also the former socialist countries, and now India (to a degree that is unprecedented since the high noon of collective imperialism in the nineteenth century), on the other hand, creates a situation in which all the countries in the region are compelled to manage the tension between the security and trade systems through their own means and in light of their own imperatives, even as East Asian community building also constitutes a way of managing this tension.

Precisely because region making in East Asia was largely driven by markets, the changes now under way will not attain institutional form until some time after the fact. Therefore, we should not limit our attention to institutional forms of community building, such as ASEAN, ASEAN+1, ASEAN+3, ASEAN+6, ASEAN+8, ARF, and APEC, even though these are important arenas for regional cooperation and dialogue. Now, more than ever, we are faced with the need to make sense of known unknowns while preparing ourselves for the unknown unknowns. The essays in this book remain useful primers for confronting this double challenge.

Takashi Shiraishi
President, Institute of Developing Economies, JETRO

List of Figures and Tables

FIGURES

TABLES

Contributors

Manolo Abella, ILO-EU Asian Regional Programme on Governance of Labour Migration, Bangkok

Hamid Alavi, Senior Economist, East Asia Poverty Reduction, Economic Management, Financial and Private Sector Development Department, World Bank

Ralph Van Doorn, Economist, East Asia Poverty Reduction, Economic Management, Financial and Private Sector Development Department, World Bank

Geoffrey Ducanes, ILO-EU Asian Regional Programme on Governance of Labour Migration, Bangkok

Masahiko Hayashi, ILO Office in Japan

Peter J. Katzenstein, Walter S. Carpenter, Jr. Professor of International Studies, Cornell University

Vikrum Nehru, Director, East Asia Poverty Reduction, Economic Management, Financial and Private Sector Development Department, World Bank

Jiro Okamoto, Senior Research Fellow, Interdisciplinary Studies Center, Institute of Developing Economies, JETRO

Takashi Shiraishi, President, Institute of Developing Economies, JETRO

Isamu Wakamatsu, Senior Economist, Overseas Research Department and Senior Coordinator (ASEAN and South Asia), Planning Department, JETRO

*The position and affiliation of the contributors are at the time of the international symposium held in December 2008.

1

Introduction

Takashi Shiraishi
Jiro Okamoto

The Institute of Developing Economies-Japan External Trade Organization (IDE-JETRO) organized a symposium in December 2008 on the
theme, "Engaging East Asian Integration: States, Markets and the
Movement of People". It was held in the wake of the Lehman Brothers
collapse and in the midst of the deepening global financial crisis that
originated in the United States.

The crisis reminded us of other historic events that marked turning
points in the history of East Asian region making. One was the Plaza
Accord in 1985 which marked the beginning of the region's economic
development and regionalization. The yen appreciated enormously in
the wake of the Plaza Accord, forcing Japanese firms — above all,
electronics, machinery, and automotive firms — to move abroad and
deploy their production facilities regionally to remain competitive in
the world market. South Korean, Taiwanese, and Hong Kong as well
as Southeast Asian ethnic Chinese business also went transnational
and became regionalized. This expansion and deepening of business
networks and production chains led to *de facto* economic integration.

It was against this background of regionalization that people such as Mahathir Mohamad, then prime minister of Malaysia, and Takeshita Noboru, prime minister of Japan, started to talk about East Asia as we do now when referring to the region extending from Japan and South Korea through China, Taiwan, and Hong Kong to Southeast Asia. It was also in those years that China transformed itself from socialism to a socialist market economy while being integrated into the regional and global economy.

A crisis that marked another turning point in the history of East Asia was the Asian economic crisis in 1997–98. In the midst of this crisis, the first ASEAN plus 3 (Japan, China and South Korea) summit meeting was held in 1997. The summit meeting was institutionalized in 1998, which also saw the establishment of an East Asia Vision Group to map out the future of the region. A year later, in 1999, the Chiang Mai Initiative laid the foundation for currency cooperation at the bilateral level among states in the ASEAN plus 3. Through these steps, there emerged a regional political project of building an East Asia community in the wake of the 1997–98 Asian economic crisis, in part to create a mechanism for regional cooperation, especially in currency, as a hedge against the kind of U.S. intervention that Indonesia, Malaysia, South Korea, and Thailand had experienced, and, in part, to promote trade and investment in the region in view of stalling WTO negotiations and the transformation of regional triangular trade. China's emergence as an economic powerhouse was also crucial in changing the pattern of triangular trade that had hitherto anchored the regional system. In the wake of the Asian economic crisis, Japanese, South Korean, Taiwanese, and other firms reorganized their production systems. Producing capital and intermediate goods in their home countries and their production bases in Southeast Asia, they assembled final products in China for export to the United States and other markets. As a result the triangular trade system, which had consisted of Japan, Asia (minus Japan), and the United States, came to be reorganized with China, Asia (minus China) and the United States as its three mainstays. This change led to the expansion of Chinese exports to the United States and the European Union, while the intraregional trade in capital and intermediate goods expanded between China and the rest of Asia. Following the 1997–98 crisis, East Asia also saw the flourishing of regional institutions. ASEAN has been at the centre of this development, providing venues for ASEAN plus 3 and the East Asia Summit (ASEAN plus 6) processes. ASEAN members ratified the ASEAN Charter in 2008. The IDE-JETRO has also played its part by contributing to the establishment of the Economic Research Institute for ASEAN and East Asia (ERIA).

The current global financial crisis will no doubt mark yet another turning point in the making of East Asia. And this is the reason the symposium was organized with Professor Peter J. Katzenstein — the leading scholar of regionalism — as the keynote speaker.

Let us look at some long-term forecasts about the region in order to gauge the scale of changes in store. According to the long-term economic outlook released by the Japan Center for Economic Research in 2007, the size of the Chinese economy surpassed that of Japan in 1994, based on year 2000 purchasing power parity. It forecasted that the Chinese economy would grow to four times larger than the Japanese economy by 2020, and five times larger by 2030. The Indian economy would be more than twice the size of Japan's by 2030 and, in the same year, the ASEAN economies combined would be larger than Japan's. People can debate the accuracy of these forecasts, but there can be no question that the global and regional distribution of wealth and hence national power will change enormously over the coming twenty years. Japan will not be in the same league as the United States, China, the European Union, and India.

Major demographic changes are also taking place in East Asia. By the year 2030 more than 60 per cent of the population in East Asia (minus Japan) will be living in urban areas; by country, the percentage of urban population will be: South Korea 87 per cent, the Philippines 78 per cent, Indonesia 62 per cent, China 61 per cent, and Thailand 46 per cent. Yet most of these countries will not be able to create a strongly middle-class society. While more than two thirds of the population of the region will be living in urban centres in twenty years' time, the social divide between urban middle class and urban poor, as well as between urban middle class and rural poor, will remain a major political issue, which probably means that the politics of economic growth will remain an imperative in the region in the years to come.

Recent developments in East Asia need to be placed against the above long-term trends. The rise of China, the U.S.-originated global financial crisis, and the changing pattern in regional cooperation do not necessarily signal the end of U.S. hegemony and the making of a Sino-centric regional order. The region of East Asia finds itself between two superpowers. The global financial crisis has accelerated China's rise, military modernization, and influence in regional affairs. China's economic rise beckons states and firms in the region. But China's neighbours have also come to be increasingly concerned about its assertiveness in the South China and East China Seas in recent years. The United States, finally ending its imperial overextension in the Middle East and Central Asia, has also become more actively re-engaged in East Asia. In his November 2009 speech in Tokyo, President Barack Obama reconfirmed U.S. engagement in East Asia as a Pacific nation. Since then the United States has responded by beefing up its military presence and making the Trans-Pacific Partnership (TPP) — in which Japan will soon participate in negotiations — its major trade initiative as an approach to the Free Trade Area of the Asia Pacific (FTAAP).

The global financial crisis has also provided an opportunity for states (and firms) in East Asia to assess the direction of the regional trade system. When the crisis hit in 2008, the argument arose that East Asia was at a crossroads and would have to shift its model of economic growth from that of export-oriented economic development to one of domestic demand-led growth. The U.S. market would remain depressed for quite some time and could not be expected to serve as the engine for East Asian economic growth on the demand side. The Chinese Government pumped in a huge amount of money to stimulate domestic demand following the collapse of Lehman Brothers in 2008. The Chinese economy overcame the crisis in less than a year and was back on the path of growth. But it is now clear that China's domestic demand has not translated into expanding exports from the rest of Asia. China's market for final goods from the rest of Asia remains as small as South Korea's. Its industrial upgrading has led to expansion in the domestic production of intermediate goods at the expense of imports from its neighbours, especially ASEAN countries. This means another transformation for the pattern of triangular trade that had developed in the wake of the 1997–98 crisis, one where China may become more self-sufficient while the Unite States remains the important market that it has been.

ASEAN has been insisting on having a central role in regional cooperation and region making, whether through ASEAN plus 3, or the East Asia Summit processes. An interesting development in 2010 was that ASEAN decided to expand the East Asia Summit to include the United States and Russia, in addition to the previous ASEAN plus 6. ASEAN has also sought to develop a regional security architecture, such as the ASEAN Regional Forum and more recently the ASEAN Defence Ministers' Meeting-Plus (ADMM-Plus) process, which puts ASEAN in a position to set the agenda and to make decisions. Key Southeast Asian states have reacted by adopting self-help measures to strengthen their defence capabilities, while aligning themselves with the United States and its allies to pursue hedging strategies as a response to the geopolitical transformation now unfolding in the Asia Pacific. Japan has also reaffirmed its alliance with the United States after Prime Minister Yukio Hatoyama briefly flirted with the idea of an East Asian Community as a way to make the triangular relations among Japan, China, and the United States "equilateral". This is clear from Prime Minister Naoto Kan's January 2011 foreign policy speech in Tokyo in which he reaffirmed the Japan-U.S. alliance as the cornerstone of Japanese foreign policy without even referring to Hatoyama's East Asian Community initiative.

All of these developments have led to a recent shift in the framework for regional cooperation from East Asia back to the Asia Pacific. In 1997 the ASEAN plus 3 started to promote regional cooperation in response to the currency crisis and heavy-handed U.S. intervention, the group seeing itself evolving as a major mechanism for regional cooperation while keeping the United States out. Now, however, China's assertiveness has caused concern for many states in the region — especially those that have territorial disputes with China — leading them to strengthen their relations with the United States and its allies while expanding the framework for regional cooperation back to the Asia Pacific, which includes the United States.

Things may change if China redefines its position on territorial sovereignty issues. Although this is not the place to examine why China puts such importance on territorial sovereignty, one wonders whether tranquillity in the South China and East China Seas is more important to its long-term national interest than its sovereignty over the maritime sphere. For now, however, tension has mounted between the regional security system, on the one hand, and the regional trade system, on the other, as China becomes more assertive on territorial issues. More worrying is the fact that it briefly employed trade (the export of rare earth) as a foreign policy instrument to impose its will on Japan in a territorial sovereignty issue. As tension mounts, U.S. allies as well as some others have affirmed their relations with the United States while also engaging China multilaterally and seizing opportunities offered by China for economic gains. Meanwhile China is promoting economic and trade cooperation in order to break what it calls "containment". This underlines the fact that China's rise is mainly economic. The states in its vicinity certainly want to gain from its economic rise, but as soon as they feel threatened by China, they align themselves with the United States and its allies. The regional framework for cooperation is flexible enough to swing back and forth between East Asia, where the United States is excluded, and the Asia Pacific, where it is included. Ultimately, East Asian regionalism has been shaped by a history of small and middle powers having to negotiate between at least two great powers. The benefits of the regional system in East Asia/Asia Pacific give it much staying power despite its inherent structural tensions.

*****

This book is a compilation of the papers presented at the aforementioned symposium and the proceedings of the panel discussion.

In Chapter 2 Peter J. Katzenstein analyses current world politics from the perspective of U.S.-centred regionalism (American imperium). He argues that the American imperium has been having a significant effect on regions by not only acting to shape the world, but also by reshaping America itself. He analyses the effects that U.S. policy initiatives, such as the "Nixon Doctrine" and regional economic integration efforts in North America, have had on the world of regions and explains how the impacts have emerged in different regions. He also argues that globalization and internationalization have made contemporary regionalism considerably "porous" and no region making process can be built solely on any one national model. Therefore, the rapid rise of China does not imply that the regional integration process in East Asia is the "Sinicization" of the region; it will not become a "Sino-centric" region.

Chapter 3 deals with the economic aspect of East Asian regional integration. Focusing on regional trade and investment, Hamid Alavi, Ralph Van Doorn, and Vikram Nehru first review the development of economic integration in East Asia and point out that Japan and China have been playing a major role in making the regional economies dynamic and increasingly integrated. The chapter goes on to examine the remaining agenda for regional integration. It shows that integration efforts in the areas of trade facilitation (logistics in particular), services trade, and finance are important, but still limited. If the region is to take full advantage of economic integration, the authors argue, cooperation in these areas urgently needs to be advanced. The chapter concludes with an emphasis on the need for coordinated risk management policies in the region to cope with crises, rather than slowing down the pace of economic integration or going back to old protectionism.

In Chapter 4 Isamu Wakamatsu focuses on the development of FTA networks in East Asia over the past decade and discusses Japan's strategy. First, he reviews the development of East Asian economies into the "world's growth center". Second, he focuses on regional FTA networks. He points out that the establishment of FTA networks centred on ASEAN, such as ASEAN plus 1 FTAs (with China, South Korea, India, and Japan) and bilateral FTAs of individual ASEAN members, has had the effect of increasing intra-regional trade further in East Asia. The networks, however, still need to promote trade facilitation measures such as the harmonization of customs clearance procedures, convergence of rules of origin, and logistics cooperation. Liberalization in investment and migration is also required for further regional economic integration. Third, he argues that for Japan, with its ageing society and declining birthrate, to maintain its standard of living, the county must remain outward looking and utilize resources in East Asia. Japan should work towards realizing an East Asian FTA, help develop an Asian Bond market, and support infrastructure development in the region, so that the East Asian economies as a whole can play a role in stimulating the global economy through greater regional demand.

Chapter 5 focuses on the involvement of the states in regional cooperation and integration in East Asia, and explains characteristics of the East Asian integration processes. Jiro Okamoto reviews the development of East Asian integration processes, arguing that they have a "flexible", "inclusive", and "multi-layered" nature. These characteristics have emerged because individual East Asian states are seeking practical benefits from regional integration efforts. The states have not limited themselves to East Asia to realize these benefits, and they are sensitive to the dominant influence of a power in the region. Okamoto then points out that the characteristics of East Asian integration can be explained in sharp relief through the success and failure of Australia's Asian engagement policy over the last twenty years. The chapter concludes with a discussion of some implications for the future: the characteristics of East Asian regional cooperation/integration are likely to remain unchanged; thus the convergence of the policy goals of individual states to create a community in the region will not happen for some time at least.

In Chapter 6 Manolo Abella and Geoffrey Ducanes discuss the cross-border movement of professional workers (skilled human resources) within East Asia in the era of regional integration. They pose a number of critical questions regarding the topic: Is there a redirection of flows of professional migration towards destinations in East Asia? Are immigration policies likely to induce significant redirection of flows? They answer these questions by analysing data from the past decade. First, they conclude that skilled human resources in East Asia still largely go outside the region, particularly to North America. Japan (and South Korea) still has not introduced large numbers of foreign professionals into its labour markets. Second, they argue that the immigration policies of Japan and South Korea, the two developed economies in the region with rapidly declining workforces, are less competitive in winning skilled migrants than those of countries in North America and Western Europe. They predict that in the near future pressures will mount in the East Asian countries to improve access for professionals, as these people are vital for replacing their ageing workforce and for their remaining competitive in the global economy.

Chapter 7 is a transcript of the panel discussion by the speakers that followed their presentations at the symposium. Because of the diverse topics of the presentations, the panel concentrated on discussing several questions that came up during the presentations, rather than trying to summarize all the presentations or draw definitive conclusions from them. Questions raised and discussed include: How does the global financial crisis affect the American imperium? Can ASEAN remain at the centre of regional integration processes? How effective can regional integration institutions in East Asia be in dealing with the global financial crisis?

PART I

Evolution of
East Asian Integration

2

Japan and East Asia in the American Imperium[1]

Peter J. Katzenstein

The United States plays the central role in a world of regions. Gone are the clearly demarcated, rival blocs of East and West. Since the end of the Cold War, the collapse of socialism has made anachronistic the distinction between a First and a Second World. And even before the disintegration of the Soviet Union, the Third World had ceased to exist as a cohesive force in world politics. The distinction between an industrialized North and a non-industrialized South became outdated with the rapid industrialization of numerous poor countries, while the gap in income and wealth within and between North and South has widened. The American imperium is now the hub in a wheel with many regional spokes. In short, world politics has undergone a huge shift from bloc bipolarity to an American-centred regionalism.

In this chapter, I wish to develop three interrelated arguments. First, through actions that mix its territorial and non-territorial powers, the American imperium has been having a profound effect on regions.

The American imperium is not only an actor that shapes the world, but it is also a system that reshapes America. Although regions are conceptualized, alternatively, in materialist, ideational, and behavioural terms, my understanding of the term draws on all three traditions in an eclectic manner, trading in a false sense of precision for an encompassing sense of family resemblance between different instances of this thing we call region. Each of the world's major regions has at its core either supporter states, such as Japan or Germany, or regional pivots, such as France and Britain, China and Indonesia, Nigeria and South Africa, or Brazil and Argentina. I call Japan and Germany supporter states because they were the only major powers that challenged the Anglo-American world order through war in the twentieth century, suffered total defeat, and only then came to support the global order. Pivot states do not share this historical experience, but instead a structural affinity in terms of the distribution of material capabilities in different world regions.

A second argument points to regional policy initiatives and regional institutional orders. During the last half century, two U.S. policy initiatives in particular have made regions an important aspect of world politics. In the late 1960s and early 1970s President Nixon set about implementing the "Nixon doctrine", which took account of the relative decline of American power, illustrated by the losing American effort in the Vietnam War. The Nixon doctrine sought to shift the military burden of fighting communist aggression to American allies who were at risk, and more generally, it looked to supporters or pivots, such as Germany or Iran, to help maintain regional stability. Beyond Vietnamization of the war effort, in East Asia the Nixon doctrine was central for the opening to China, for a redeployment of American troops from the Korean peninsula, and for attempts, successful only in the 1980s, for Japan to assume a bigger defence role. Spurred by Japan's economic rise, starting in the late 1980s, a second policy initiative of the U.S. Government aimed at strengthening regional trade integration in North America and throughout the world. The eventual result was a set of "minilateralisms" which have come to compersate to some extent stalled attempts at multilateral efforts to reduce trade barriers. Finally, different world regions reflect not just policy initiatives, but distinct regional orders. In the case of East Asia, and in contrast to Western Europe, after 1945, bilateralism rather than multilateralism was constitutive of the region's future evolution. Furthermore, ethnic capitalism in Japanese and Chinese trading networks operating in highly competitive markets made Asian regionalism very different from the partial pooling of sovereignty through law and politics that has defined Europe during the last half century.

Third, the process of region making extends well beyond the relevance of any one national model of institutionalized practices. Globalization and internationalization are important for making contemporary regionalism porous and open to developments in the larger world. But in a regional setting, processes and practices take a specific form and content, discussed here under the headings of Japanization, Sinicization, and Americanization. These processes tend to be open-ended and two way streets in which Japan, China, and the United States project their practices into the larger region and, in turn, are affected — at times deeply — by the effects the region has on them. Illustrations drawn from technology and production networks, as well as internal and external security, illustrate the distinctiveness of these processes in East Asia compared with those in Western Europe.

I end with a brief reflection of the implications of this chapter's arguments for our understanding of the rise of China. Rather than stressing sharp changes — rupture of the American imperium and a world of regions or return to a refurbished Sinocentric world — this chapter's argument points to recalibration of power and purpose in a world which will continue to be marked by the interaction between imperium and region.

I. AMERICAN IMPERIUM AND A REGIONAL WORLD

Imperium is a concept I use for analytical rather than historical reasons. Its meaning has shifted historically. This is how I use the concept here: the conjoining of power that has both territorial and non-territorial dimensions. Regions have both material and symbolic dimensions, and we can trace them in patterns of behavioural interdependence and political practice. Regions reflect the power and purpose of states. They are made porous by the cumulative impact of globalization and internationalization.

American Imperium

In its decisive victories over fascism in World War II and over communism in the Cold War, the United States has demonstrated the entwining of its political, military, economic, and ideological powers, the foundations of its pre-eminence in world politics. The source of American strength is reflected in the character of the American imperium, which combines two different types of power. Territorial power was at the centre of the old land and maritime empires that collapsed at the end of the three great wars of the twentieth century. The far-flung network of U.S. bases that encircled the Soviet Union during the Cold War, and that has spread greatly after the attacks of September 11, points to the territorial dimension of the American imperium. According to statistics released by the Department of Defense, in September 2001 the United States deployed a quarter of a million military personnel in 153 countries. Adding civilian employees and dependents doubles that figure to more than half a million. The United States had significant military bases in thirty-eight countries.[2] The non-territorial dimension of American power is analysed by Michael Hardt and Antonio Negri, who argue that "Empire is not a weak echo of modern imperialism but a fundamentally new form of rule".[3] In this view, there exist political logics in world politics that operate at levels other than that of the traditional nation state. Non-territorial politics is characterized by a fluid instability that manifests itself in hybrid identities, flexible hierarchies, multiple exchanges, and the production of new forms of authority and coercion across boundaries. Territorial "empire" and non-territorial "Empire" are analytical opposites or ideal-types.

In different political contexts, "imperium" designates both formal and informal systems of rule, and a mixture of hierarchical and egalitarian political relations. The American imperium is creating a world politics that is both enabling and constraining. The relative importance of its territorial and non-territorial power has waxed and waned, shaped by domestic political struggles between conflicting coalitions. Victory and defeat in these domestic struggles have affected the reactions of American foreign policy to porous regions in world politics.

Regional World

Broadly speaking there exist three different approaches: materialist, classical theories of geopolitics; ideational, critical theories of geography; and behavioural theories. I believe that materialist and ideational theories contain important, partial insights that I merge in a perspective of regional orders, defined by their distinctive institutional forms, which both alter and are altered by behaviour or political practice.

In different national and political contexts, all of the *materialist theorists* of geopolitics believed that interstate war over territory was inevitable. Some made a fundamental distinction between the strategic imperatives governing land and sea power. For Alfred Thayer Mahan, for example, naval power was the key to America's future rise to the status of a great power. Space was intimately tied to strategy and the dynamics of power competition.

Other theorists of geopolitics focused exclusively on territoriality. Before World War II, Karl Haushofer saw three rising powers — the United States, Germany, and Japan — challenging British world hegemony. Each was emerging as the dominant power in its sphere of influence, the United States in Latin America, Germany in Europe and, by extension, Africa and the Middle East; and Japan in the western Pacific. For Haushofer these emerging "pan-regions" were becoming the essential building blocs of world politics. In his novel *1984*, George Orwell gave a chilling description of this world of regional blocs, marked by total mobilization and perpetual war between Oceania, Eurasia, and Eastasia.

Events turned out differently. In line with the analysis of American geostrategists, bipolarity prevailed over tripolarity. Western Europe and East Asia, the rimlands of Eurasia, were strategic regions of overwhelming importance for the United States, as George Kennan famously argued in 1947.[4] Classical geopolitical analysis was revived — with a twist. In the implementation of America's new Cold War strategy, the meaning of the term, *containment*, was no longer restricted to geography. Instead it became a label for protecting the religious and civilizational values of an entire way of life.

The central point of *ideational theories of geography* is simple: regions are politically made. Regional designations are collective symbols chosen by groups to dominate specific places in the natural world. Space is

not given by nature. It is a social construct that people invent for
political purposes. This is well illustrated by the different understandings
of bodies of water. Philip Steinberg depicts "a non-territorial 'Indian
Ocean' construction in which the sea is understood as an asocial space
between societies; a highly territorial 'Micronesian' construction in
which the sea is perceived and managed as an extension of land-
space; and a complex 'Mediterranean' construction in which the sea
is defined as non-possessible but nonetheless a legitimate arena for
expressing and contesting social power".[5] What is true for water is
also true for land. Conflicts over sacred spaces illustrate a global
phenomenon. Land is not natural and undifferentiated; it means
different things to different people. The more central and exclusive
holy places are to different communities, the greater the challenge for
a peaceful resolution of territorial conflicts. Thus the sacredness of
place and the distances between land masses may differentiate land
from sea into fundamentally different spheres for human cooperation
and conflict.

The third perspective that concerns us are *behavioural theories of
geography.* They focus on how regions are shaped and reshaped by practice.
Regions are material and ideational structures that have behavioural
effects. Space and imagination have behavioural properties. Consider
the maritime-territorial distinction. In the analysis of domestic politics,
scholars have applied the same basic insight into the importance of
water in subtle analyses of developments within rather than between
states. Once merchants began to exploit the economic opportunities of
sea transport, the inhabitants of seaports and riverine ports cultivated
outward-looking, commercial, river-basins along the littorals. These
differed starkly from inward-looking, mercantilist, and landlocked
regions. This argument has been profitably applied to China, France,
and England. Numerous findings show that geography has direct and
indirect behavioural consequences. Geographical distance, for example,
shapes the intensity of economic exchanges and the likelihood of war.
In statistical studies, economists have demonstrated the importance of
geographical distance for the intensity of international trade flows. A
distance of 2,500 miles reduces trade by 82 per cent, equity flows by
69 per cent, and FDI by 44 per cent; the corresponding figures for
4,000 miles are 97, 83 and 58 per cent.[6]

In sum, materialist, ideational, and behavioural theories of geography all contain helpful partial insights. I integrate them here in a perspective that stresses the importance of the distinctive institutional forms of different regional orders, which both shape and are reshaped by political practice. Regions have material and symbolic aspects, and create among different groups of countries marked behavioural interdependencies over a wide range of different issues. I argue in this chapter that regions are made porous by a variety of processes, vary greatly in their institutional form, and differ in having (or not having) core states that support U.S. power and purpose.

Region States

Japan in Asia and Germany in Europe offer prime vantage points for exploring how regions operate in the American imperium. In the interest of containing the Soviet Union and preventing future wars through liberalizing the world economy, U.S. post-war policy anchored Japan and Germany securely in the American imperium. Other world regions mattered less. In both South Asia and Africa, for example, the United States failed to establish close partnerships with key regional states. In South Asia, containment of Soviet influence in Afghanistan drove U.S. policy to engage Pakistan, especially in the 1980s. The inevitable result was poor relations with India. In Africa, no core state emerged as a possible regional leader. Apartheid prevented South Africa from translating its economic and military strength into regional leadership. Nigeria remained hobbled by civil war, military rule, and economic failure.

In sharp contrast, Germany's and Japan's unconditional surrender and occupation by the United States created two client states that eventually rose to become core regional powers. Although it is of vital interest to the United States, the Middle East resembles South Asia and Africa in lacking regional core states that are both consistent supporters of the United States and central to regional politics. In the Middle East, Saudi oil and Israeli security have engaged vital U.S. interests. But the overwhelming importance of territory, claimed by three monotheistic religions, has voided the non-territorial dimensions of American power. The political values of the Saudi regime are antithetical to America's, and Israel's central position in American domestic politics has stopped the United States, in the eyes of Arab states, from curtailing Israeli power. This is in sharp contrast to the political restraints that NATO, the U.S.-Japan security treaty, and international economic institutions imposed on Germany and Japan, thereby reassuring their nervous neighbours.

The United States has had vital interests in the Americas for much longer than in the Middle East. Yet here too no viable regional intermediary state or group of states has emerged. In its own backyard American power and influence have been too direct and too strong. Although the United States has had strong strategic interests in four areas — the Americas and the Middle East, South Asia and Africa — none has developed stable regional intermediaries. Even though no one region defines the norm against which we can measure the performance of other regions, the role of Japan and Germany in supporting the imperium and the porousness of East Asia and Western Europe are clearly very distinctive.

II. REGIONAL POLICY INTIATIVES AND REGIONAL INSTITUTIONAL ORDERS

The role of regions in the American imperium is supported by U.S. initiatives and by the policies and practices of regional state and non-state actors.

Regional Policy Initiatives

The U.S. Government has taken two major policy initiatives in the last generation that have had the clear and intended effect of strengthening regional forces in world politics. First articulated by President Nixon in 1969, the Nixon doctrine stated that the United States would keep all its treaty obligations, provide nuclear guarantees to allies whose survival was deemed vital to American security, and, in other kinds of aggression, would furnish economic and military assistance, if requested, but not manpower. The adoption of the doctrine was necessitated by the draw-down of U.S. commitment in Vietnam and the Vietnamization programme. The Nixon doctrine was also central in the opening towards China and in the withdrawal of the Seventh Infantry Division from South Korea, coupled with a new security assistance programme to modernize South Korea's military. After successful negotiations over the return of Okinawa to Japan, American policy remained largely unsuccessful — until the 1980s — in affecting a shift in Japanese policy to accommodate the Nixon doctrine.

A second policy initiative of the United States has stemmed from the increasing economic rivalry with Japan and the growing erosion of the threat posed by the Soviet Union. Since the mid-1980s, capitalist rivalry and socialist bankruptcy have reinvigorated regional politics. A change in U.S. policy has directly strengthened regions as important arenas for world politics. Seeking to shore up its international position, under both Republican and Democratic administrations, the United States developed regional initiatives to complement its traditional preference for worldwide liberalization. This new policy move encouraged the formation of economic regions that remained open to the world economy, with the United States joining several of them. Levelling the playing field in the name of "fair trade," the U.S. Government sought to protect both its vulnerable and strategic industries, such as textiles and microelectronics, and to open up European and Asian markets through concerted political pressure and the creation of the North American Free Trade Agreement (NAFTA). At the turn of the century the United States remained committed to both the WTO's Doha round of trade negotiations and the U.S.-led plan to create a Free Trade Area of the Americas (FTAA).

In a world of increasingly permeable borders, large numbers of regional organizations are dealing with both economic and security affairs. The 1990s saw an explosion of regional initiatives, including the adoption of NAFTA; the creation of the European Economic Area (EEA) which liberalized trade between the European Union (EU) and the European Free Trade Association (EFTA); the Miami Declaration of a Free Trade Area for the Americas; and the Declaration of Bogor of the Asia Pacific Economic Cooperation (APEC). The thirty-three regional trade agreements signed between 1990 and 1994 constitute the largest number for any five-year period since the end of World War II.[7] A decade later, regional trade agreements continue to spread. In 2004 the United States signed an agreement with the states of Central America and Australia; seven South Asian states signed a free trade agreement; the South American customs union, Mercosur, was closing in on a free trade agreement with the EU while half-heartedly continuing negotiations with the United States over a free trade agreement for all of the Americas.

Regional trade arrangements have spread quickly since the 1980s. Between 1948 and 1994, GATT received 124 notifications of the creation of such arrangements, and between 1995 and 2000 the WTO received an additional ninety, covering trade in goods and services. Of 214 agreements signed, 134 were in force in the year 2000, about a threefold increase during the 1990s.[8] In the early 1990s, about ninety per cent of all GATT signatories were reported to be participating in regional trading arrangements.[9] Debates about the character of these arrangements encompass both Lester Thurow's analysis of a tripolar regional world, and Jagdish Bhagwati's defence of a worldwide free trade regime.[10] Between these two positions, most analysts steer a middle course, arguing that regional trading arrangements tend to be open, not closed, and that regionalization can be a source of both conflict and cooperation.

For decades regionalism and regionalization have been hitched to the wagon of multilateral negotiations on a global scale. As a result, between two thirds and four fifths of total world trade and investment flows occur both within and between the economies of North America, Europe, and East Asia. In recent years, bilateral deals between states located in these three major regions and those in other, less important areas, have begun to create systems of "minilateralisms" to complement existing multilateral ones. The launching of the multilateral Doha world trade round has initiated a rush to create new regional free trade agreements (FTAs) liberalizing trade, investment, and government regulations.

Corporations grow most in the regions closest to their national home market. Microeconomic factors thus push corporations to organize their activities along regional lines. Throughout the Third World, export processing zones have become favored sites for economic development. Two such zones existed before the mid-1960s, and there were twenty in ten countries in 1970; by 1986 those numbers had increased, to 175 and more than fifty respectively; in 2002 there existed about 3,000 such zones. Thirty of the thirty-seven million workers employed in these zones are Chinese.[11] Operating across national borders, large corporations create specific forms of dependence with suppliers, subcontractors, and customers. The tendency of foreign investment and operations to take place in adjacent regions, and the appearance of regional production complexes in Europe and Asia, illustrate how new spatial constellations, both within and above the nation state, create regions that are open.

Regional Institutional Orders

Actions that the United States took in the late 1940s were crucial in bringing about the regional institutional orders that have characterized Asia and Europe during the last half-century. Markets and law were the two key institutions through which Asian and European regions organized. In Asia regionalism has been shaped by the powerful impact of ethnic capitalism in markets that are typically organized through networks. In Europe, law and judicial institutions are embedded in a variety of political institutions that link countries together in a European polity. The comparison of Europe and Asia highlights two important facts. European networks are embedded in a legal context that profoundly shapes their operations; Asian states seek to ride markets that are evolving in broader networks. The fact that similar institutions, in part emanating from U.S. influence, can be found in both regions takes nothing away from the more important argument that I develop here: the distinctive institutions that shape Europe and Asia differ greatly.

In the first decade after the end of World War II the United States had succeeded in creating in Europe and Asia a strong anti-communist, cross-regional coalition to balance against the Soviet Union and China. In an open international system, the United States enjoyed a preponderance of power in relations with its European and Asian allies. Germany in Europe, and Japan in Asia, were the two most important staging areas for the Cold War. And porous regionalism made Europe and Asia the sites where the American imperium reached its fullest maturation.

Seen as a potential cause of World War III, Germany was at the core of the Cold War. In 1945 neither Soviet nor U.S. decision makers recognized the existence of a clear bipolar system. Instead, they saw a variety of possible configurations of power. Europe figured prominently in their calculations, with the possibility that it might emerge as a third power containing a revived Germany and thus decisively affecting the geostrategic balance. Competition between the two superpowers occurred in a system that was latently tripolar. In this situation, the United States did not follow a unilateral, isolationist strategy, devoting all its resources to strengthening its own military power. Instead, it pursued in Europe a multilateral strategy that invested heavily in allies.

In Asia, at about the same time, the U.S. Government built an anti-communist alliance under very different regional circumstances. Rebuilding and stabilizing Southeast Asia, the Truman Administration hoped, would both contain China and restore Japan. Like Germany in Europe, Japan was the linchpin of an anti-communist coalition. The victory of the Chinese Communists in 1949 consolidated the U.S. commitment to Japan. For Japan to prosper required U.S. involvement in Southeast Asia, an area historically of no more than marginal U.S. interest. Southeast Asia was important for two additional reasons. It was in the grip of a revolution in which nationalism and communist insurgency were closely intertwined. And Southeast Asia offered some hope, especially in the case of British Malaya, for reducing Britain's stifling dollar debt through a triangular trade involving the United States, Britain, and Malaya that would discriminate against U.S. producers.

Although the combustible mixture of nationalism and communism varied from country to country, by late 1949 U.S. policymakers had articulated a rudimentary domino theory for East and Southeast Asia that suggested the establishment of a series of bilateral defence arrangements. The loss of China and fear of a French defeat in Indochina made it imperative to stem what U.S. officials increasingly viewed as successful Soviet expansion on a worldwide scale. Communist subversion in Southeast Asia and Japan was a particularly nefarious and threatening prospect that required a vigorous response. Between the middle of 1949 and the spring of 1950, several events occurred that galvanized the United States to action. The Soviet Union exploded its first nuclear bomb, ending the U.S. nuclear monopoly. In China, the U.S.-supported Kuomintang regime collapsed, and the Communists seized power, raising the spectre of increased insurgency throughout Southeast Asia. And the economic recoveries in Europe and Japan were stalling. In the face of these developments, the United States chose to take a stand. When North Korean troops attacked South Korea on 25 June 1950, the Truman Administration responded quickly and forcefully, in line with the anti-communist policy that it had adopted over the previous years. American ground troops were sent into battle, and previously limited aid programmes for the region were ramped up quickly. The economic stimulus of the Korean War would be decisive for the economic revitalization of Japan and Asia.

The anti-communist alliance that the United States assembled in the late 1940s and early 1950s took different institutional forms in Europe and in Asia. Economic openness, political pluralism, and a broad range of legal institutions defined the imperium into which the United States attempted to bind others, while committing itself with considerable caution. Yet the wide range of views entertained in Washington makes it clear that the architects of America's evolving imperium, in the words of John Ikenberry, "were trying to build more than one type of order".[12]

Different policy objectives, geopolitical realities, and material capabilities made U.S. policy favour different institutional forms in Europe and Asia — forms that were shaped also by policy makers' differing levels of identification with these newly constructed regions. In dealing with its North Atlantic partners, the United States preferred to operate on a multilateral basis, with its Southeast Asian partners, in bilateral settings. U.S. policymakers saw in their European allies relatively equal members of a shared community. Potential Asian allies, in contrast, were inferior and part of an alien community. Broadly speaking, the United States was willing to create in Europe multilateral institutions that would restrain U.S. power in the short term only to enhance that power in the long term. It was eager to build bilateral institutions in Asia, where the concept of binding institutions did not seem as attractive as locking in the advantages of America's preponderant power through bilateral relations.

An important reason for this difference in institutional form was prevailing perceptions of power and status in world politics. American officials believed, quite correctly, that despite the reduction in capabilities inflicted by World War II, their European allies would soon regain their strength, whereas their Asian allies would remain permanently weak. Measured in relative terms, American power after 1945 was much greater in Asia than in Europe. In 1950, the combined GNP of the four major European states equaled 39 per cent of that of the United States; in 1965, the combined GNP of the seven major East and Southeast states was only 15.9 per cent of U.S. GNP. It would increase, on the strength of Japan's economic ascendance, to 79.8 per cent by 1989.[13] It was not in the interest of the United States to create institutions in Asia that would constrain Washington's ability to make independent decisions. Nor was it in the interest of subordinate states in the Asia-Pacific to enter institutions in which they had minimal control, while foregoing opportunities for free riding and the reduction of dependence. Status also mattered. Europe was the home of the traditional great powers in world politics. Most Southeast Asian states in the late 1940s were only at the threshold of gaining full national sovereignty.

The military and civilian leaders of the United States were in general agreement that Southeast Asia was less important and less threatened than Europe. In Asia, the primary issue for the United States was fighting communist insurgencies. In Europe, NATO was designed to hold off a massive Soviet offensive. The variety of the internal subversive threats faced by different Southeast Asian states made a "one-size-fits-all" multilateral defence arrangement such as NATO's inappropriate. In one of the few references to SEATO in his memoirs, Eisenhower approvingly quotes Churchill's belief that "Since sectors of the SEATO front were so varied in place and conditions, he [Churchill] felt it best to operate nationally where possible".[14]

Although power, status, and threat perceptions were important, ultimately the different forms of alliance politics in Asia and Europe were rooted in the self-conception of the United States, which identified more with Europe, less with Asia. The U.S. preference for a multilateral approach in Europe and a bilateral approach in Asia was thus due to a complex mix of political, material, institutional, and identity factors. Undeniable was the central fact that the different policies the United States adopted in the late 1940s had important institutional consequences for the evolution of European and Asian regionalism.

The multilateral and bilateral mechanisms through which anti-communist coalitions in Europe and Asia were linked to the centre of the American imperium also had a strong effect on Germany and Japan after 1945 — both domestically and in their interactions with their regional partners. U.S. occupation after 1945 brought about a political process of "creative destruction" in both countries. In eliminating discredited elites and redirecting outmoded institutional practices, the U.S. Government prepared the ground for new political and economic institutions, in Germany more so than in Japan. U.S. policies also set in motion processes that affected profoundly how German and Japanese elites exercised power, domestically, in Europe and Asia, and in the world at large. What emerged from these policies, both imposed from without and set free from within, were German and Japanese polities that were fundamentally altered in some ways, moderately changed in others, and unreconstructed in still others.

Ethnic Capitalism in Asian Market Networks vs. Law and Politics in a European Polity

China and Japan are important centres of the new Asian regionalism, but in ways that differ from the regionalism of Japan's Co-Prosperity Sphere of the 1930s and 1940s. The old regionalism emphasized autarchy, the new one relies on open networks. East Asia's regional networks are linked tightly to the world at large. Asian regionalism takes two different forms. Japanese capitalism is the result of indigenous economic developments and a conscious political strategy, orchestrated jointly by government and business elites (Hatch 2010). At the regional level, by contrast, Chinese capitalism lacks both an integrated, indigenous political economy and a coherent political strategy. It is almost unlimited in its flexibility.

Asian regionalism is institutionalized in different business networks, with national Japanese and ethnic Chinese identities playing an important role. The benefits of cultural affinities and old familial and business ties in overcoming problems of trust and reliability offer some advantages to a Chinese mode of organizing that contrasts with the dynamic technological efficiencies created in more hierarchical Japanese networks. While Chinese networks are excellent for rent-seeking behaviour and quick returns on capital, Japanese ones control the flow of aid and technologies, and provide producers in other countries with capital and intermediate inputs. South Korea and Taiwan, though closing the development gap quickly, specialize in somewhat less sophisticated goods and remain dependent on Japanese imports of key technologies and intermediate products. Thus, they have taken their place between Japan and Southeast Asia, which currently provides raw materials and markets and are upgrading industrial platforms for assembly and increasingly indigenous production.

The overlay of Japanese and Chinese business networks is evident in the case of Thailand. On the basis of his field research, Mitchell Sedgwick concluded that "Japanese multinationals in Thailand have reproduced an atomization of labor and strong centralization of decision-making authority. Beyond internal plant dynamics, however, the strict centralization is also reflected in the position of subsidiaries vis-à-vis headquarters. Subsidiaries in Thailand are part of a tightly controlled and rigorously hierarchical organizational structure extending down from Japan."[15] Thailand's Chinese-dominated business community, in contrast, has taken different forms over time; but in the last three decades, younger Chinese entrepreneurs have responded to the internationalization of the Thai economy by running their businesses along traditional Chinese lines and maintaining close contacts with the Chinese business communities in Hong Kong, Singapore, Taiwan, and China. Thailand illustrates that rapid corporate growth can result from the horizontal and open networks of the overseas Chinese, as much as the vertical and closed ones typical of Japan.

Although today these Japanese and Chinese variants of Asian regionalism take the form of ethno-nationalist business networks and subregional zones, their historical sources differ greatly. Japanese capitalism flowered between 1870 and 1930 in an era of state and empire building; Chinese capitalism, developing at the same time, bears the marks of imperial and state collapse. Since the mid-nineteenth century, the population of overseas Japanese has been dwarfed by the Chinese diaspora; and Chinese business networks are more extensive and have deeper historical roots than do their Japanese counterparts. Japanese officials have built up Japanese networks in full awareness of the severe limitations that Japanese firms face in Asia. Different historical origins have thus shaped the characters of China's and Japan's current economic extensions into Asia.

This general pattern is evident in specific industrial sectors. Japanese networks of firms rely substantially on known Japanese suppliers with comparable technical capacities. Overseas Chinese firms work through networks that draw on the increasing technical specialization of small- and medium-sized firms scattered throughout Asia. Japanese networks are closed, vertical, Japan-centred, and long-term. Chinese networks are open, horizontal, flexible, and ephemeral. In vertical organizations, groups are controlled by shareholding ownership, whereas horizontal networks favour family ownership and partnerships. Within a group, vertical networks control through cross-shareholding and mutual domination; horizontal ones manage through multiple positions held by core personnel. Vertical systems organize between group networks with cross-shareholding; horizontal ones favour loans and joint ventures by individuals and firms. In the former, subcontract relations are structured or semi-formal; in the latter, they are informal and highly flexible. Growth patterns are differentiated by bank financing in vertical systems, and informal financing and reinvestment in horizontal ones.

In sum, Asian markets do not consist of a series of unconnected and atomized individual transactions. "Interlinked commodity chains," Gary Hamilton writes, "simultaneously are embedded in the social and political institutions of locales and are extremely sensitive to such global conditions as price and currency fluctuations".[16] At the regional level, these social and market links typically follow ethnic Chinese or national Japanese lines. Both types of business network avoid formal institutionalization as Japanese *keiretsu* structures and Chinese family firms bring about economic integration without formal political institutions. In the 1990s, regionalism and regionalization in Asia was porous to developments in the world economy; its economic form was network-like; and its political shape was multicephalic.

European regionalism differs greatly in its institutional form from Asia's. For example, EU membership rules stipulate the centrality of the values of liberal democracy. The rule of law, private property in a market economy, the rights of democratic participation, and respect for minority rights and social pluralism all derive from the liberal human rights which are central to the European Union. They are embedded in a system of multilateral arrangements of states committed to a peaceful resolution of all conflicts. Since 1957, these values have been cast in legal language and are specified in various treaties that European governments have signed and ratified. They were restated succinctly by the European Council in its 1993 Copenhagen meeting.

With the passing of time, regional integration in Europe has changed from a system of bargaining between governments to a polity in which, among others, governments also bargain. Governance in Europe is driven by functional needs, has a large bureaucratic component, and occurs at multiple levels that link subnational, national, and European institutions. Groups, parties, and government bureaucracies are drawn into a polity that is acquiring legitimacy while remaining contested. This process is leading neither to unification through the creation of a European superstate, nor to fragmentation into a plethora of nationalistic states.

Institutionalization in Europe is a pervasive phenomenon affecting many dimensions of social and political life. Yet, compared with Asia, it is the constitutionalization of the European treaty system, more than the adoption of a European constitution, that is the distinctive trait of the evolving European polity. Consensus decision making occurs in a multitiered political system that fuses and separates power and is always open to serious conflicts of interest, pitting national governments against one another. Joseph Weiler draws our attention to the principle of constitutional *tolerance*. Very different European states are committed to coming together in an ever closer union. They are connected through a growing number of ties that invite, more than oblige, the submission of national power to the decisions of a political community — one in which other states, not a democratic public, exercise authority. "European federalism," Weiler concludes, "is constructed with a top-to-bottom hierarchy of norms, but with a bottom-to-top hierarchy of authority and real power".[17] These intersecting political processes direct our attention to Europe as a problem-solving, deliberative polity that complements the alternative political logics of state sovereignty and societal associability.

American policy has had some influence over the core differences in Europe's and Asia's regional orders. After 1945 multilateralism was an institutional innovation that American policymakers pursued vigorously in Europe, but not in Asia. Washington thus nudged the two regions onto institutional trajectories that were rooted in long-standing institutional norms and practices which are reflected in ethnic capitalism in Asian markets, and law embedded in various European political arrangements. These differences are consequential both for the American imperium, and for Japan and Germany, which play central roles in two of the world's most important regions.

III. REGION MAKING BEYOND NATIONAL MODELS

One crucial feature of contemporary regionalism is its porousness. Journalists and politicians often use the concept of regional "blocs". In their view traditional international politics is replicated among a much smaller number of much larger and more powerful regions. Nothing could be further from the truth. Globalization and internationalization processes make regions porous, often in accordance with the power and purpose of the American imperium.

Globalization and Internationalization

Since the end of the Cold War, globalization and internationalization have dominated public discussion and scholarly writings. Although the terms are often used interchangeably, I see a vast difference.[18] I define *globalization* as a process that transcends space and compresses time. It has novel transformative effects on world politics. I define *internationalization* as a process that refers to territorially based exchanges across borders. It refers to basic continuities in the evolution of the international state system. Globalization highlights the emergence of new actors and novel relations in the world system; internationalization, the continued relevance of existing actors and the intensifications of existing relations. Territorially-based international processes permit continued differences in national practices. Non-territorial global processes push towards convergence of national differences, and also towards a wide variety of local processes of specific adaptations to global changes. In a global economy, for example, transnational corporations undercut national public policies and tend to move corporate practices to one preferred global standard; but global corporate policies also give rise to a wide variety of supportive and oppositional local responses. In an international economy, by way of contrast, government policies continue to adapt the national economy to the operations of multinational corporations pursuing different strategies.

Globalization and internationalization make today's regions porous. Their effects are transformative in the case of globalization, incremental in the case of internationalization. Interacting with each other they strengthen porous regions and undermine closed regions.

Both theories update earlier insights, specifically yesterday's writing about "international interdependence". Then, as now, analytical concepts are deeply contested both analytically and normatively. In the 1970s, careful analyses of increasing levels of international interdependence, understood both as growing sensitivities and vulnerabilities of societies and states, pointed to their wide-ranging, powerful effects on world politics. Liberals saw an era in which traditional centres of authority would be challenged by new, non-state actors. Marxists pointed to the inherent instabilities that growing international interdependence was creating for capitalism, both at home and abroad. And realists and students of domestic politics argued that even a sharp increase in levels of interdependence would not be strong enough to transform world politics.

Today's disagreements are similarly strong. They focus, for example, on the benefits of increasing efficiency and the costs of increasing inequality that come in the wake of globalization. Similarly, the spread of a global popular culture has energized many political counter movements that insist on the political primacy and moral superiority of nation states or transnational religious communities. Disagreement centres also on what many consider to be an outmoded organization of the international state system, with its inadequate response to challenges such as global warming and genocide. States are criticized for being too small for many of the big problems, and too big for many of the small ones. In domestic politics, what is increasingly needed is not heavy-handed state intervention, but the light-footed tap dance of public-private partnerships.

A regionalism made porous by globalization and internationalization remains available for processes that create ever larger regions, illustrated since the mid-1990s by the enlargements of NATO, the European Union, and ASEAN. Regional enlargements go hand in hand with new forms of interregional engagement. Since 1996, for example, European and Asian leaders have met periodically in high-level talks. And the building of closer links between the European Union and Latin America's Mercosur is under active consideration. Often the result of American power and purpose, globalization creates changes in world politics that transform the capacities of territorial states and other actors. Internationalization is an incremental process of increasing national openness that does not touch the core competencies of territorially-based states. Neither process shapes world politics to the exclusion of the other. While trade data lend support to the relative importance of internationalization, financial flows point to the pervasiveness of globalization. A devoted advocate of globalization and author of a best-seller on the topic, Thomas Friedman combines the two dynamics in his characterization of world politics: "a new international system has now clearly replaced the Cold War: globalization".[19] Not quite. I argue that globalization and internationalization coexist and complement one another. They make regions porous and embed them deeply in America's imperium.

Japanization, Americanization, Sinicization

The concept of Japanization is an abstraction that refers to diverse empirical patterns. Japanization does not offer fixed benchmarks by which to measure its spread. Rather, it involves open-ended processes of diffusion, emulation, and the adoption of distinctive patterns of production, consumption, and behaviour. It thus does not yield clear copies of a template replicated in different national or local settings. The combining of patterns can result from deliberate organizational design, from ongoing gradual change in shared cognitive schemas and normative orders, and from political conflicts driven by competing interests. The most intensively studied instance of Japanization — the American automobile industry — indicates the importance of all three mechanisms. What holds for the Japanization of the U.S. car industry also holds for the Japanization of East Asia.

In the 1980s Japanization became a term to characterize the shift from an old to a new paradigm of production that bought Japan another decade (Hatch 2010). It referred to the particular talent of Japanese firms to create large productivity gains in the export of manufactured goods, such as cars, auto parts, and electrical products. It also described the setting up of Japanese factories abroad, which revolutionized the global car industry. More generally, "the notion of Japanization has become a label for a fairly open-ended agenda of investigation rather than a set of strong claims about the scope and character of the spread of Japanese production techniques".[20] Yet the awareness of a "Japanese model" increased with the spread of its direct foreign investment, especially after the mid-1980s. East Asian governments and automobile producers sought out Japanese investment, and they actively encouraged the introduction of new products and processes. The threat of U.S. protection encouraged Japanese firms to create new production platforms outside Japan. Furthermore, the Japanese Government favoured direct foreign investment as an attractive way of recycling Japan's large trade surplus. In the 1980s various actors with complex motivations pushed the process of Japanization.

Throughout East Asia during the 1990s a new wave of Japanization occurred that had little to do with the earlier one. Japanese popular culture has been increasingly embraced by the newly affluent younger "middle mass" in all of East Asia's major metropolitan areas. Japan's affluence and technological prowess have made deep inroads, and Japanese department stores and supermarkets have altered consumer cultures. In the 1990s the products of Japan's popular culture industries — songs, dramas, comics, toys, Pokemon games, fashion, and food — swept across East Asia with truly astounding speed. Japanese today is the most popular foreign language in Singapore. No longer is it viewed as a passport to a job with a Japanese company. It is instead the magic key that opens the door to Japan's popular culture. Student exchanges between Singapore and Japan have been small, but the creation of a Japanese Studies department at the National University of Singapore has served growing student demand even after Singapore's government began playing down its policy of learning from Japan. The department's pedagogical mission has been to learn about Japan from Singapore's cultural context rather than simply fostering the transplanting of Japanese social practices.

Today, Japan's popular culture has global appeal. "Hello Kitty" is Western so she will sell in Japan, and she is Japanese so she will sell in the West. Part of the attraction of Japan's culture industries is their flexible and absorptive character. Japan's cultural products and idiom facilitate regional spread, and not conveying a distinctly Japanese message is their greatest commercial strength. Ann Allison concludes that "Japan's cultural industries have touched a pulse in the imaginations and lives of millennial children in this era of cybertechnology and postindustrial socialization. They have done this by blending flexibility and fantasy into technology that is conveniently portable, virtuality that is intimately cute, and a commodity form that is polymorphously perverse. And, as its stock in the marketplace of children's entertainment rises (slowly) around the world, Japan is moving itself closer to the center of global culture. One consequence of this is the decentering of cultural (entertainment) trends once hegemonized by Euroamerica (and particularly the United States)".[21]

Singapore's various experiences with Japanization reveal some regularities in the ups and downs of Japanization. Initial assistance from Japan and at times close emulation of Japanese institutions and social practices yield eventually to modifications to suit local circumstances and, later, to growing indifference. Far from worrying about the pervasive influence of Japanization, Leng Than and S.K. Gan conclude, "it is paradoxical that Japanese influence is extremely modest when compared with the prominent Japanese presence in Singapore since the 'learn from Japan' era".[22] More generally, the movement to learn from Japan slowed dramatically in the second half of the 1990s. T.J. Pempel writes that "there is widespread skepticism in much of Asia about the wisdom of emulating any alleged 'Japanese model,' following Japan's leadership, or allowing Japan to be Asia's main bridge to the West."[23] In a nutshell, in the making of an East Asian region, "flying-geese-style Japanization" is out, "beyond Japanization" is in.

What is true of Japanization is also true of Americanization. More than a century ago William Stead (1901) argued that the New World was having a big impact on the Old. Even then Stead's argument contained only a half truth: America was indeed affecting the world, but the world was also affecting America. Webster's *Third International Dictionary* defines "Americanization" as the process by which immigrants were made into Americans. Not any longer. The processes that link the United States, East Asia, and the world have become increasingly complex in fusing different national influences. Americanization is a close cousin to globalization and Westernization, but it is analytically distinct. Americanization is marked by the legacy of two hundred years of Anglo-American preponderance in world politics. Preponderance can be measured in terms of both material capabilities and institutional and ideological appeal. This is true as much of American preponderance in East Asia today as it was half a century ago. But distinctive of the present is the growing importance of processes no longer defined by the logic of traditional power politics.

In the area of technology, for example, the United States emerged from World War II as undisputed global leader. In the 1970s and 1980s, one study reports, about two thirds of the international supply of disembodied proprietary technology had been of U.S. origin, with the United Kingdom running a distant second.[24] And after a Japanese surge in the 1970s and 1980s, the technology gap between the United States and Japan has again widened since the mid-1990s.

Americanization refers also to the appropriation of American popular culture by different social strata, groups, and generations, each creating specific subcultures and all together constituting a national culture. Research into the Americanization of the young, everyday life, gender roles, generational change, literature, popular music, film, and television, gives us insight into complex processes of cultural and social change in East Asia. Americanization has both positive (affluence, modernity, tolerance, enlightenment) and negative (non-Asian, culturally inferior, superficial, materialist, profit-hungry) connotations. Positive and negative connotations are indelibly fused in the concepts of democracy and capitalism. In the 1950s and 1960s the American Way of Life became accessible to a few thin strata in East Asia. A generation later pervasive changes in the major metropolitan areas in East Asia have transformed accessibility into familiarity. Students of popular culture use concepts such as "cultural creolization" to underline the active role that local actors play in the selection and appropriation of American mass culture. "Self-Americanization" is not a bad way to capture the repertoire of practices open to numerous recombinations by those who operate not in homogeneous national societies, but in complex networks of variegated cultural affinities.

Americanization is neither a unified nor unifying process. Hollywood, for example, is to a substantial degree owned by non-Americans and many of its most famous directors and actors are non-American. Paralleling developments in the recording industry, in the early 1990s only three of the seven major Hollywood studios were controlled by U.S. corporations: Disney, Paramount, and Warner Brothers. Yet national ownership had little impact on the way films were conceived and made in Hollywood. Indeed, the influx of foreign movie makers stretches back to the 1920s and 1930s. In terms of ownership and artistic talent, Hollywood is the world. Like "Self- Americanization", the "Other-Americanization" of the contemporary U.S. popular culture industries illustrates the hybridity and polymorphism of the United States and its global entertainment industry.

In East Asia the processes of Japanization and Americanziation have fused to create regionalization that goes beyond any one national model. In the 1960s and 1970s American GIs, the first demands for the liberalization of trade and capital, growing direct foreign investment, jazz and chewing gum, cartoons and Disney animation, sitcoms and chocolates, Coca-Cola and Lucky Strikes, all spread the promise of the American Way of Life. The growing relative power of the United States in world politics, increasing liberalization in trade and capital flows, the spread of cross-border production networks and technology flows, environmental degradation and the political countermovements it spawned, fast-food chains, Hollywood action movies, and American pop music, deepened the Americanization of East Asia in the 1980s and 1990s.

Over time Americanization has fused with Japanization. Japan's underlying cultural similarity with other East Asian societies and Japan's longer exposure to Americanization have given it a central role in mediating connections between East Asia and the United States. Japan's popular culture industry, for example, often acts to rework Western sensibilities to fit East Asia. This is true also in fashion, where Japan translates American and European ideas into East Asian tastes and emotions. Because of its special relationship with the United States, Japan also mediates the geostrategic and commercial demands and expectations of U.S. governments in East Asia. In this mediation, Japanization leaves a less clear imprint on individual consciousness and collective ideology. Japan's popular culture products, for example, are perfect vessels for transporting a common cultural experience across East Asia. Japanese comics are becoming East Asian comics. The mixing of Americanization and Japanization is not transmitting distinctive national models as much as it is helping spark a hybrid Asian regionalism.

The rise of China and East Asia's "Sinicization" is reinforcing and enriching that fusion of Japanization and Americanization. Sinicization refers here to both the growing importance of China *and* the social, economic, and political reassertion of the Chinese populations living in Southeast Asia. In the last two decades China has made great strides, and today a growing number of observers are speculating about the coming of a *Pax sinica*. East Asian states will not balance against China, but jump on its bandwagon as China rises. The recent track record of such speculations does not inspire confidence. An impending *Pax nipponica* ended when the financial bubble burst; *Pax americana* yielded in a few short years to a deficit-addicted, nervous

United States trapped in a war of its own choosing, and a financial meltdown of historic proportions. China's sheer size is having a large effect on East Asia, it is true, and that effect is growing quickly. Yet Sinicization is not remaking East Asia in the likeness of China. The Sinicization of Southeast Asia, for example, has worked itself out in different ways in different countries.[25] Ethnic Chinese make up large parts of the professional classes in Southeast Asia and control large segments of the business sector in various countries. The influx of Japanese capital after 1985 affected these Chinese strata differently, yielding a Sinicization that has proved remarkably variable at the regional level. Sinicization is important because it results in a hybrid regionalism that makes it virtually impossible to disentangle different national strands. The important role that the overseas Chinese play in East Asia reinforces the hybrid nature of the region.

The overseas Chinese suffered greatly in the middle of the twentieth century. They were devastated by the effects of the Great Depression, the Pacific War, Japanese occupation, and nationalist anticolonial revolutions. Politically cut off from China between the 1950s and the 1970s, the Chinese in Southeast Asia were subject to assimilationist policies that Southeast Asian governments imposed as part of nation building. The economic power of Chinese businessmen began to grow once again in the 1960s as they eventually moved beyond national into regional and global markets, increasingly as trusted supporters of, rather than despised pariahs in, Southeast Asian polities. In a carefully calibrated strategy, Chinese businessmen invested in roughly equal proportions in Southeast Asia, China, and the United States. Upper and upper-middle class Chinese, especially in Indonesia and Thailand, began sending their children to high schools in Hong Kong and Singapore for better training in Mandarin and English, and to the United States and the United Kingdom, for university and professional education. Even though they retain Hokkien, Cantonese, or Teochew as their mother tongues, Chinese businessmen no longer rely on local dialects for business. Nor does this new generation of Chinese use clan or regional ties to build social networks. Trilingual in Mandarin, English, and a mother tongue, they use their Chineseness as the key to their networks. Sinicization is a market-driven phenomenon intimately tied up with the rise of China, for the overwhelming share of the foreign investment that has helped catapult China forward is owned by ethnic Chinese who live in Southeast Asia.

Taiwan and the overseas Chinese have been central in creating and sustaining East Asia's regional production networks. This development was spurred less by Chinese initiatives and more by shifts in the competitive position of Japanese and American firms in specific sectors. Still the rise of the Chinese electronics industry, as a base for export production, as a sophisticated growth market, and as a source of innovation and specialized skills, is likely to have lasting effects on East Asia. In electronics China will contribute to the synergistic processes that are central for the continued expansion of Japanese exports and economic growth. These will define East Asian regionalization beyond any specific national model. China's market size and dynamic adjustment have also played a large role in the reorganization of East Asia's ecology, displacing to China, in some instances in only a few years, the large ecological shadow Japan once cast over Southeast Asia. China's trade with Japan in resource-intensive products, from poultry to furniture, and its vegetable exports have increased disproportionately, creating a serious problem for Japan's traditional agro-export zone in Southeast Asia. It also saddles China with serious ecological problems. Finally, with the opening of China's popular culture market, the emergence of an East Asian popular culture is well under way — complementing rather than substituting the Japanization that has rapidly altered East Asia's urban landscape, especially among the young.

What is true for popular culture is true more generally. In the emergence of East Asia it is impossible to untangle Japanization, Americanization, and Sinicization. North of Beijing, for example, upscale homes at the Orange County development cost upwards of half a million U.S. dollars. And Japanese-style convenience stores (konbini) are spreading rapidly in South Korea. International markets versus state control, cultural cosmopolitanism versus post-colonial nationalism, urban versus agricultural life, maritime-coastal versus interior-continental geographies — such oppositions do not capture the hybrid East Asia that is emerging. Instead we should think of East Asian regionalism as being increasingly based on new, urban-based social foundation. Admittedly that urban space represents only a fraction of one per cent of the region's land area and less than 7 per cent of its total population; but collectively it accounts for about

80 to 90 per cent of the region's international activities, projecting a bubbling consumerism that reflects, "a networked regionalism which in turn rests on global capitalism".[26] National models no longer supplant one another in sequential fashion. Instead they fuse and yield unexpected regional patterns. Such hybridity undermines established preconceptions about the differences that separate Japan from China, or Orient from Occident. From Tokyo and Los Angeles, to Singapore and Seattle, from Shanghai to Ho Chi Minh City, extending beyond all national models and fusing into a new regionalism, East Asia offers us a glimpse of a future marked by unexplored opportunities and new challenges.

IV. EPILOGUE:
CHINA'S RISE, EAST ASIA, AND THE
AMERICAN IMPERIUM

The three interrelated arguments that I have advanced in this chapter have implications for how we might think about the effect of China's rise on East Asian regionalism. I do not see either America's prolonged war in Iraq and Afghanistan or the unfolding global financial crisis as the end of this imperium. Nor do I believe that the election of Barack Obama is a transformational change ringing in a radically new beginning. Rather, following Churchill's quip, I see both as an affirmation that Americans tend to do everything wrong before doing the right thing. I readily acknowledge that the two terms of President Bush have done enormous damage to American values, interest, and power. Yet America's imperium rests on foundations that even a uniquely reckless and astonishingly incompetent president could not dismantle in eight years. The overall structure of world politics will surely be adjusting to China's rise and America's slide. But it will do so within an established structure that this chapter has attempted to elucidate. Not rupture with but recalibration within the imperium and East Asia's regional order is the most likely consequence of China's rise.

To some extent this implication follows from my view of China as more than the territory and the citizens of the Peoples Republic of China. The overseas Chinese were crucial in providing the lion's share of the starting capital that set China on its economic path. And China's unique economic openness (measured as the proportion of foreign trade to GDP) — unique, that is, in comparison to Japan, India, the European Union, and the United States — makes it structurally available for and interested in the liberal economic bent that the American imperium has pursued with great consistency in the last half century.

The failed expectations of other rising powers suggest that we should expect gradual not dramatic change and regional recalibration, not rupture. In the 1970s, for example, Germany was proud of its institutional model. Others in Europe were afraid that the Bundesbank would succeed where Nazi Germany's armies had failed: dominating Europe. Yet even before national unification it had become clear that Europe was not to be dominated by any one country. And in many dimensions a united Germany has proven to be a weaker not a stronger Germany. In the 1980s it was Japan's turn to expect that its economic rise and emergence as a technological superpower would set the stage for a glorious twenty-first century. Yet the bursting of the Japanese bubble and a decade and a half of slow growth and an eroding sense of self-confidence ended that dream. Next it was the turn of the United States, after its unexpectedly quick victory in the Afghan war, to dream of being the New Rome, of creating new realities rather than heeding existing ones. Yet that brief period of megalomania was over in half a decade. Given these shattered hopes and expectations, those looking to China (and soon India) as the next superpower are in for some disappointments. There are, inevitably, the challenges that especially the downward cycles of capitalism create for authoritarian governments. Furthermore, besides coping with the downward cycles of capitalism that are particularly risky for authoritarian governments whose legitimacy depends largely on delivering the dividends of growth, one, if not *the* greatest, preoccupation of all Chinese governments during the next half century will be how to care for one of the most rapidly ageing populations in the world.

Region making, I have argued, is always a two-way street. Sinicization is not only China remaking Asia, but Asia remaking China. Analyses of Japanization and Americanization processes show as much. Regional networks realign and readjust. Global and regional developments are complex and fast. They require a more fully developed conceptualization of power than is typical for those who see China's rise leading to dramatic change. Rather than focusing only on the visible and behavioural aspects of power which operate in directly targeted ways, we need also to look at the invisible and non-behavioural or structural aspects of power which operate indirectly and diffusely. In the process of region making, rising powers seek to project specific institutional models and practices. But in the process of doing so, they and the models and practices they seek to project, are altered — often beyond recognition. This dialectic led to the disappointment of German, Japanese, and American hopes and expectations. And this dialectic will undermine unrealistic Chinese or Indian hopes and expectations. China's rise often elicits breathless adulation or great worry, even fear. Both are unwarranted. History will not end either in a liberal nirvana or in a civilizational clash (Fukuyama 1989. Huntington 1993). And contra Marx, history does not repeat itself as farce. Instead history rhymes. China's rise is likely to be an integral part of regional dynamics, most of which it will not be able to dominate. In brief, China's rise will occur in and help shape regional contours that are embedded in the American imperium.

Notes

1. Except for minor stylistic corrections and improvements, this chapter is printed here in the form in which the author submitted it, on time, in January 2009. This chapter is based substantially, without most of the references to extant scholarship, on excerpted and adapted material from chapters 1 and 2 of Katzenstein (2005) and Katzenstein (2006).
2. Johnson 2004, 4, 154–60.
3. Hardt and Negri 2000, xii, 146.
4. Kennan 1947, 1994.
5. Steinberg 2001, 207–08.
6. Hirst and Thompson 2002, 258.
7. Mansfield and Milner 1999, 601. Frankel 1997, 4.
8. <http://www.wto.org/english/tratop_e/regfac_e.htm> (Chase 2005, 1–2).
9. Mansfield and Milner 1999, 600.
10. Thurow 1992. Bhagwati 1992.
11. Yuan and Eden 1992, 1026. ILO 2002, 1.
12. Ikenberry 2001, 184.
13. Crone 1993, 503, and note 7, 510.
14. Eisenhower 1963, 368.
15. Sedgwick 1994, 8.

16. Hamilton 1999, 52.
17. Weiler 2000, 244, 240.
18. Hirst and Thompson 1996, 185 and also 8–13.
19. Friedman 1999, 110.
20. Elger and Smith 1994, 7.
21. Allison 2004, 47–48.
22. Thang and Gan 2000, 21.
23. Pempel 1997, 76.
24. Ernst and O'Connor 1989, 29.
25. Shiraishi 2006.
26. Rohlen 2002, 8, 9.

References

Allison, Anne. "Cuteness as Japan's Millennial Product". In *Pikachu's Global Adventure: The Rise and Fall of Pokemon*, edited by Joseph Tobin. Durham: Duke University Press, 2004.

Bhagwati, Jagdish. "Regionalism versus Multilateralism". *The World Economy*, Vol. 15, No. 5 (September 1992): 535–55.

Chase, Kerry A. *Trading Blocs: States, Firms, and Regions in the World Economy*. Ann Arbor: University of Michigan Press, 2005.

Crone, Donald. "Does Hegemony Matter? The Reorganization of the Pacific Political Economy". *World Politics*, Vol. 45, No. 4 (July 1993): 501–25.

Eisenhower, Dwight D. *The White House Years: Mandate For Change: 1953–1965*. Garden City: Doubleday and Company, 1963.

Elger, Tony and Chris Smith. "Introduction". In *Global Japanization? The Transnational Transformation of the Labour Process*, edited by Tony Elger and Chris Smith. London: Routledge, 1994.

Ernst, Dieter, and David O'Connor. *Technology and Global Competition: The Challenge for Newly Industrialising Economies*. Paris: Organization for Economic Cooperation and Development, 1989.

Frankel, Jeffrey A. *Regional Trading Blocs in the World Economic System*. Washington, D.C.: Institute for International Economics, 1997.

Friedman, Thomas L. "Dueling Globalizations: A Debate Between Thomas L. Friedman and Ignacio Ramonet". *Foreign Policy*, No. 116 (Fall 1999): 110–27.

Fukuyama, Francis. "The End of History?". *The National Interest*, No. 16 (Summer 1989): 3–16.

Hamilton, Gary. "Asian Business Networks in Transition: or, What Alan Greenspan Does Not Know about the Asian Business Crisis". In *The Politics of the Asian Economic Crisis*, edited by T.J. Pempel. Ithaca: Cornell University Press, 1999.

Hardt, Michael and Antonio Negri. *Empire*. Cambridge: Harvard University Press, 2000.

Hatch, Walter F. *Asia's Flying Geese: How Regionalization Shapes Japan*. Ithaca: Cornell University Press, 2010.

Hirst, Paul and Grahame Thompson. *Globalization in Question: The International Economy and the Possibilities of Governance*. Cambridge: Polity Press, 1996.

———. "The Future of Globalization". *Cooperation and Conflict*, Vol. 37, No. 3 (September 2002): 247–65.

Huntington, Samuel P. "The Clash of Civilizations?". *Foreign Affairs*, Vol. 72, No. 3 (Summer 1993): 22–49.

Ikenberry, G. John. *After Victory: Institutions, Strategic Restraint, and the Rebuilding of Order after Major Wars*. Princeton: Princeton University Press, 2001.

ILO (Committee on Employment and Social Policy, International Labour Organization). *Employment and Social Policy in Respect of Export Processing Zones (EPZs)*. Geneva: International Labour Organization, 2002.

Johnson, Chalmers. *The Sorrows of Empire: Militarism, Secrecy, and the End of the Republic*. New York: Henry Holt, 2004.

Katzenstein, Peter J. *A World of Regions: Asia and Europe in the American Imperium*. Ithaca: Cornell University Press, 2005.

———. "East Asia-Beyond Japan". In *Beyond Japan: The Dynamics of East Asian Regionalism*, edited by Peter J. Katzenstein and Takashi Shiraishi. Ithaca: Cornell University Press, 2006.

Kennan, George F. (Mr X). "The Sources of Soviet Conduct". *Foreign Affairs*, Vol. 25, No. 4 (July 1947): 566–82.

Kennan, George F. "The Failure in Our Success". *New York Times*, 14 March 1994, A17.

Mansfield, Edward D. and Helen V. Milner. "The New Wave of Regionalism". *International Organization*, Vol. 53, No. 3 (Summer 1999): 589–627.

Pempel, T.J. *The Politics of Economic Reform in Japan*. Canberra: Australia-Japan Research Centre, Australian National University, 1997.

Rohlen, Thomas P. *Cosmopolitan Cities and Nation States: Open Economics, Urban Dynamics, and Government in East Asia*. Stanford: Asia/Pacific Research Center, Stanford University, 2002.

Sedgwick, Mitchell W. "Does the Japanese Management Miracle Travel in Asia? Managerial Technology Transfer at Japanese Multinationals in Thailand". Paper delivered at the Workshop on Multinationals and East Asian Integration at MIT Japan Program, Cambridge, 18–19 November 1994.

Shiraishi, Takashi. "The Third Wave: Southeast Asia and Middle-Class Formation in the Making of a Region". In *Beyond Japan: The Dynamics of East Asian*

Regionalism, edited by Peter J. Katzenstein and Takashi Shiraishi. Ithaca: Cornell University Press, 2006.

Steinberg, Philip E. *The Social Construction of the Ocean*. Cambridge: Cambridge University Press, 2001.

Thang, Leng Leng and S.K. Gan. "Deconstructing 'Japanization': Reflections from the 'Learn from Japan' Campaign in Singapore". Paper delivered at the International Conference on the Japanese Model, the Malaysian Association of Japanese Studies, Kuala Lumpur, 29–30 March 2000.

Thurow, Lester C. *Head to Head: The Coming Economic Battle between Japan, Europe, and America*. New York: William Morrow, 1992.

Weiler, John H.H. "Federalism and Constitutionalism: Europe's Sonderweg". *Jean Monnet Working Paper* No. 10. New York: Jean Monnet Center for International and Regional Economic Law & Justice NYU Law School, 2000.

Yuan, Jing-dong and Lorraine Eden. "Export Processing Zones in Asia: A Comparative Study". *Asian Survey*, Vol. 32, No. 11 (November 1992): 1026–45.

3

Building a Neighbourhood — One Policy at a Time: The Case for Deeper Economic Integration in East Asia[1]

Hamid Alavi
Ralph Van Doorn
Vikram Nehru

I. INSIGHTS ON THE BENEFITS OF EAST ASIAN INTEGRATION

The benefits of regional integration are greater than previously realized. This section summarizes the main benefits of regional integration as documented in the literature on this, and discusses recent work that suggests that regional integration can be even more beneficial than previously realized, especially if the potential associated risks of integration are managed properly.[2]

The Benefits of Regional Integration

Conventional Analysis Stresses Specialization as the Driver of Benefits

The conventional analysis of the benefits of regional integration focuses on trade in goods and emphasizes trade and location effects. The preferential reduction in tariffs through regional agreements induces a shift in demand towards exports from partner countries at the expense of domestic production (trade creation) and away from exports from non-member countries (trade diversion). According to this view, trade creation improves welfare, trade diversion reduces it.[3] Changes in trade flows induce changes in the location of production between member countries of a regional agreement based on static comparative advantage (specialization).

New Insights Identify Economies of Scale and Agglomeration Economies as the Key Driver

The new economic literature — sometimes called the "new international trade theory" — summarized in *An East Asian Renaissance* (Gill and Kharas 2007) and *World Development Report* (World Bank 2009), emphasizes the increasing role of economies of scale and agglomerations economies as central forces driving international trade, the geographical concentration of economic activity, and economic growth. While this theory was developed in the late 1970s (Krugman 1979), empirical support has been more recent. The premise of the new thinking is that when trade barriers fall, firms gain access to bigger markets, allowing them to expand production and reap economies of scale. But openness also exposes them to competition from rival foreign firms, paring their margins. As such, some firms may go out of business, but between the domestic survivors and the foreign entrants, consumers will have more variety of goods to choose from. Thus the main gains from trade arise not from specialization, but from economies of scale, fiercer competition, and increased consumer choice that regional integration and, eventually, globalization provide. These economies of scale are usually of three kinds — the internal economies of scale within a plant or factory, localization economies of scale that arise from a large number of firms in the same industry and the same place, and urbanization economies that arise from a large number of different industries in the same place (Krugman 1991).

Features of East Asia's Experience[4]

Regional Integration Has Spurred East Asia's Growth

The region's GDP has climbed on average 8 per cent a year for over two decades, higher than any other region in the world (Figure 3.1). At the same time, intraregional trade has increased by almost 12 per

FIGURE 3.1
Growth of Regional GDP per Capita
(index = 100 in 1990)

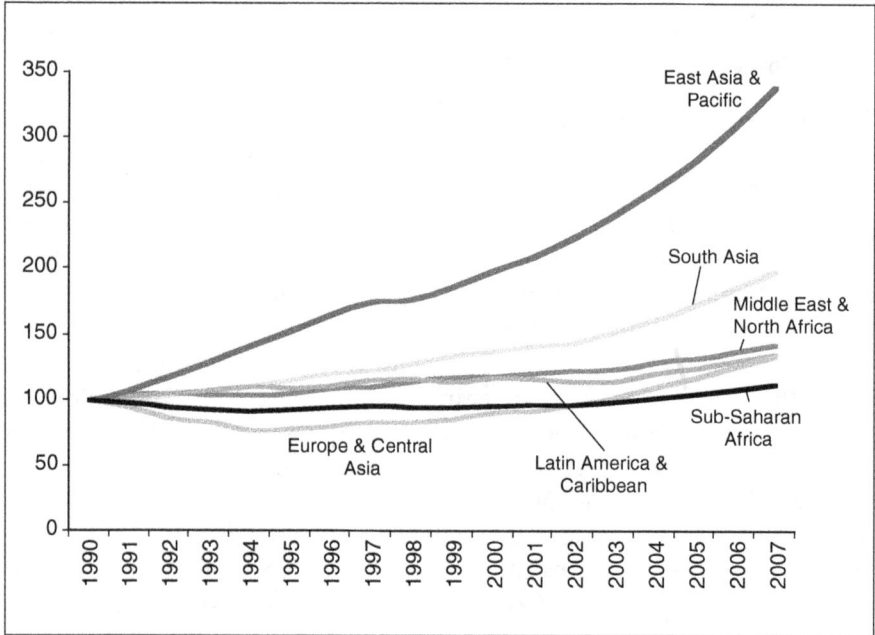

Note: These numbers refer to low- and middle-income countries only according to The World Bank's country classification. In this chart and the next few charts, East Asia & Pacific (EAP) includes the ASEAN+3 countries, Hong Kong, Mongolia and Papua New Guinea.
Source: World Development Indicators.

cent annually, growing faster than trade with the world, which grew only 9 per cent annually in the same period. Figure 3.2 shows a strong correlation between intraregional trade flows and regional GDP per capita growth.

In fact, East Asia's intraregional trade as a share of total trade is far above that of any other developing region, and is closer to that of high-income countries. The region has overtaken NAFTA in terms of intraregional trade as a share of total trade of the region with the world, and has been catching up with the European Union (Figure 3.3).

Within the East Asian region, all countries with a few exceptions (notably Papua New Guinea) have increasingly imported from within the region, although in terms of exports the picture is more mixed (Figure 3.4). This suggests that these countries have become more integrated with regional *production* networks while benefiting from access to global markets for their exports

FIGURE 3.2
Intraregional Trade Has Led East Asia's Growth

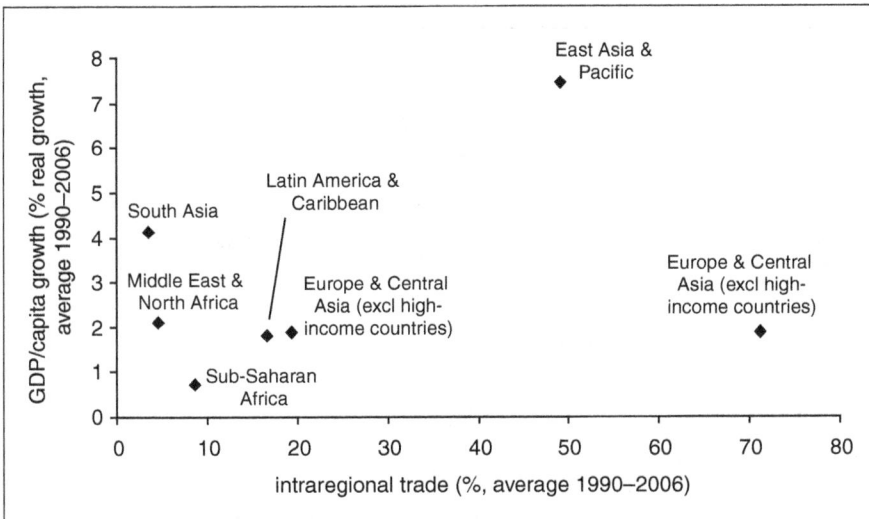

Note: For East Asia & Pacific, intraregional trade includes Japan and Korea as well, whereas the GDP/capita growth excludes these countries. For Europe & Central Asia intraregional trade is shown both including and excluding high-income countries (mainly the individual European Union countries).
Source: UN Comtrade statistics, World Development Indicators.

FIGURE 3.3
Intraregional Trade in EAP, Compared with NAFTA and the European Union
(share of total trade within the region as a percentage of total trade)

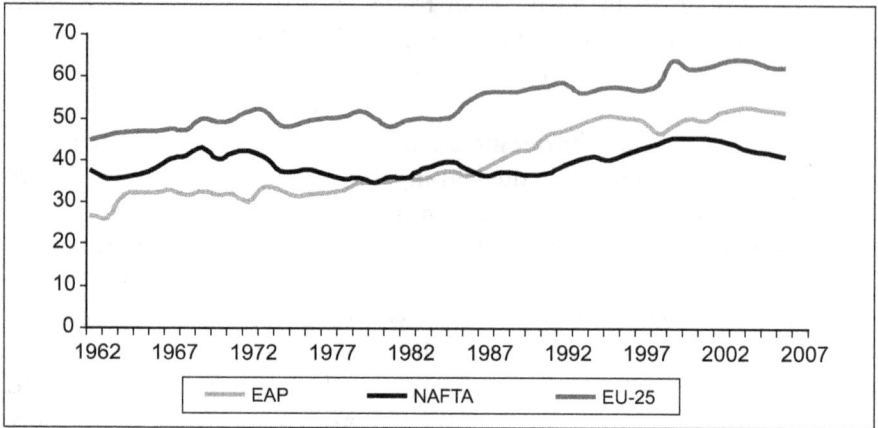

Source: UN Comtrade statistics.

FIGURE 3.4
Intraregional Exports and Imports in 1990 and 2006
(percentage of total exports or imports for each country)

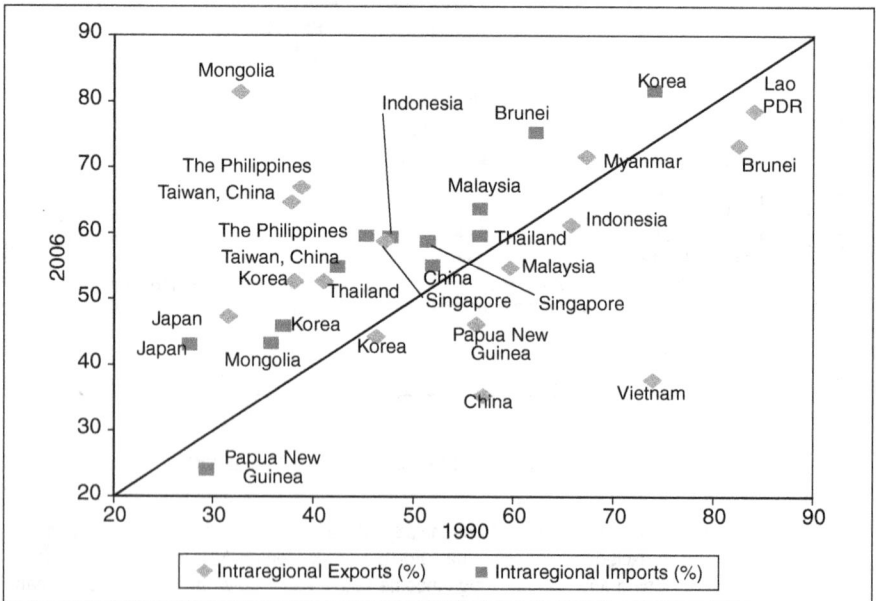

Source: UN Comtrade statistics.

Central Role of Japan and Now China

Japan and China have played a central role in energizing regional integration by absorbing a large share of East Asia's trade (Figure 3.5). A key reason for this has been the development of regional production networks (or supply chains) led initially by Japan in the early 1980s.[5]

More specifically, one of the major factors in the concentration of intraregional trade has been the remarkable increase in international production sharing, as reflected in the growth of intra-industry trade (see next section).

While Japan remains an important centre of production sharing operations in East Asia and is the origin of about one third of all regional exports of components for assembly, China is increasingly a central player in production networks. High and middle-income East Asian economies have found their niches within China's markets (Figure 3.6). Interestingly, this is not the case for low-income countries in the

FIGURE 3.5
China's and Japan's Imports from ASEAN+3
(percentage of total ASEAN+3 imports from ASEAN+3)

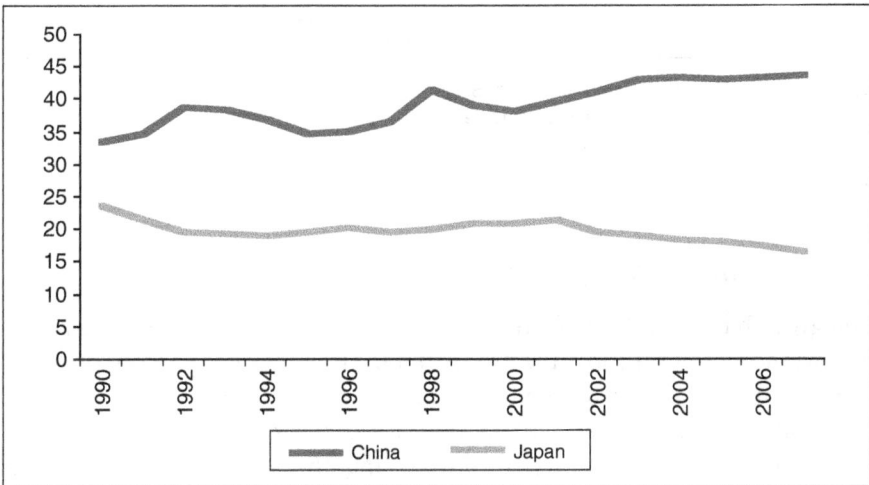

Source: IMF Direction of Trade Statistics.

region where exports are mainly destined for the U.S. market (mostly through subcontracting arrangements), suggesting that these countries are not as integrated as the high and middle-income countries in the region (Figure 3.7).

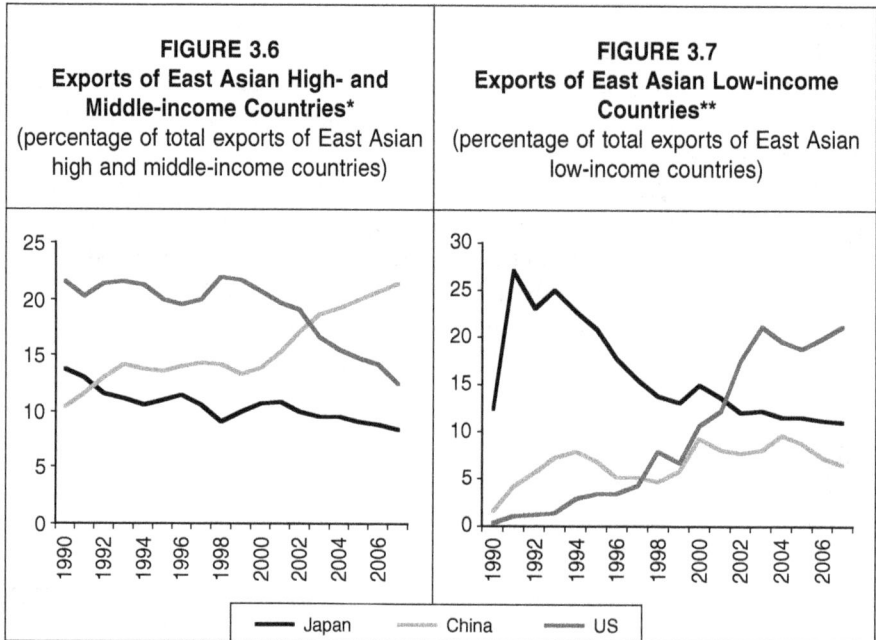

FIGURE 3.6
Exports of East Asian High- and Middle-income Countries*
(percentage of total exports of East Asian high and middle-income countries)

FIGURE 3.7
Exports of East Asian Low-income Countries**
(percentage of total exports of East Asian low-income countries)

— Japan   China   — US

Notes: * China, Hong Kong, The Philippines, Singapore, Indonesia, Thailand, and Malaysia.
       ** Vietnam, Cambodia, Myanmar and Lao PDR.
Source: IMF Direction of Trade Statistics.

Rise of Intra-industry Trade

The growth of intra-East Asian trade has been accompanied by the rising importance of intra-industry trade (IIT), or two-way trade within the same industry. While the share of inter-industry trade in the regional total halved from 45 per cent in 1990 to 22 per cent in 2004, the share of IIT rose from 55 to 78 per cent during the same period (Gill and Kharas 2007, p. 55).

Table 3.1 below shows that in 2006, ten out of thirteen East Asian countries demonstrated that intra-industry trade is most prevalent with other East Asian countries and Japan. By comparison, in 1985 only seven out of thirteen had the most intensive IIT with East Asian developing countries and Japan.[6]

TABLE 3.1
Intra-industry Trade of East Asian Countries in 2006
(Each country is in the column of the region with which it has the most intensive intra-industry trade, i.e. highest IIT index)

Country has highest IIT with region	East Asia		NAFTA	EU-15
	East Asia excl Japan	Japan		
1985	China Indonesia Malaysia Singapore Thailand	Korea, Rep. of Taiwan, China	The Philippines Lao PDR	Brunei Hong Kong Cambodia Vietnam
2006	China Cambodia Indonesia Lao PDR Malaysia Singapore Thailand	Korea, Rep. of Taiwan, China Vietnam	The Philippines	Brunei Hong Kong

Source: UN Comtrade statistics.

A key reason for the increase in IIT is the rapid development of regional supply chains and production networks.[7] An indication of the sophistication of these supply chains is the importance of parts and components in intraregional trade. Figure 3.8 shows how the share of parts and components in intraregional manufactured trade has increased for most East Asian countries between 1985 and 2006, with the exception of Myanmar, Cambodia, and Lao PDR.

FIGURE 3.8
Intraregional Trade in Parts and Components Has Increased*
(percentage of total intraregional trade in manufactured products**)

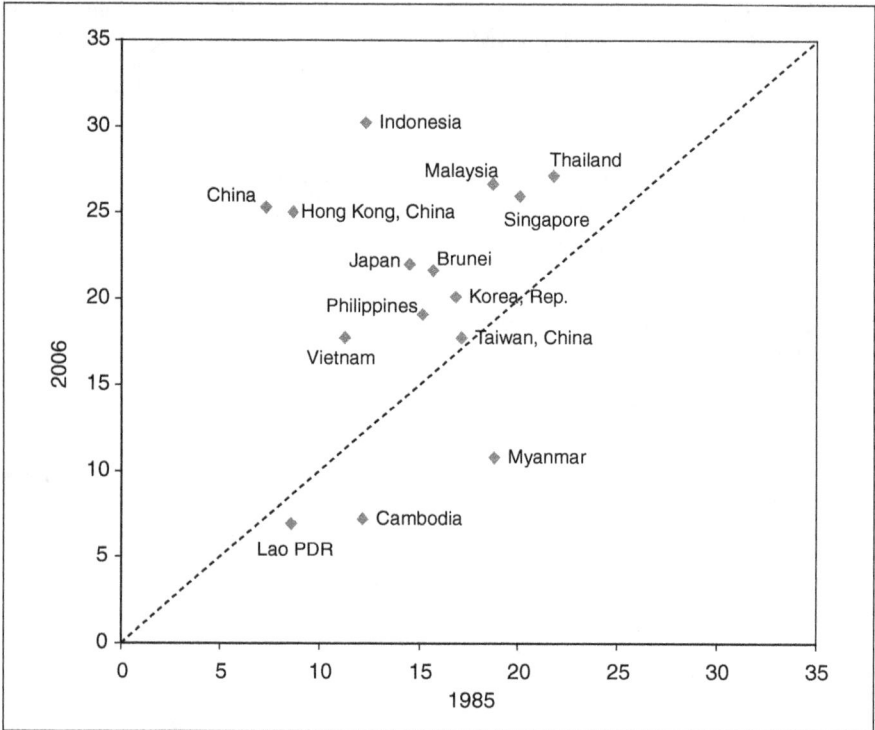

Notes: * Parts and components defined as 3, 4, and 5-digit products in the SITC Rev. 2
          classification.
       ** Trade in manufactured product excluding chemicals (SITC Rev. 2 categories 6, 7 and 8).
          All definitions based on Table 17.1 in Ng and Yeats (2003).
Source: UN Comtrade statistics.

Increasing Returns

There is also some tentative evidence that growth in exports from East
Asia has taken place in sectors that are subject to increasing returns to
scale (Figure 3.9), another feature consistent with the new thinking in
international trade theory, although other factors such as preferential
trade agreements in certain sectors might have played a role as well.

FIGURE 3.9
East Asian Exports Share in Sectors in Increasing
Returns to Scale and Constant Returns to Scale
(percentage change in export share, 1994–2004)

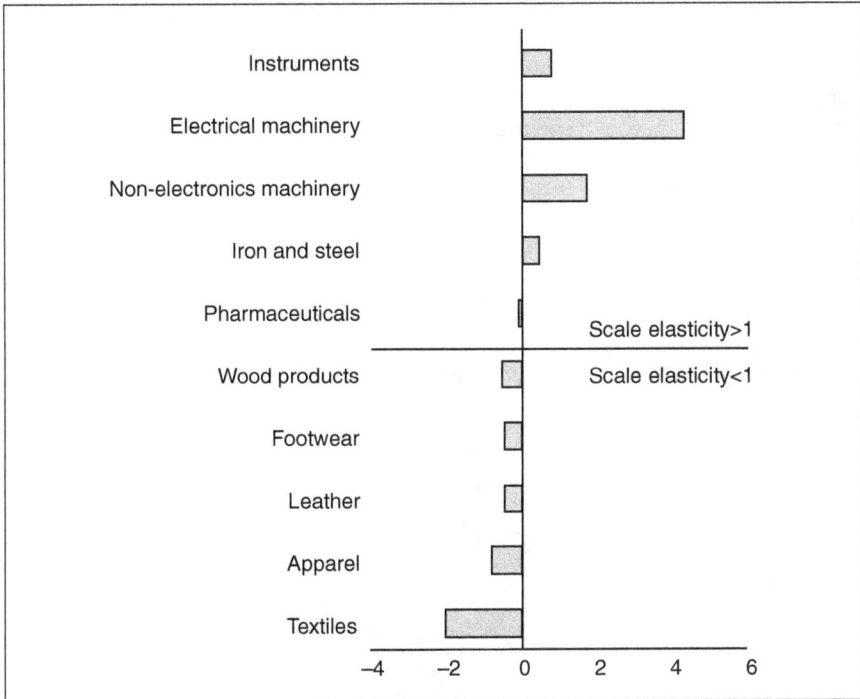

Source: Gill and Kharas (2007), based on Antweiler and Trefler (2002), and export data by the authors.

The increase in foreign direct investment across the East Asia region has been the vehicle that has driven intra-industry trade. The benefits of vertical integration in production chains were reinforced through economies of scale in production, with the allocation of production processes to countries according to their comparative advantage.[8] This process intensified after the East Asian crisis. Although there is considerable heterogeneity in intra-East Asian FDI flows across countries, the levels have been quite high (Table 3.2), with the most intensive FDI activity between China and Hong Kong (Figure 3.10).

TABLE 3.2
Regional FDI Patterns
(intraregional FDI as a share of total FDI, selected countries,
1985–2004, average share in per cent)

Country	Definition	1985–89	1990–94	1995–99	2000–04
China	Inward FDI flows	76.5	83.2	73.2	61.4
Indonesia	Inward FDI approvals	40.6	47.1	38.0	41.8
Korea	Inward FDI approvals	53.1	29.7	26.3	25.8
Malaysia	Inward FDI flows	—	48.5	28.4	28.6
The Philippines	Inward FDI registered	25.9	38.9	43.3	41.9
Thailand	Inward FDI flows	71.0	62.3	51.9	94.4

Note: — = no data are available.
Sources: Gill and Kharas (2007); based on China: National Bureau of Statistics (various); Indonesia: Investment Coordinating Board; Korea: UNCTAD (2000) (for data up to 1997), Ministry of Commerce, Industry and Energy (for data from 1998); Malaysia: BNM (various); the Philippines: Central Bank of the Philippines; Thailand: Bank of Thailand.

FIGURE 3.10
FDI Flows within East Asia

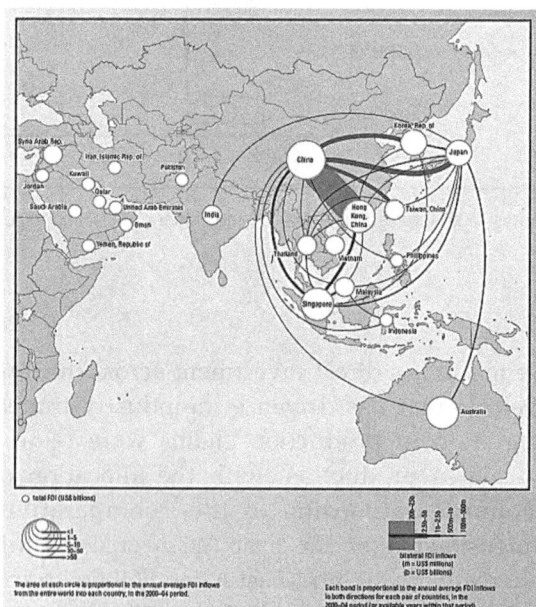

Source: Gill and Kharas (2007, p. 194).

For the ASEAN subgroup, most FDI still originates from outside ASEAN. Figures 3.11 and 3.12 show that although the EU-25 has been the largest single source of FDI into ASEAN countries, the combined share of Japan, ASEAN, Hong Kong, Korea, Taiwan, China, and China was 36.1 per cent of total inflows during 2004–06. Intra-ASEAN FDI flows are still limited at about 10 per cent of total flows, although Cambodia received 31.8 per cent of its FDI from ASEAN countries on average in 2004–06. Manufacturing, financial intermediation and services, and trade/commerce were the largest recipients of FDI in 1999-2006 (Figure 3.13), which suggests that a large share of FDI is meant to support the production networks.

FIGURE 3.11
Major Sources of ASEAN Foreign Direct Investment Inflows
(percentage of total inflows)

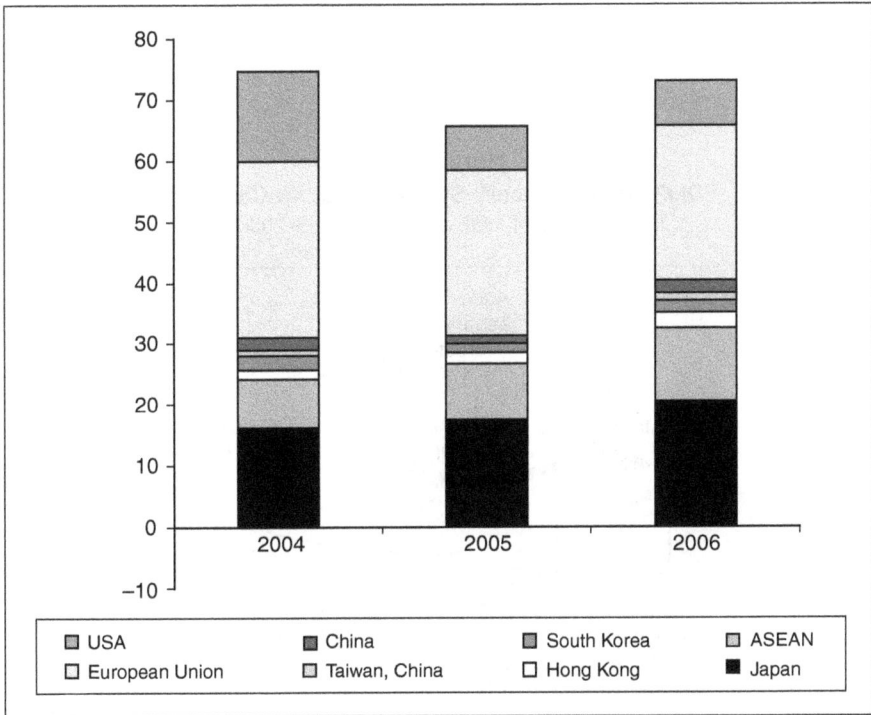

Source: ASEAN Foreign Direct Investment Statistics. At <http://www.aseansec.org/18144.htm>.

FIGURE 3.12
Intra-ASEAN FDI Net Inflows
(percentage of total net inflows, average 2004–06)

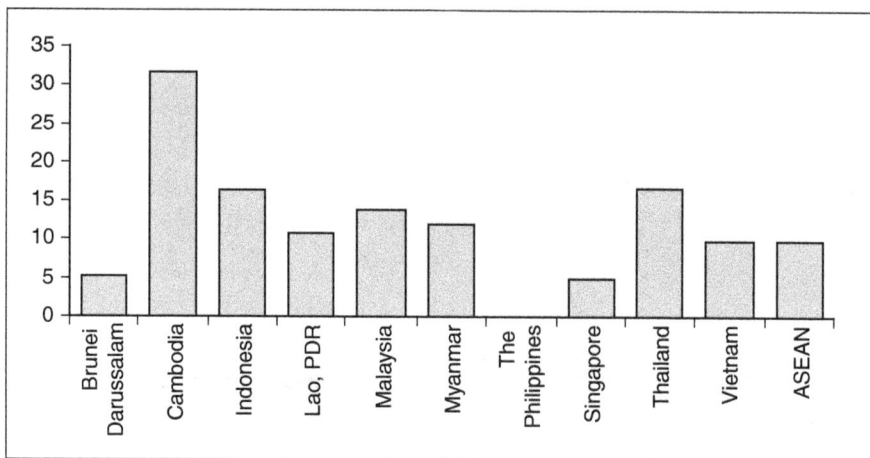

Source: ASEAN FDI Statistics at <http://www.aseansec.org/18144.htm>.

FIGURE 3.13
FDI Flows to Economic Sectors in ASEAN Countries
(percentage of total, average of 1999–2006)

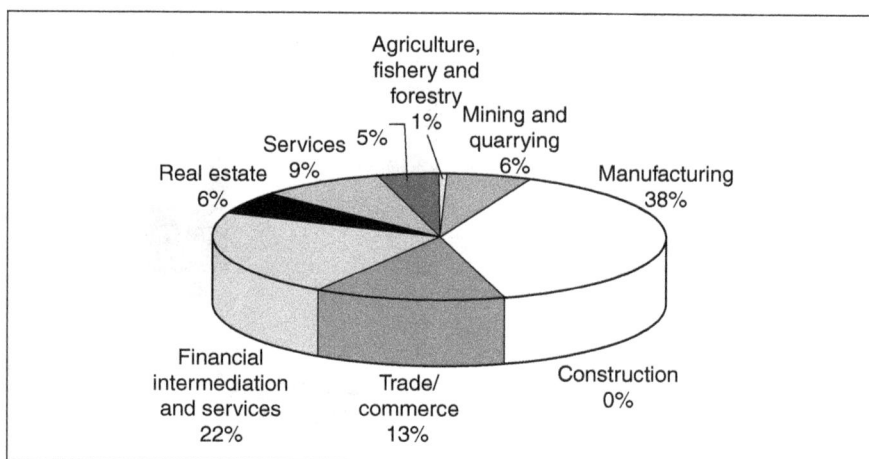

Source: ASEAN FDI Statistics, 2007.

II. REMAINING INTEGRATION AGENDA

Despite the role regional integration has played in generating growth and economic dynamism in the region, integration overall remains low and the region is not taking full advantage of the opportunities available for further trade and investment links. The greatest welfare gains are likely to come from addressing the deeper integration agenda, in particular, the benefits from liberalizing trade in services and overcoming behind-the-border barriers to trade — benefits that are likely to be many times those from reducing border barriers alone. And while it may be unfashionable to note this in the middle of the world's greatest financial crisis, there are benefits to be gained from financial integration as well, provided, of course that, such integration is properly monitored and subject to prudential rules and regulations.

Room for Further Regional Integration

East Asia has achieved a high degree of market-driven regional integration, but regionalism — more formal economic cooperation and economic integration arrangements and agreements between countries — has been limited. Exceptions have been the ASEAN Free Trade Area (AFTA), established in 1993, and dialogue under the Asia-Pacific Economic Cooperation (APEC). As regional integration progresses, it should in theory lead to convergence of incomes across the member countries. While this has indeed been the case in East Asia, the region remains far behind the level of integration that has been achieved in the European Union, where the incomes converged dramatically between 1960 and 1972 (Figure 3.14).

The Remaining Agenda in Trade Integration

A feature of regional agreements in East Asia is that they have extensive provisions to exclude "sensitive" sectors. This may be well justified in the case of certain sensitive goods, such as arms and ammunitions, goods of an artistic and historic nature, and the like. For others, however, such as unprocessed agricultural goods, such exclusions can reduce potential welfare gains from regional agreements. For example, Krumm and Kharas (2004) show that a free trade agreement of ASEAN with

FIGURE 3.14
Dispersion of Per Capita Income in Western Europe and East Asia
(coefficient of variation in per capita income, 1960–2006)

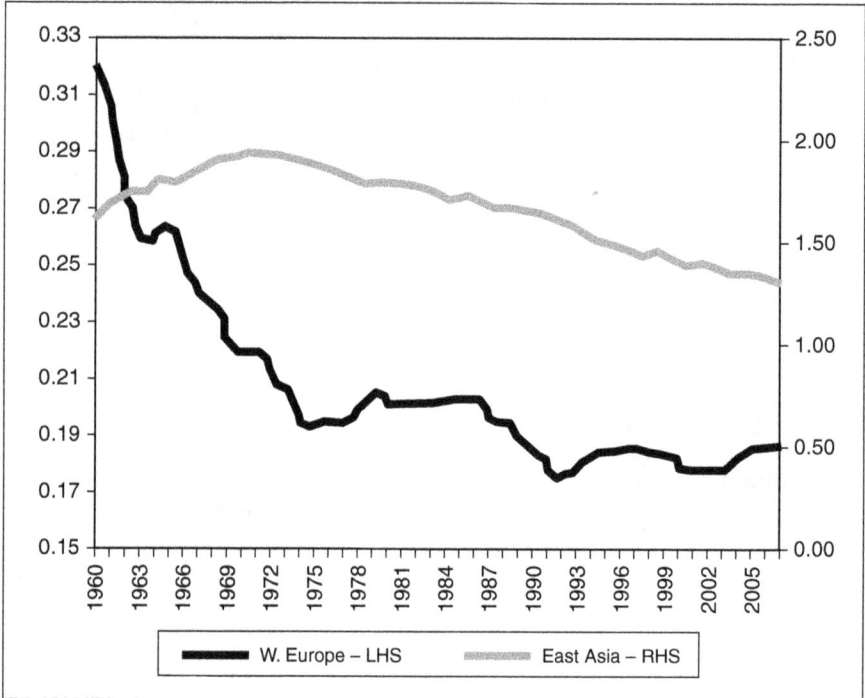

Source: The World Bank.

a combination of China, Japan, Korea, Australia, and New Zealand would double the gains from integration for ASEAN countries, if it liberalized agricultural trade (see Table 3.3, first column).

Furthermore, although tariffs have been significantly reduced in the last few years (Freudenberg and Paulmier 2006), compared with the European Union and NAFTA, there is still scope for further reductions, which is the ASEAN FTA's aim by 2010 (2015 for the newer ASEAN members). For example, for textiles and agricultural products, intra-ASEAN tariffs are 5.2 per cent and 6.6 per cent respectively, 0.05 per cent and 3.2 per cent for intra-NAFTA respectively, and zero for intra-EU tariffs.

TABLE 3.3
Net Effects on Economic Welfare of Various Regional Trade Proposals
(percentage of GDP; in parentheses: percentage of GDP excluding agricultural liberalization)

Proposal	ASEAN	China	Korea	Japan	USA
China+Korea+Japan	−0.26 (−0.16)	+0.1 (−0.2)	+1.0 (+0.6)	+0.1 (+0.2)	+0.0 (+0.0)
ASEAN–China	+0.9 (+0.5)	+0.0 (+0.1)	−0.1 (−0.1)	+0.0 (+0.0)	+0.0 (+0.0)
ASEAN–Japan	+1.1 (+0.2)	−0.1 (−0.1)	−0.2 (−0.1)	+0.0 (+0.1)	+0.0 (+0.0)
ASEAN+3	+1.5 (+0.6)	+0.1 (−0.2)	+1.1 (+0.8)	+0.2 (+0.2)	−0.1 (+0.0)
ASEAN+3+CER	+1.3 (+0.6)	+0.0 (−0.1)	+1.1 (+0.9)	+0.2 (+0.2)	−0.1 (+0.0)
APEC liberalization (MFN)	+0.7	+0.5	+0.7	+0.4	−0.0
APEC preferential liberalization	+0.8	+0.6	+0.9	+0.4	+0.0

Note: Calculations for ASEAN include only Indonesia, Malaysia, the Philippines, Singapore, Thailand, and Vietnam. CER (Australia-New Zealand Closer Economic Relations Trade Agreement) includes Australia and New Zealand.

Source: Krumm and Kharas (2004), Table 1, p. xxiv.

Remaining Trade Facilitation Issues

Efficient trade logistics — getting goods to markets fast — plays a key role in creating production and distribution networks that are at the heart of East Asia's economic prosperity. For some countries such as Lao PDR and Mongolia that are landlocked, effective regional logistics cooperation is crucial, and the benefits of efficient trade logistics go beyond trade. Lao PDR, in particular, has greatly benefited from regional initiatives such as the Greater Mekong Subregion (GMS) project, which enables the country to take advantage of its geographical location. The benefits of the GMS have gone beyond the development of transport corridors to include institutional and regulatory reform for trade facilitation, as well as addressing social issues (e.g. HIV/AIDS) that can be better addressed as a result of better infrastructure.

Trade Logistics Issues

Superior logistics and low transport costs have been an important part of East Asia's outward orientated growth. This is particularly so in the region's most impressive long-term performers – Singapore, Taiwan (China), Hong Kong (China), Japan, Korea — but also in a number of developing countries — Malaysia, Thailand, China, and the Philippines (see Figure 3.15). But continuous logistics improvements will be required to increase the prosperity that many East Asian countries have enjoyed from trade, and bring prosperity to more of East Asia's citizens. In a region where regional production networks require the goods to cross national boundaries several times before the final shipment reaches consumers, these cross-border transactions become all the more crucial in terms of efficiency and competitiveness.

Improved logistics reduces the difference between prices paid by consumers and received by producers. Imported goods become cheaper to inland consumers, raising real disposable income. A greater variety of goods become competitive, raising living standards through increased choice and greater specialization. Expanded input variety in manufacturing can raise productivity. Ex-factory or ex-farm prices increase, as do associated land values and wages. Exports of a wider range of products to a wider range of markets become possible.[9] Larger and larger areas of inland East Asia become connected to international

FIGURE 3.15

In the Most Open Economies of the Region, Logistics Costs Are Typically Much Lower

(trade openness and accessibility, East Asia)

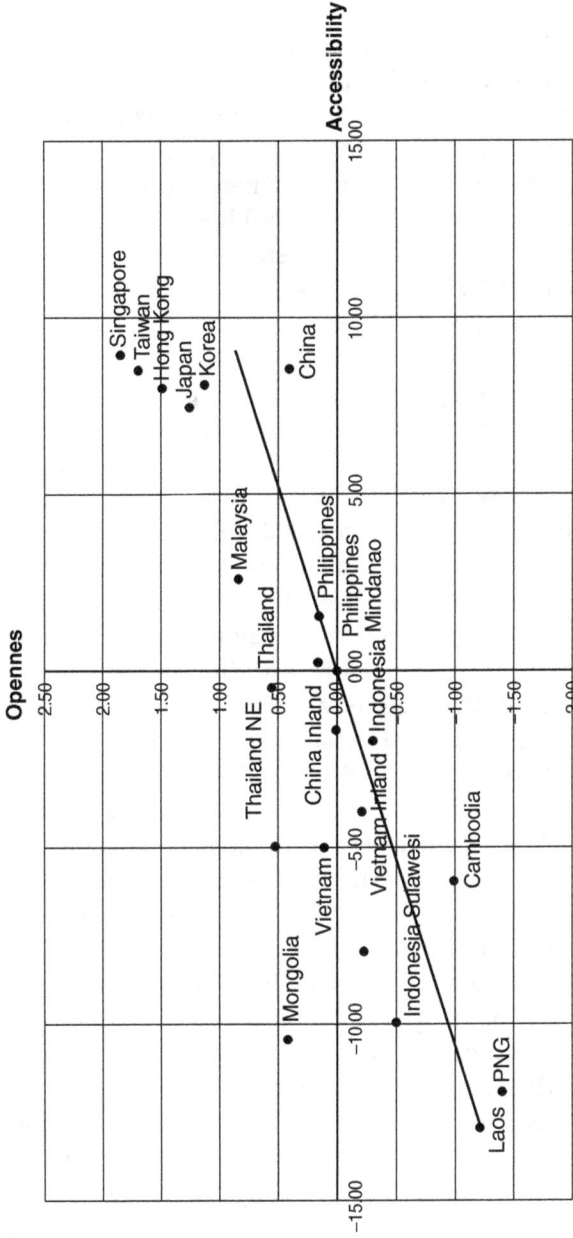

Note: The measures of trade openness are based on those indicated in the Global Competitiveness Report, 2001–02 (World Economic Forum 2002). Values for countries not included in the Global Competitiveness Report have been added using The World Bank assessment, in keeping with those of the World Economic Forum. All values have been normalized for the countries of East Asia. The measure of accessibility is based on the cost of transporting a standard TEU from the metropolitan region of the largest port to Hamburg. For inland regions, the land transport cost to the metropolitan region has been added.

Source: Carruthers et al. (2003).

markets and coastal domestic markets. Improved logistics is also a form of risk management that opens up new economic possibilities. Product diversification protects incomes against volatile prices for specific commodities. For agricultural commodities, efficient logistics allows surplus regions to sell to deficit regions, dampening price and income fluctuations. This is particularly important in countries such as Lao PDR, Cambodia, and Vietnam where agriculture constitutes a large share of GDP and rural poverty is high.

Recent research has shown that there remains a large agenda on logistics and cross-border trade in East Asia (ADB et al. 2005; Krumm and Kharas 2005). The speed with which the value of East Asia's exports has grown has outpaced the speed with which the logistics industry has developed in the region. Specifically, the costs of logistics in this region are about double the equivalent costs of logistics in more advanced countries. For example, in terms of averages for all products, logistics accounts for about 8 per cent of landed costs from East Asia — this compares with about 4 per cent in the developed world (Krumm and Kharas 2005). In places such as China, the costs of logistics are nearly prohibitive in areas distant from coastal areas. For example, 63 per cent of the cost of transporting goods from Chonqing to the west coast of the United States is incurred before arriving at the Chinese port of export (Figure 3.16) (Carruthers et al. 2003).

High logistics costs in East Asia stem from inadequate transport infrastructure, underdeveloped logistics and transport services, technical control regulations, and bureaucratic (and sometimes corrupt) import and export procedures. Much of the problem is "behind the border", and indeed beyond the port. The cost of internal access to ports is greater than the costs associated with the ports themselves or with maritime transport. This has limited the spread of the benefits of trade-induced growth to areas beyond those adjacent to ports, and has created congestion near the ports. More than 90 per cent of the FDI in export-oriented industries in China has gone to the four main coastal provinces. Similarly, the multiplier effect of the textile export boom in Cambodia has been limited mainly to areas easily accessible to the Sihanoukville port (ADB et al. 2005). With respect to port congestion, a study of Bangkok estimated that moving port-related activities away from the downtown area would result in a 10 per cent reduction in peak hour trips.

FIGURE 3.16
Exports to Los Angeles: Logistics Costs of Transport Containers
($/container)

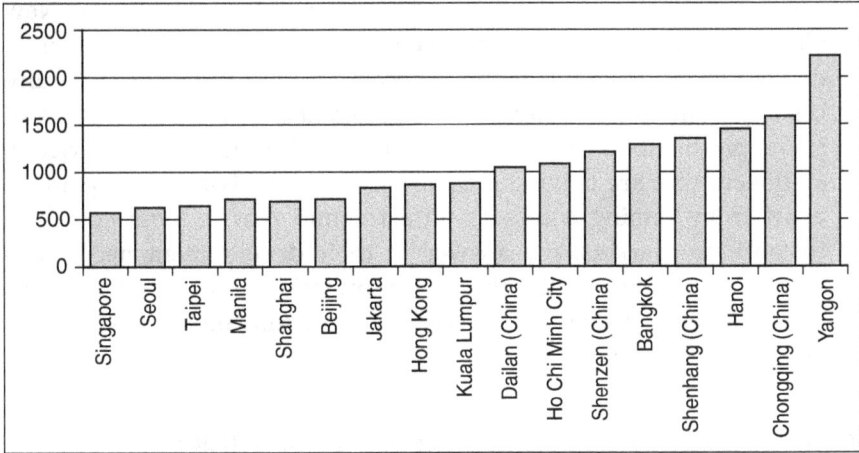

Note: Export rate is for a 40-foot container.
Source: ADB et al. (2005).

East Asian countries differ in their logistics capabilities, and therefore their logistics challenges. One logistics study attempts to classify them into four groups (Carruthers et al. 2003, Box 2.5):

(1) Outward oriented economies that are highly accessible, that is, have low transportation costs and superior logistics (Singapore, Hong Kong [China], South Korea, and Taiwan [China]). For these countries, the challenge is to build greater connectivity in knowledge-intensive activities as they try to gain comparative advantages with high knowledge barriers to entry.
(2) Countries that have open trade, but face serious logistics challenges (Thailand, the Philippines, Malaysia, China, Indonesia). Policies and institutions in this group of countries need to encourage multimodal transport and improve transport infrastructure in some parts of these countries, especially from areas of economic concentration and trade to the hinterland.
(3) Less open, but accessible countries (Lao PDR, Cambodia, and Vietnam), where infrastructure is the key constraint to regional

integration, but where location and trade policies are ideal for foreign direct investment and integration into regional production and value chains.

(4) The landlocked and island economies (e.g. Mongolia, Papua New Guinea, Timor Leste, and the Pacific island states) that are mainly commodity dependent exporters economically and geographically distant from markets, and cut off from the mainstream forces of trade, production networks, economic concentration, and knowledge spillovers that are driving growth in East Asia. For these countries, apart from gaining access to infrastructure that reduces economic distance to markets, the answer to their development needs also partly lies in connectivity through information and communications technologies that shrink their competitive disadvantage arising from location (see below).

Improving Transparency in Trade Policy and Trade Facilitation

Logistics is not the only improvement that can be made, improving transparency in trade policy and trade facilitation can also potentially yield significant intraregional gains in trade and welfare. The principle of transparency can influence the efficacy of a wide range of policies affecting border and "behind-the-border" procedures and rules. Transparency has two elements: predictability and simplification (Helble et al. 2007). Making trade policy more *predictable* reduces uncertainty, and therefore costs for business, and could include such measures as: (a) binding tariff rates through the WTO; (b) adopting "flatter" tariff structures; (c) making import and export delays less variable; (d) lowering uncertainty surrounding unofficial payments; and (e) reducing favouritism in administrative decision making. *Simplifying* trade policy makes it easier, and therefore less costly, for importers and exporters to identify, assess, and comply with regulation. Examples of simplification include: (1) streamlining documentary requirements for import/export transactions; (2) reducing the number of border agencies with which firms must interact; (3) removing "hidden" trade barriers; and (4) limiting unofficial payments.

A recent study (Helble et al. 2007) constructs data on the above indicators to produce summary measures of import and export transparency for APEC countries and assesses the increase in trade flows resulting from transparency reforms, using a standard gravity model. The analysis covers three scenarios involving policy reform to the regional average in relation to tariffs, non-tariff barriers, and transparency. The largest intraregional trade impact comes from transparency reform (see Figure 3.17), and amounts to 7.5 per cent of baseline 2004 trade.

Another recent study (Abe and Wilson 2008), using transparency indices for East Asian members of APEC, constructed through principle factor analysis on eleven variables,[10] concludes that overcoming transparency issues will significantly increase exports and welfare in East Asia. Specifically, the study uses gravity and CGE models, and estimates the impact on trade and welfare, based on enhancing transparency of trade to the average of APEC (Figure 3.18).

FIGURE 3.17
Transparency Reforms
(change in trade as percentage of 2004 baseline)

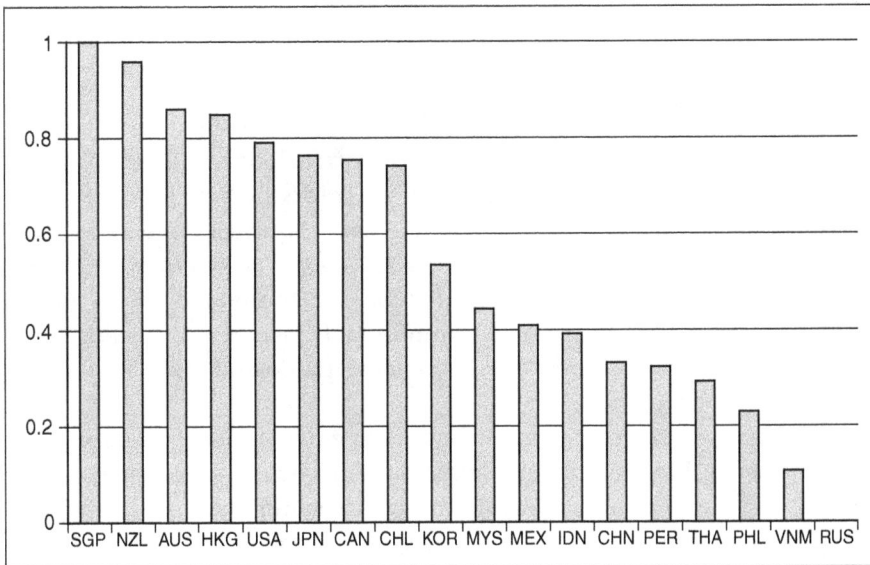

Source: Helble et al. (2007).

FIGURE 3.18
Impact on Welfare in APEC as a Result of Improvements in Transparency
(percentage change of real GDP)

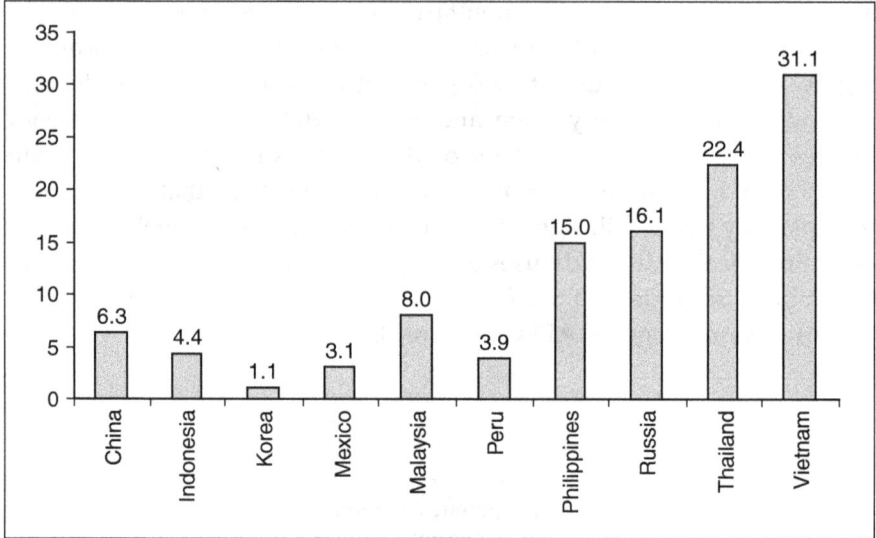

Source: Abe and Wilson (2008).

Services Trade Liberalization

A remarkable feature of the recent wave of regional trade agreements (RTAs) worldwide is the inclusion of trade in services in many agreements. Since the mid-1990s East Asian countries have negotiated twenty-five free trade agreements (FTAs) with a services component. There are important architectural differences in these agreements, which ultimately affect their value in promoting transparency, fostering the credibility of trade policies, and advancing market opening in services (Fink and Molinuevo 2008).

The rising interest in services trade agreements reflects a number of developments. First, as tariff barriers have declined, governments have turned their attention to other barriers restricting trade. In East Asia, the growth of intraregional trade in goods through the emergence of international production networks have highlighted the importance of an efficient services infrastructure — whether in telecommunications, finance, logistics, or legal advice. Second, just as in manufacturing, technological progress has vastly expanded the range of services that can be traded and has allowed final services to the client to be broken down into subtasks that can be completed around the world by firms that hold a comparative advantage. The outsourcing phenomenon has led to the emergence of new, dynamic export industries in services. Location has ceased to be a handicap and the economic distance between geographically distant countries has shrunk. Third, many governments have transferred the provision of infrastructure services to the private sector, expanding the scope for foreign participation in services. In fact, services FDI has grown faster than total FDI in recent years, as service providers from high and middle-income countries seek new commercial opportunities in foreign countries (Finks and Jansen 2007).

East Asia has lagged behind other regions in terms of its openness and efficiency in the services sector (Figure 3.19).[11] The current record also shows that East Asia has not kept pace with the required reforms and preconditions for services sector liberalization (Figure 3.20).

FIGURE 3.19
East Asia's Services Sector Can Be More Efficient

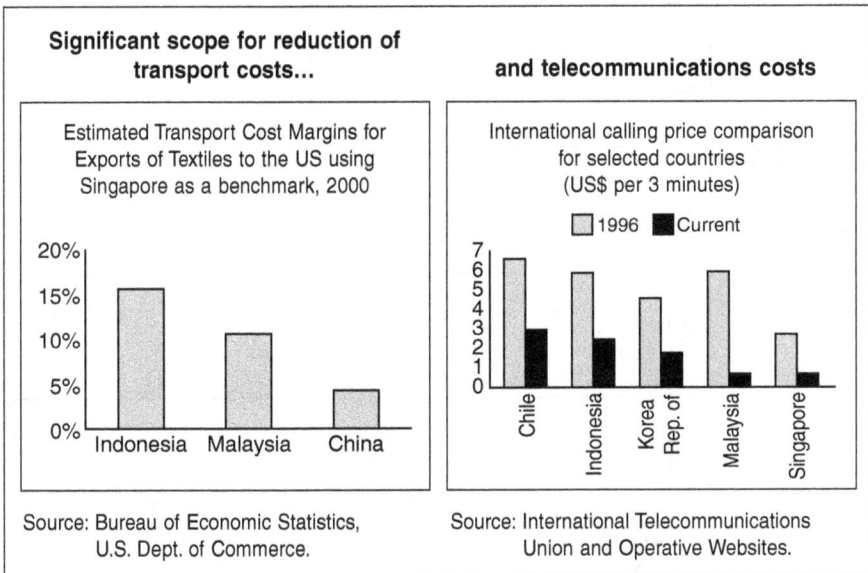

Significant scope for reduction of transport costs...

Estimated Transport Cost Margins for Exports of Textiles to the US using Singapore as a benchmark, 2000

Source: Bureau of Economic Statistics, U.S. Dept. of Commerce.

and telecommunications costs

International calling price comparison for selected countries (US$ per 3 minutes)

Source: International Telecommunications Union and Operative Websites.

FIGURE 3.20
Time-line of Reforms and Privatization in Selected Countries

Regulatory and competition reforms have not kept pace with privatization
Sequence of fixed-line telecom reforms in selected Asian countries

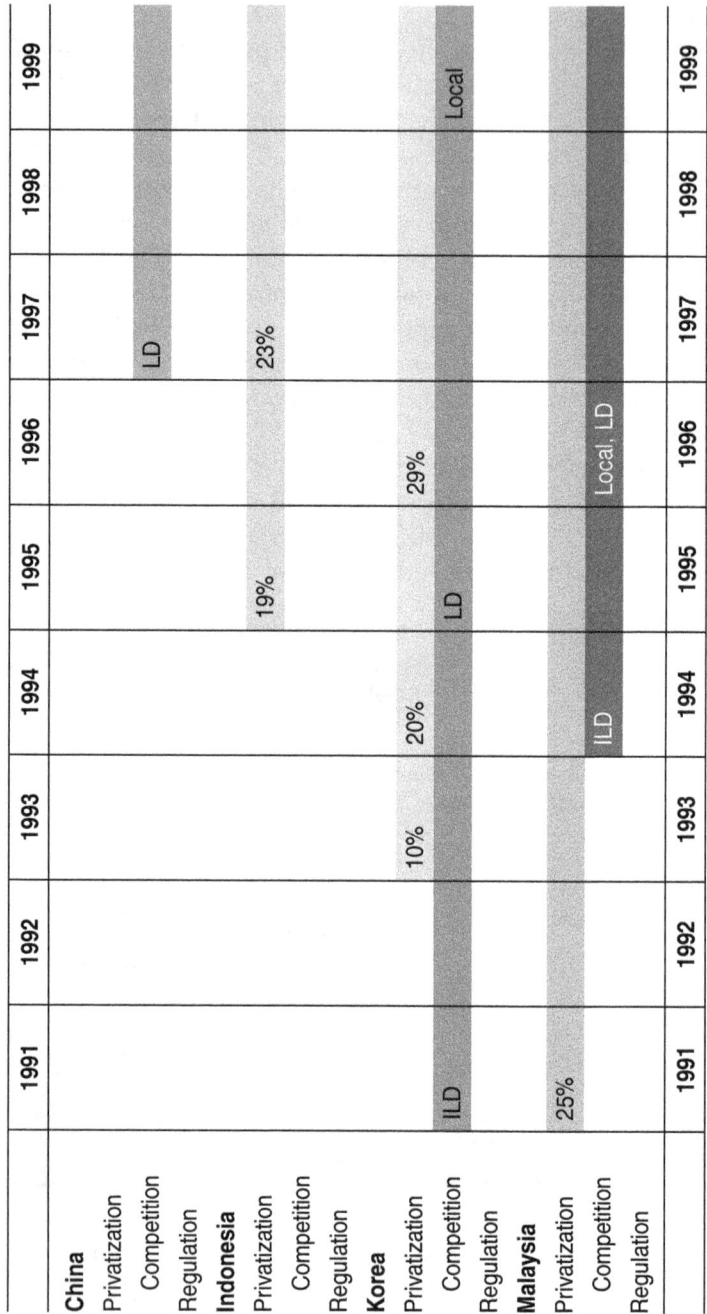

	1991	1992	1993	1994	1995	1996	1997	1998	1999
China									
Privatization							LD		
Competition									
Regulation									
Indonesia									
Privatization					19%		23%		
Competition									
Regulation									
Korea									
Privatization			10%	20%		29%			
Competition	ILD				LD				Local
Regulation									
Malaysia									
Privatization	25%								
Competition				ILD		Local, LD			
Regulation									

Source: Fink et al. (2002).

Liberalizing Services Trade Yields Large Benefits

The benefits from integrating trade in services and addressing technical barriers to trade are likely to be many times those from reducing border barriers.[12] For East Asia, recent estimates indicate that these benefits are large, a finding consistent with modelling results for other countries and regions. For example, static gains for developing East Asia and Korea from services liberalization throughout the developing world are estimated at about US$270 billion, or 10 per cent higher income, by 2015 (World Bank 2002). If there could be improvements in the efficiency of the services sector — and we think that the kinds of measures that are discussed in broader trade agreements could yield those kinds of efficiency improvements, then the gains not only occur within the services sectors, but also within other sectors because services are a key input into their production processes. As such, services trade liberalization is increasingly important for goods trade integration. As regional production networks become the basis for manufacturing strength and greater competitiveness, there's a realization that weaknesses in the services side can seriously undercut competitiveness more broadly.

Regional Integration Can Be a Stepping Stone for Services Trade Liberalization

Even though governments can initiate services sector reforms unilaterally, regional engagement can play an important catalytic role (Hoekman and Eschenbach 2005). Enlarging services markets through regional agreements can lead to gains arising from a combination of scale and competition effects. In a market of a given size, there is trade-off between scale economies and competition: when firms are larger, there are fewer firms and markets are less competitive. Enlarging the market makes it possible to have larger firms and more competition simultaneously (World Bank 2000). Regional agreements can also act to attract FDI. Specifically, if such agreements create large markets and do not impose stringent ownership-related rules of origin, they can attract FDI when economies of scale matter. In effect, regional trade agreements can be considered an attractive first step to global liberalization. They can be a form of gradual liberalization, exposing firms to competition first in the more sheltered confines of a regional market, and thereby preparing firms for global competition.[13]

Such liberalization, however, is not easy, as demonstrated by recent experience in ASEAN and there are a number of preconditions that need to be met, although these vary by sector.[14] Preferential treatment in services trade is granted not through tariff reductions, but by relaxing restrictions on the movement of labour and capital (e.g. share of foreign ownership) and a variety of domestic regulations (e.g. those related to technical standards, licensing, and qualification requirements). As such, regulatory convergence and the development of appropriate regulatory institutions can be important for effective services trade liberalization within East Asia. Challenges exist in introducing genuine competition, building the regulatory institutions that are needed to remedy market failures, appropriately sequencing services-sector reforms, and establishing mechanisms that promote the availability of essential services.

Financial Integration

Financial Integration

This is an aspect of services trade liberalization focused on the delivery of financial services. As is the case when goods trade is liberalized, larger markets, the possibility of economies of scale, and increased competition, not only serve to increase efficiency, but also deepen markets which, with proper government oversight, and regulation, can foster financial stability.

Cross-border Capital Flows

Before the Asian crisis cross-border capital flows consisted mainly of short-term trade finance and FDI from Japan, Europe, and the United States in the form of long-term financing for production networks. Since then, East Asian NIEs[15] have overtaken Japan in their share of total portfolio finance in the region and have become the largest portfolio equity investors in absolute terms in developing East Asia (Figure 3.21). In addition, an increasing share of FDI into ASEAN is originating from within the East Asian region.

FIGURE 3.21
Source of Portfolio Finance into NIEs[1] and Developing East Asia[2] (left)
and into Developing East Asia (right)

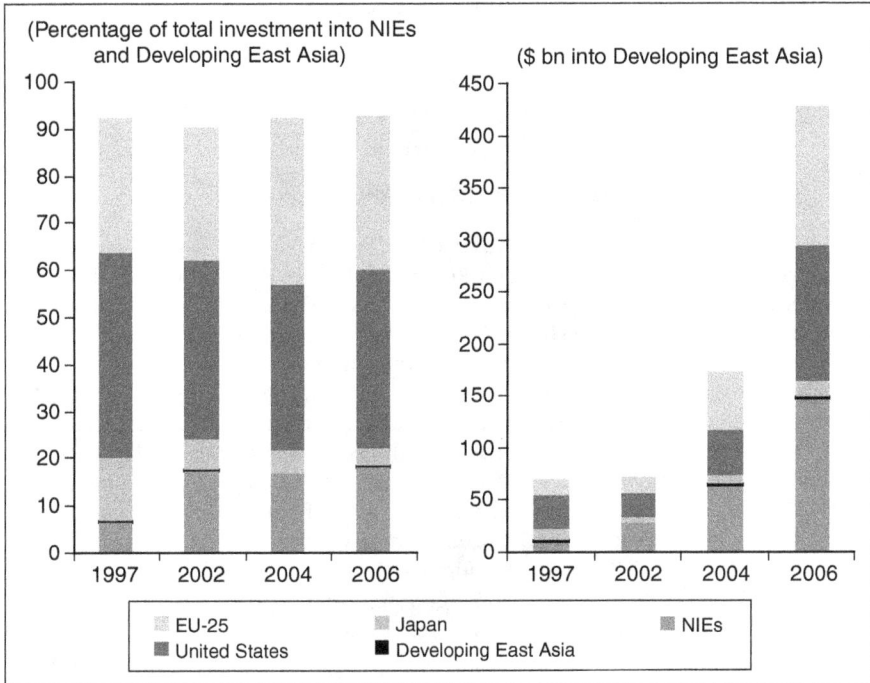

(Percentage of total investment into NIEs
and Developing East Asia)

($ bn into Developing East Asia)

EU-25 · Japan · NIEs
United States · Developing East Asia

Notes: (1) NIEs: Hong Kong, Korea, Singapore, and Taiwan, China.
       (2) Developing East Asia: Cambodia, China, Indonesia, Lao PDR, Malaysia, Myanmar,
           the Philippines, Thailand, and Vietnam.
Source: IMF Coordinated Investment Portfolio Survey.

The Asian Bond Market Initiative

This offers low-cost entry to foreign investors and identifies impediments
to bond market development in the East Asian (see Box 3.1). By any
measure, its total size of $3 billion is small relative to the total value
of East Asian local-currency bonds outstanding, which was $3.7 trillion
at the end of 2008 (ADB 2008*b*) and, at the same time, a substantial
amount of East Asian savings are still channelled into U.S. Treasuries.[16]
In order to facilitate cross-border investments within the region and
assist further financial market integration, remaining impediments

need to be addressed.[17] When asked how to improve market liquidity, a survey conducted by ADB (2008b) suggests that market players in Asia, Europe, and the United States worried most about the lack of diversity of investors, availability of hedging products, and intraday price transparency.[18]

BOX 3.1
The Asian Bond Market Initiative

The Asian Bond Market Initiative (ABMI) is a tentative start to offer low-cost entry to Asian bond market to foreign investors and to identify impediments to bond market development in East Asia. The ABMI was started in 2003 by the EMEAP (Executives' Meeting of East Asia-Pacific Central Banks) to create a local government bond market in order to mitigate some of the causes of the Asian crisis: high Asian savings were recycled by mainly G3 institutions and returned to Asian firms and banks as short-term FX loans and portfolio inflows, which proved volatile and caused both maturity and currency mismatches on the balance sheets.

The Asian Bond Fund 1 had an initial size of about US$1 billion, and was invested in a basket of US$-denominated Asian sovereign and quasi-sovereign bonds in EMEAP economies (China, Hong Kong, Indonesia, Korea, Malaysia, the Philippines, Singapore, Thailand), passively managed by the BIS according to a specific benchmark. In 2005 a second bond fund, ABF2, was launched, investing in local-currency bonds of the same issuers as ABF1. It consisted of two components, each of US$1 billion: a Pan-Asian Bond Index Fund (PAIF) and a Fund of Bond Funds (FoBF). The PAIF is a single bond fund and the FoBF is a parents fund investing in eight single-market funds. As the central banks' FX reserves are invested, the ABFs only invest in government and quasi-government bonds, as investment in corporate bonds would lead to moral hazard.

The purpose of the ABMI is to provide low-cost access to Asian bond funds and to learn from the experience and identify impediments to bond market development in the East Asian countries and to be a catalyst for regulatory reforms and improvements to market infrastructure.

Sources: Ghosh (2006), EMEAP (2006), EMEAP website at <http://www.emeap.org>.

But Financial Integration Remains Limited

Focusing on financial market outcomes rather than inputs, Fung et al. (2008) assessed the integration of East Asia's equity and bond markets using a variety of methods based on high-frequency data on equity and bond returns. Their findings suggest that generally both bond and equity market indicators in Asia are only weakly integrated. They attribute this to the lack of links between the financial infrastructure of countries in the region (such as payment, clearing, and settlement), absence of harmonized standards, and unnecessary restrictions on access of foreign financial intermediaries to domestic financial markets.

Entry of Foreign Banks

This can lead to substantial benefits to customers, although recent European experience in primarily Hungary and the Baltic states has shown that there are substantial risks if this is not well managed (see next section). They tend to bring best practices and increased competition and efficiency in the banking sector. This encourages better risk management, competitive pricing and, in the medium run, more efficient allocation of credit.[19] Although foreign banks tend to focus on large clients, they also force local banks to look for new niches and reach small clients that otherwise cannot gain access to credit.

The Chiang Mai Initiative

A further aspect of financial integration in East Asia is the Chiang Mai Initiative. Following the Asian Financial Crisis in 1998, the countries of East Asia expanded this insurance arrangement which is unique to East Asia. This ASEAN+3 framework for regional financial stability is designed to reduce the risk of sudden stops or capital flow reversals (see Box 3.2 and Figure 3. 22). The current financial crisis is a test of the framework, and it is indicative that so far it has not been used even as some members of the Chiang Mai Initiative (Singapore and Korea) have arranged swap arrangements with the U.S. Federal Reserve. Currently the amount of liquidity available to an individual country under either the ASEAN Swap Arrangement or the Bilateral Swap Arrangement is relatively small, given the severity of the current financial crisis. Although the total amount of bilateral swap arrangements under the Chiang Mai Initiative is around US$80 billion,[20] the maximum amount available for each country is still significantly less than their foreign exchange needs at this time — for example, Korea has access to US$23 billion, Thailand to US$9 billion and Indonesia to US$12 billion.[21]

BOX 3.2

The Existing Framework for Regional Financial Stability

In 1977 the five original ASEAN countries agreed to create the ASEAN Swap Arrangement (ASA), with an initial amount of US$200 million, which a member state with temporary international liquidity problems could draw from. A major drawback of the ASA was the "equal partnership" condition, specifying that when a member state requested a swap, all other countries would contribute equally. Moreover, each country has the right to refuse to provide the swap at its discretion. The swaps were not used at all during the Asian Crisis. In November 2000, the ASA was extended to the five new ASEAN members and the swap amount was augmented to US$1 billion (and the yen and euro became available besides the U.S. dollar) and to US$2 billion in 2005.

At a meeting in 2000 in Chiang Mai, Thailand, the ten ASEAN member states, the People's Republic of China, Japan, and the Republic of Korea agreed to develop a system of much larger bilateral swaps; typical swap values range between US$1–3 billion (and up to US$7 billion between Japan and Korea) and are mostly against the U.S. dollar (and yen in some cases). Besides the BSAs, the meeting agreed to exchange data on capital flows and to develop an early warning system as a safeguard against future crises. When a disbursement exceeds 10 per cent of the maximum amount of the swap, an agreement with the IMF is needed. At a 2005 meeting, they agreed to raise the bar to 20 per cent and a step towards a collective decision making process was taken. There was also agreement to institute a more comprehensive mandatory surveillance mechanism for all ASEAN+3 members.

At subsequent meetings the bilateral swap amounts were further raised to a total of about US$80 billion, the countries stated their intention to take steps towards making the CMI framework multilateral by clarifying the activation process and by devising a collective decision making mechanism, and to strengthen the Economic Review and Policy Dialogue. At the Asia-Europe summit (ASEM) on 24 and 25 October in Beijing, the ASEAN+3 countries recommitted to set up an $80 billion multilateral swap scheme by mid-2009, to pursue a regional surveillance agency, and to accelerate bond market development by boosting a regional bond settlement mechanism.

On 29 October 2008, in response to the ongoing difficulties in obtaining US$ funding, the US Federal Reserve established temporary swap lines of US$30 billion each with the central banks of Korea, Singapore, Brazil, and Mexico and, separately, the IMF announced the establishment of a Short-Term Liquidity Facility which can be quickly disbursed to countries with a good track record, facing temporary liquidity problems (see Figure 3.22).

Sources: Park and Wang (2005), Ghosh (2006), Kenen and Meade (2008), press releases by Japan's Ministry of Finance, the US Federal Reserve Board of Governors, and the IMF and Reuters news (2008).

FIGURE 3.22
East Asian Swap Arrangements

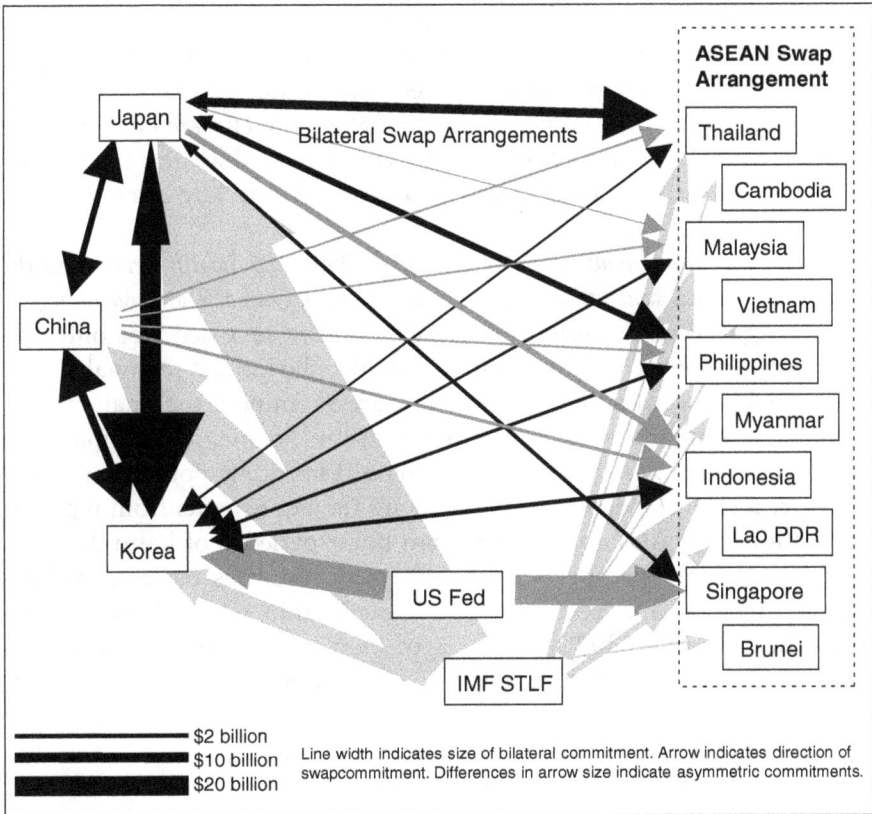

Source: Japan Ministry of Finance, IMF, press releases, The World Bank.

III. MANAGING RISKS

Regional Integration

While regional integration is shown to be a major source of growth, dynamism, and job creation in East Asia, it is also an important source of contagion risks. The current global financial crisis spread rapidly from its epicentre in the United States to the four corners of the world with unusual speed, highlighting the financial integration that binds countries and banking systems today. Financial instability is only one kind of contagion risk that countries face when integrating with the regional or global economy. Others are trade shocks, environmental disasters, and infectious diseases that can spread through cross-border labour mobility or inadequate phyto-sanitary standards in the trade of food. This section discusses some of the potential risks that could arise as a result of more open regional markets. These are associated with trade diversion, financial integration, premature service sector liberalization, climate change, food security, and social and health issues. The section does not treat all of these potential risks in detail but focuses on a few key ones.

The outbreak of financial crisis of the late 1990s and health crises shortly afterwards (SARS and avian flu) challenged the legitimacy and adequacy of existing regional arrangements. These crises have revealed not only the potential risks of regional integration, but also the limited regional efforts and capacity in dealing with them. They are a reminder that maintaining economic competitiveness and growth is by no means automatic or linear and reform efforts can be derailed. Managing potential risks is therefore a critical element of maximizing the net benefits from regional integration. East Asia could learn from the experience of Latin America which had bright prospects in the 1970s as countries entered middle-income status and were expected to benefit from regional integration. But many were derailed as a result of their responses to the financial crisis of the 1980s (Gill and Kharas 2007, chapter 1).

As the recent crisis has shown, East Asia's strong economic fundamentals and sound macro environment help inoculate it from the worst effects of external risks, but the region must nevertheless be prepared to adopt appropriate measures rapidly when shocks arise. Fiscal prudence, high savings rates, competitive exchange rates, good corporate governance, and labour market flexibility can help.

Trade and Investment Diversion Risks

Low External Tariffs

The risk of trade diversion can be mitigated if countries implement very low external tariffs to the rest of the world ("open regionalism" arrangements). East Asia has followed this approach and should not stray from these policies – especially as the current crisis intensifies. Beneficial competitive effects will be larger if low external tariff allows for a significant degree of import competition from firms outside the region. Otherwise, the dominant country within the regional arrangement can extract disproportionate benefits. Enlarging a subregional market also brings *direct foreign investment*, provided the incentive for foreign investors is not to engage in "tariff-jumping".

The Risk of Proliferating Regional Trade Agreements

Overlapping and Intraregional Bilateral Trade Agreements

A network of overlapping trade agreements with their own set of preferential access arrangements and conflicting rules of origin is very costly and difficult for exporters to comply with and could force an artificial distortion of trade.[22] One solution would be to establish a customs union with uniform external tariffs applied at the border of the union. However, this would require institutional deepening as tariff revenue needs to be collected at the external border and redistributed among the customs union countries according to some key.[23]

A network of intraregional bilateral trade agreements such as in East Asia with one or two countries at the centre might artificially tilt market access to firms in the centre, leaving firms in the outer countries at a disadvantage. These differences could become permanent, thanks to scale economies, better market access, and other agglomeration economies for firms in the centre.[24] Baldwin (2004) applies this scenario to East Asia and warns that trade relations will naturally tend to form a hub-and-spoke pattern with Japan and China as the two natural hubs and regional FTAs will reflect these patterns. He suggests that a better alternative would be a comprehensive regional free trade agreement adhering to WTO principles or a commitment that all free trade agreements between the centre and outer countries be followed by additional agreements between the outer countries.

Greater Output Volatility Associated with Trade Openness

Potential Downsides

Besides the beneficial effects of trade integration, there are also potential downsides. Ongoing research by Olaberria and Rigolini (2008) suggests that the increase in openness to trade in East Asia between the 1980s and 2001-05 has contributed not only to higher output growth, but also to higher volatility of output growth (see Figure 3.23). They argue that

FIGURE 3.23
Estimated Contribution to the Decrease in Volatility in EAP
(1980s vs 2001–05)

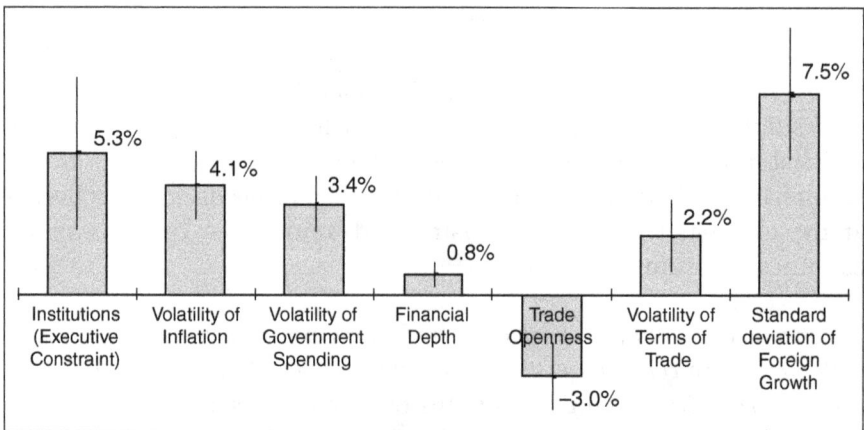

Source: Olaberria and Rigolini (2008); data from WDI, IMF, and Polity IV. For each variable, EAP is the median for countries with a population greater than one million.

the region's relatively high openness to trade encourages specialization along the lines of comparative advantage which exposes it to external shocks. Their research also shows that improvements in institutions (as measured by constraints on the executive), financial depth, and a decrease in the volatility of inflation and government spending have contributed to a decrease in the volatility of output growth, more than offsetting the negative effect of trade openness. This suggests that trade openness has a direct positive effect on East Asian countries, and the negative effect can be mitigated by improvements in institutions and domestic policies. A further simulation based on the same data suggests that additional convergence up to OECD standards (which implies a further improvement in institutions and policies) could lead to even lower output growth volatility.[25]

There are ways in which countries can benefit from greater trade openness while also dealing with the consequences of greater output growth volatility. Low exit and entry barriers, and flexible labour markets keep the price of adjustment low, while deeper product markets and broader product variety allow firms to adjust their product mix as shifts in demand occur.

Food Security

Most countries in East Asia are net importers of food staples including grains, seeds, dried beans, and rice. Policymakers in the region are understandably concerned with the whiplash effects which they have recently experienced from highly volatile global markets.[26] The unfortunate actions of some net food exporters to raise trade barriers and the consequent sharp rise in global food prices was a harsh reminder of the thinness of international food markets and the fragility of the global food chain. This has initiated a rethinking in East Asian countries of food security strategies in a bid to rely less on volatile international markets and maintain greater stability in domestic prices. The instruments to control the price and availability of food staples include trade tariffs and "buffer stocks". Many countries used these approaches in the past and discarded them as too costly, and the fact that these policies are being re-examined today spells a possible retreat from developing strong and deep international markets for food that encourage efficiency as well as reliable supplies. It is important, therefore, to look into other potential remedies which hold out the possibility of improving supply chain efficiency while improving global access to reliable food supplies. The answer lies in a multilateral trading system and global agreements to maintain open markets in net food exporting and net food importing nations.

Besides developing a global system that reduces food security risks, there are other risks related to food security that also need to be managed. Food staples have characteristics which significantly affect the efficiency with which they are moved and traded. The characteristics which provide a systematic basis for assessing the adequacy of regional public and private sector responses to increasing supply uncertainty include the following.

Low Value to Weight and Large Shipment Lot Size

These translate into high transport intensity and creating significant economies of scale and scope in the physical distribution elements of food chains. Transport costs can be significant (e.g. as much as 80 per cent of delivered price) when moving grains, seeds, beans, and rice from the point of production to where they are consumed. There is therefore a premium on the effective management of logistics activities along the chain in the region and, in part, through investment in high-capacity infrastructure along the chain. Adequate incentives for chain integrators are also important. Government policies that allow sufficient degrees of freedom for investment, or for competitive replacement of capacity constraints that force non economic lot size and other handling constraints along the chain, can become material in improving overall chain efficiency.

Degradable Quality

The quality of dried food staples deteriorates relatively fast over time, depending on the conditions under which staples are transported and stored. But preventive measures can be designed into the supply chains which carry them to market through interconnected process management of storage, transport facilities, and transfer processes along the chain.

Unstructured Trade

The efficiency with which food staples are transferred from seller to buyer is also affected directly by the nature of the trading systems through which food staples move. Unlike other commodities, trading in food commodities involve a large number of trading intermediaries, each of whom has established its own rules for procurement and its own set of trading relationships. This is particularly the case in East Asian markets. The net result is the so-called *"unstructured trade"* in which investments in the social capital required to minimize trading costs for all market participants fall well below the point where marginal social benefits exceed marginal social costs. The design and governance of regional trading systems can directly affect transaction costs for food staples because of the multiple buyers who typically participate in any specific point-to-point movement.

High Trading and Holding Risk

Holding stocks of food staples can be highly risky, not only because of price risk, quality risk, and timely supply risk in local markets, but also because of the leverage which most traders take up when they assume inventory positions. Buffer inventories of food staples have gradually eroded over the past five years. As a result global food commodity markets have become tighter and more susceptible to price fluctuations. Therefore an increased need exists to create institutions which can price these risks and buy them from market principals.

Risks Associated with Financial Integration

Financial Services

Although opening up to international portfolio investment has benefited firms looking for finance outside the domestic banking system, it has also exposed the bond and stock markets to contagion of financial crises. Since 1997 the region has witnessed a large inflow and outflow of portfolio equity and bond investments. Much of the increase can be attributed to the East Asian NIEs which have increased their bond and equity holdings in both NIEs and in developing East Asia.

The current financial crisis which has its roots in the United States and directly affected banks and financial institutions primarily in the United States and Europe, had an indirect effect on Asian markets, as foreign investors started to withdraw their funds. A sample of major international equity and bond funds suggests that most East Asian countries experienced accumulated net outflows over 2008 (Table 3.4).

TABLE 3.4
Year-to-date Cumulative Net Bond and Equity Fund Inflows by Major Fund Managers
($ million [negative is net outflow], between 1 January and 5 November 2008)

	Bond Funds	Equity Funds
China	−76.2	−1,457.9
Hong Kong	−78.3	−3,807.4
Indonesia	−681.4	−663.2
South Korea	−234.5	−5,983.8
Malaysia	−176.2	−1,314.9
The Philippines	−418.9	−203.8
Singapore	−73.6	−2,338.5
Taiwan	−1.6	−2,090.7
Thailand	−90.5	−843.2
Vietnam	−9.7	133.7

Source: EPFR, the World Bank.

In several East Asian middle-income countries, these sell-offs (by both domestic and foreign investors) led to large stock market declines, increases in interest rates, skyrocketing risk premia in international capital markets, and sharply depreciating exchange rates. While the responses of the authorities in East Asian countries have been swift and decisive and successfully protected the stability of the banking systems, the slowdown in global growth and the consequent slowdown in trade (global trade is projected to contract in 2009) is expected to test East Asian financial systems further.

The financial crisis underscored the risks associated with financial integration — be it regional or global. It highlights the simple point that even if risk management in financial systems is properly managed and regulated, countries can still be affected if other countries (especially those with large financial weight in the global financial system) are not as prudent or diligent in their regulatory oversight. This is forcing the world to re-examine what needs to be done on a global scale to mitigate some of the risks associated with financial integration and is reopening the issue of the international financial architecture.

IV. LOOKING AHEAD

The literature on regional integration has shown that it has been a key driver of growth and competitiveness in East Asia. At the same time, there is also considerable evidence that regional integration can be deepened substantially by addressing behind-the-border trade facilitation problems and the liberalization of the services sectors, including the financial sector, and easier cross-border labour mobility. But recent events have thrown into question parts of the conceptual framework that have underpinned the belief that greater openness can be an unalloyed force for the good. These events must force the economic policy community to reopen the issue of risks associated with greater openness and trigger a frank debate on what these events mean for policies encouraging integration in the future. Rather than spell a retreat for integration policies in the future, however, these events should focus the minds of academics, policymakers, and government officials on how best to manage the risks associated with greater integration while maximizing the benefits.

There is little doubt that East Asia's greater regional integration in merchandise trade has led to enormous efficiency gains, growth opportunities, technological advancement, and international competitiveness. And yes, there still remains a large agenda ahead — on policy transparency, trade facilitation, infrastructure alignment, and harmonization. At the same time, it must be recognized that when tested by trade frictions, these trading arrangements are less robust than may appear at first glance — largely because they are not underpinned by risk management policies. Nowhere was this truer than in the series of events that led to the sudden increase in the price of food, especially rice. Food exporting countries outside and inside the region adopted policies that sharply exacerbated world food prices, and forced food importing countries to re-examine their food security options — many of which include a lesser reliance on regional and world trade. The challenge to the world is to make the global food trading system more reliable and less volatile, so that net-exporting and net-importing countries do not retreat into food-autarky, but remain engaged with the world economy and, in doing so, reap the advantages of improved efficiency, technology, and competitiveness.

An equally important challenge confronts the world when it comes to the liberalization of financial services and the integration of financial systems. The recent crisis has reopened the debate on open capital accounts, the advisability of securitization, and the wisdom of mark-to-market accounting. Again, it would be unfortunate if there were a retreat from such policies — especially as they have brought enormous global gains in the efficiency of resource mobilization and allocation. At the same time, there will need to be considerable discussion and thought on when such policies are appropriate and when they are not, how such policies should be accompanied by regulatory and other policies to make them less susceptible to exogenous risks, and how and when they should be introduced. There has been an unfortunate tendency in the past to adopt such policies uncritically on the grounds that such policies are followed in the advanced countries where institutions are stronger and markets deeper.

There are two important services sector issues that are not dealt with, but should nevertheless be mentioned as important areas for further work. The first is the speed with which services industries are being integrated regionally and globally through the power of the Internet. This is yet another example of technology overtaking the ability of governments to understand and manage the risks such innovations can bring. Similarly, the chapter does not deal with the complex issue of cross-border labour mobility, which is the least advanced aspect of regional economic integration in East Asia. This is often a sensitive area for many governments — for obvious reasons. The countries of the region are dealing with cross-border labour movements in a fragmented way, either to increase national competitiveness by encouraging the entry of highly skilled workers, or by liberalizing guest worker programmes for low-skilled and services industry occupations. But there are many examples of innovative approaches being adopted in different parts of the world to deal with the question of cross-border mobility more comprehensively, harness the benefits associated with labour movement, while managing the associated social and political risks, and East Asia can adopt or adapt such models and progress towards establishing an integrated regional labour market.

Finally it is useful to consider how the current financial crisis may influence the pace of regional economic integration in East Asia. The experience of the European Union shows that free trade arrangements flourish during good times, but come under considerable stress during times of crisis. East Asia needs to guard against this as financial crisis unfolds and global growth slows; regional institutions, such as ASEAN+3, can play a useful role in ensuring that commitments to free trade are reaffirmed and that countries avoid using beggar-thy-neighbour policies to further their own ends at the expense of their neighbors. Indeed, this may be the best time to advance the agenda of regional integration, especially as East Asia will remain an important pole of growth in the world economy and strengthening intraregional links is likely to increase the region's resilience. But it will have to be done with a series of confidence building measures that are mutually supportive of the countries of the region that are all at very different stages of development and have diverse economic interests. There is no blueprint for such an approach, but here the past can be a useful guide to the future. As East Asia has done so successfully over the last thirty years, it can in the coming years continue to strengthen the neighbourhood one policy at a time.

Notes

1. This chapter was written specifically for the IDE-JETRO conference on regional integration in East Asia. The authors are grateful to Yang Dong for research assistance. Excellent comments by Deepak Bhattasali, Aadytia Mattoo, John S. Wilson, and James Seward are also gratefully acknowledged. The views expressed in this chapter are those of the authors and do not necessarily represent those of The World Bank, its senior management, or its executive directors.
2. The latter is the subject of Section III.
3. See Viner (1950), World Bank (2000), Schiff and Winters (2003), and Teunissen (1996).
4. East Asia in this chapter refers to the member countries of ASEAN, as well as China, Japan, and Korea, the so-called ASEAN+3, unless otherwise specified.

5. These East Asian production networks started to develop rapidly after the 1985 Plaza Accord when the yen appreciated sharply against the dollar and European currencies, and Japanese firms started to relocate abroad (Gil and Kharas 2007).

6. The intra-industry trade (IIT) index for country in a particular year is defined as:

$$IIT = 1 - \frac{\sum_j \left| \sum_i X_i - M_{ij} \right|}{\sum_j \left| \sum_i X_i + M_{ij} \right|}$$

where X_{ij} is exports of industry j to country i and similarly for imports M_{ij}. Industries are defined at the 3-digit level of the SITC Revision 2 classification system for manufactured goods (categories 5, 6, 7, and 8, excluding non-ferrous metals). An index of 0 means no IIT and 1 means full IIT. See also Ng and Yeats (2003).

7. Ando and Kimura (2003) provide more details of the drivers of IIT and production networks.

8. Some economies such as Japan, South Korea, and Taiwan have used FDI as alternative to labour mobility. The main destination of their FDI is China to take advantage of low labour costs (Figure 3.10).

9. Evenett and Venables (2001) show that 40 per cent of trade growth in East Asia comes from offering new products and finding new trade partners.

10. Factor analysis is a statistical technique to produce an index summarizing performance across a number of correlated indicators. The indicators used by Abe and Wilson (2008) include three variables on predictability of customs administration (time spread for import, standard deviation of irregular payments, and favouritism), four variables of predictability and the simplification of trade policy (percentage of bound tariff lines, tariff dispersion, hidden barriers, and e-readiness), and four variables on simplification of customs administration (clearance time of imports, number of agencies involved in import clearance, number of documents required for import, and irregular payment).

11. See also Mattoo et al. (2001).

12. See Hoekman and Konan (1999) for the European Union and Egypt, and Brenton and Manchin (2002) for the European Union and Russia.

13. See Mattoo et al. (2007).

14. Annex 1 in Mattoo et al. (2007).

15. Newly Industrialized Economies: Singapore, Hong Kong, Taiwan, and Korea.

16. The combined holding of U.S. Treasuries by the governments of China, Japan, Hong Kong, Taiwan, Korea, Singapore, and Thailand (which are

among the thirty largest holders of U.S. Treasuries) amounted to $1.4 tn as of September 2008. See U.S. Treasury website at <http://www.ustreas.gov/tic/mfh.txt>.

17. See Ghosh (2006, chapter 2) for a general overview of the situation up to 2006, and Takeuchi (2005) for specific issues such as taxation in the region up to 2005.

18. The survey was conducted in August and September 2008 just before the collapse of Lehman Brothers.

19. See Box 4.6 of Ghosh (2006) for empirical evidence in emerging markets.

20. As of May 2007, see the Japanese Ministry of Finance website at <http://www.mof.go.jp/english/if/as3_070505.htm>.

21. In contrast, their foreign exchange reserves are: Thailand $100 bn (end of September 2008), Korea $212 bn, Indonesia $51 bn (end of October). Source: Haver Analytics.

22. "Rules of origin" specify how customs officials can determine from which country a product originates and which tariff to apply. Under any preferential trade agreement, the absence of such rules would provide an incentive for importers in a country with high external tariffs to import via a low-tariff country and then to re-export to its own country duty-free (Baldwin 1994).

23. See, for example, Baldwin (2006).

24. Baldwin (2004) refers to this as hub-and-spoke bilateral regionalism, where the countries at the centre of the bilateral agreements form the hub, and other countries the spokes, and applies it specifically to the case of East Asia.

25. It is important to note that although the "median" OECD country is characterized by better institutions, lower volatility of inflation and government spending, and more financial depth, it is also less open to trade than a "median" East Asian country, which is unusually open to trade.

26. For example, the negative effects of disruptions in supply from rice exporting countries such as Vietnam and India.

References

Abe, Kazutomo, and John S. Wilson. "Governance, Corruption, and Trade in the Asia Pacific Region". Policy Research Working Paper, No. 4731, The World Bank, September 2008.

ADB. *Asian Development Outlook 2006*. Manila: Asian Development Bank, 2006.

———. *Emerging Asian Regionalism: A Partnership for Shared Prosperity*. Manila: Asian Development Bank, 2008a.

————. *Asia Bond Monitor 2008*. Manila: Asian Development Bank, November 2008*b*.

ADB Institute and IOM. *Managing Regional Public Goods: Cross-border Trade and Investment, Labor Migration, and Public Health*. Tokyo: Asian Development Bank Institute, 2005.

ADB, JBIC, and World Bank. *Connecting East Asia: A New Framework for Infrastructure*. Manila: Asian Development Bank, Japan Bank for International Cooperation, and The World Bank, 2005.

Ando, Mitsuyo, and Fukinari Kimura. "The Formation of International Production and Distribution Networks in East Asia". *NBER* Working Paper, No. 10167, National Bureau of Economic Research, 2003.

Antweiler, Werner, and Daniel Trefler. "Increasing Returns and All That: A View from Trade". *American Economic Review*, Vol. 92, No. 1 (March 2002): 93–119.

ASEAN. ASEAN website at <http://www.aseansec.org/64.htm>. 2008.

APEC. APEC website at <http://www.apec.org/apec/about_apec/achievements_ and_benefits.html#top>. 2008.

Baldwin, Richard E. "Towards an Integrated Europe". Centre for Economic Policy Research, 1994. At <http://hei.unige.ch/~baldwin/PapersBooks/ pets/tie.html>.

————. "The Spoke Trap: Hub-and-spoke Bilateralism in East Asia". *CNAEC Research Series 04-02*. Korea Institute for International Economic Policy, December 2004.

————. "Multilateralising Regionalism: Spaghetti Bowls as Building Blocs on the Path to Global Free Trade". *The World Economy*, Vol. 29, No. 11 (November 2006): 1451–518.

Brenton, Paul, and Miriam Manchin. "Making EU Trade Agreements Work: The Role of Rules of Origin". *The World Economy*, Vol. 26, No. 5 (May 2003): 755–69.

Carruthers, Robin, Jitendra N. Bajpai and David Hummels. "Trade and Logistics in East Asia: A Development Agenda". *EASTR* Working Paper, No. 3. The World Bank, June 2003.

De Brouwer, Gordon. "Institutions to Promote Financial Stability: Reflections on East Asia and an Asian Monetary Fund". *Treasury* Working Paper *2004–02*, Department of Treasury, Australia, September 2004.

EMEAP. *Review of the Asian Bond Fund 2 Initiative*. Executives' Meeting of East Asia-Pacific Central Banks, Working Group on Financial Markets, June 2006.

Fink, Carsten, and Martín Molinuevo. "East Asian Free Trade Agreements in Services: Key Architectural Elements". *Journal of International Economic Law*, Vol. 11, No. 2 (February 2008): 263–311.

Fink, Carsten, and Marion Jansen. "Services Provisions in Regional Trade Agreements: Stumbling or Building Blocks for Multilateral Liberalization?". Paper presented at the Conference on Multilateralising Regionalism. Centre for Economic Policy Research, Geneva, September 2007.

Frost, Frank, and Ann Rann. "The East Asia Summit, Cebu, 2007: Issues and Prospects". E-Brief, Parliament Library, Parliament of Australia, December 2006. At <http://www.aph.gov.au/library/INTGUIDE/FAD/eastasia_summit2007.htm>.

Freudenberg, Michael, and Thierry Paulmier. "A Comparison of De Jure Economic Integration in East Asia: Is East Asia Discriminating against Itself?". In *East Asia's De Facto Economic Integration*, edited by Daisuke Hiratsuka. Basingstoke: Palgrave Macmillan, 2006.

Fung, Laurence Kang-por, Chin-sang Tam and Ip-wing Yu. "Assessing the Integration of Asia's Equity and Bond Markets". Proceedings of the first workshop of the Asian Research Network for Financial Markets and Institutions on Regional Financial Integration in Asia: Present and Future. Bank of International Settlements and Hong Kong Institute for Monetary Research, Hong Kong, 21 January 2008 (also available as *BIS Paper*, No. 42, Bank for International Settlements, October 2008).

Ghosh, Swati R. *East Asian Finance: The Road to Robust Markets*. Washington D.C.: The World Bank, 2006.

Gill, Indermit, and Homi Kharas. *An East Asian Renaissance: Ideas for Economic Growth*. Wachington D.C.: The World Bank, 2007.

Helble, Matthias, Ben Shepherd and John S. Wilson. "Transparency, Trade Costs, and Regional Integration in the Asia Pacific". Policy Research Working Paper, No. 4401. The World Bank, November 2007.

Hew, Denis, and Hadi Soesastro. "Realising the ASEAN Economic Community by 2020: ISEAS and ASEAN-ISIS Approaches". *ASEAN Economic Bulletin*, Vol. 20, No. 3 (December 2003): 292–96.

Hoekman, Bernard, and Felix Eschenbach. "Services Policy Reform and Economic Growth in Transition Economies, 1990–2004". Presentation for World Bank Institute, The World Bank, 2005.

Hoekman, Bernard, and Denise Eby Konan. "Deep Integration, Nondiscrimination, and Euro-Mediterranean Free Trade". Policy Research Working Paper, No. 2130. The World Bank, May 1999.

Kaplan, Ethan, and Dani Rodrik. "Did the Malaysian Capital Controls Work?". *NBER* Working Paper, No 8142. February 2001 (also published as a chapter in *Preventing Currency Crises in Emerging Markets*, edited by Sebastian Edwards and Jeffrey Frankel. Chicago: University of Chicago Press for the NBER, 2002).

Kawai, M. and G. Wignaraja. "ASEAN+3 or ASEAN+6: Which Way Forward?". *ADB Institute* Discussion Paper, No. 77, 2007.

Kenen, Peter B. and Ellen E. Meade. *Regional Monetary Integration*. Cambridge: Cambridge University Press, 2008.

Krumm, Kathie, and Homi Kharas (eds.). *East Asia Integrates: A Trade Policy Agenda for Shared Growth*. Washington D.C.: The World Bank, 2003.

Krugman, Paul R. "Increasing Returns, Monopolistic Competition, and International Trade". *Journal of International Economics*, Vol. 9, No. 4 (November 1979): 469–79.

———. "Increasing Returns and Economic Geography". *Journal of Political Economy*, Vol. 99, No. 3 (June 1991): 483–99.

Mattoo, Aaditya, Randeep Rathindran, and Arvind Subramanian. "Measuring Services Trade Liberalization and Its Impact on Economic Growth: An Illustration". Policy Research Working Paper Series, No. 2655. The World Bank, 2001.

Mattoo, Aaditya, Robert M. Stern, and Gianni Zanini (eds.). *A Handbook of International Trade in Services*. Oxford: Oxford University Press, 2007.

Ng, Francis, and Alexander Yeats. "Major Trade Trends in East Asia: What Are Their Implications for Regional Cooperation and Growth?". Policy Research Working Paper, No. 3084. The World Bank, June 2003.

Olaberria, Eduardo, and Jamele Rigolini. "Macroeconomic Volatility in East Asia: What Do We Know, and What Can Be Done?". University of Maryland and the World Bank, draft mimeo, 2008.

Park, Innwon. "Regional Trade Agreements in East Asia: Will They Be Sustainable?". *Munich Personal RePEc Archive*, February 2008.

Park, Yung Chul, and Yunjong Wang. "The Chiang Mai Initiative and Beyond". *The World Economy*, Vol. 28, No. 1 (January 2005): 91–101.

Polachek, SW. "Conflict and Trade: An Economics Approach to Political Interactions". In *Economics of Arms Reduction and the Peace Process*, edited by W. Isard and C.H. Anderton. Amsterdam: North-Holland, 1992.

Schiff, M. and L. A. Winters. *Regional Integration and Development*. Washington D.C.: The World Bank, 2003.

Takeuchi, Atsushi. "Study of Impediments to Cross-border Bond Investment and Issuance in Asian Countries". Paper prepared for discussion at the working group under the ASEAN+3 Asian Bond Fund Initiative, December 2005.

Teunissen, J.J. *Regionalism and the Global Economy, The Case of Africa*. The Hague: FONDAD, 1997.

UNCTAD. *Trade in Services and Development Implications*. United Nations Conference of Trade and Development, 2006.

Viner, J. *The Customs Union Issue*. New York: Carnegie Endowment for International Peace, 1950.

World Bank (The). *Trade Blocs: A World Bank Policy Research Report*. New York: Oxford University Press, 2000.

———. *Global Economic Prospects*. Washington D.C.: The World Bank, 2002.

———. "Winners without Borders: Integrating Poor Countries with World Markets". In *World Development Report*. Washington D.C.: The World Bank, 2009.

PART II

States, Markets and
the Movement of People

4

Economic Integration in East Asia and Japan's Strategy

Isamu Wakamatsu

I. INTRODUCTION

Triggered by the bankruptcy of the investment banking giant Lehman Brothers, the financial crisis that originated in the United States instantly spreaded across the global economy. There was a string of bailouts of troubled financial institutions not only in the United States, but also in Europe, and the global recession deepened at a pace not seen since World War II, as symbolized by the simultaneous decline of world stock markets and the struggling Big Three. There were signs of a slowdown in the real economy of East Asia as well. However, the impact of the crisis was slighter in this region than among Western countries, so expectations for East Asia to drive the growth of the global economy grew ever more.

In this chapter, I provide an overview of the current situation of East Asia, the world's growth centre, where economic integration is *under way*, and present an analysis of the impact of FTAs — which are being rapidly put into effect in recent years — on trade within the East Asia region. I then consider the challenges Japan should take on to promote the integration of the East Asian economy further and ensure sustainable growth.

II. THE GROWING ASIAN MARKET AND ONGOING ECONOMIC INTEGRATION

Asia, the World's Growth Centre

The East Asian economy (Asian NIEs, ASEAN, and China) has been growing at a rate of around 8 to 9 per cent for the past few years. This is almost double the world's average growth rate, which explains why the region is called the "world's growth centre". The contribution ratio of the East Asian economy (including India) to the world economy reached 40.3 per cent in 2007 (see Table 4.1).

In addition, Australia and New Zealand have been strengthening their economic relationships with East Asia in recent years. Adding Japan, India, Australia, and New Zealand to East Asia results in a huge business block with a population of about 3.2 billion and a total GDP of US$10 trillion.

Affected by the financial crisis in the United States, the East Asian economy faced the inevitable slowdown in 2009. But although the IMF forecasted that developed countries as a whole were going to slip into negative growth for the first time since World War II, Developing Asia (China, India and ASEAN-5[1]) was nevertheless expected to grow at 4.8 per cent.[2]

East Asia has also expanded its presence in global markets. In the automobile market, automobile sales in the Asia region reached 21.40 million units in 2007, exceeding that in North America (19.37 million), and matching Europe (22.93 million). The expanding middle class in Asia with purchase power is considered to be behind this development. Although there is no formal definition of middle classes and it is therefore difficult to grasp their precise nature, the following descriptions are taken as characteristics: (1) highly educated people such as university graduates; (2) "managerial/administrative workers" such as managers of companies, "professional and technical workers" such as engineers, accountants, and lawyers, and relatively highly paid

TABLE 4.1
Trend of GDP Growth Rate and Contribution Ratio by Country and Region

(%)

	2006		2004		2005		2007	
	Growth rate	Contribution rate	Growth rate	Contribution rate	Growth rate	Contribution rate	Growth rate	Contribution rate
United States	3.6	16.9	3.1	15.7	2.9	12.8	2.2	9.7
EU-27	2.7	13.5	2.1	11.3	3.3	15.3	3.1	14.4
Japan	2.7	4.0	1.9	3.1	2.4	3.4	2.1	2.9
East Asia	8.3	26.2	8.1	29.5	8.8	29.3	9.1	32.0
China	10.1	17.7	10.4	21.3	11.1	21.2	11.4	23.4
South Korea	4.7	1.8	4.2	1.8	5.1	1.9	5.0	1.9
ASEAN-10	6.3	4.7	5.6	4.8	6.0	4.5	6.4	5.0
Vietnam	7.8	0.5	8.4	0.6	8.2	0.5	8.5	0.6
India	7.9	6.3	9.1	8.4	9.7	8.2	9.2	8.3
Latin America	6.2	10.1	4.6	8.5	5.5	8.9	5.6	9.4
Brazil	5.7	3.3	3.2	2.1	3.8	2.1	5.4	3.1
Central and Eastern Europe	6.9	5.4	6.1	5.3	6.6	5.2	5.8	4.7
Russia	7.2	4.3	6.4	4.3	7.4	4.5	8.1	5.1
Middle East	5.9	4.3	5.7	4.8	5.8	4.3	5.8	4.4
Africa	6.5	3.8	5.7	3.8	5.9	3.5	6.3	3.8
World	4.9	100.0	4.4	100.0	5.0	100.0	4.9	100.0
For reference								
Developed countries	3.2	39.3	2.6	34.7	3.0	35.0	2.7	31.1
Developing countries	7.5	60.0	7.1	64.5	7.8	64.2	7.9	67.8
BRICs (Incl. South Africa)	8.3	32.3	8.3	36.8	9.0	36.8	9.5	40.6
BRICs (Excl. South Africa)	8.5	31.6	8.4	36.0	9.2	36.1	9.6	39.9

Note: [1] The world's growth rates were calculated by the IMF with PPP weight.
[2] The contribution ratios for each country or region were calculated with price/PPP weight in 2007.
[3] East Asia refers to ASEAN-10, China, South Korea, Hong Kong, and Taiwan.
[4] Figures may vary from other tables due to revisions and differences in original statistics.
[5] The definition of developing countries complies with that of WEO (IMF).
Source: Japan External Trade Organization (2008b)

employees such as white-collar workers at foreign-owned companies;
(3) those who own durable consumables such as TVs, washing machines,
and refrigerators, and can afford to buy a car; (4) those who invest
substantial amounts in housing, leisure, and education; and (5) those
who receive benefits from urban lifestyles such as the use of mobile
phones and PCs and shopping in department stores and malls (Japan
External Trade Organization [JETRO] 2003, p. 37).

JETRO provided an estimate of the scale of the middle classes in
major East Asian countries in its 2003 White Paper on international
trade and foreign direct investment. They are the "income class
possibly deemed to be a marketing target of foreign-owned companies".
Based on the judgment standard of "whether one can afford to buy a
car" used for income-level calculations, JETRO estimated that China,
Thailand, Malaysia, Indonesia and the Philippines have middle-class
populations of 40.9 million, 4.8 million, 5.7 million, 5.0 million and
2.5 million, respectively. Given the fact that ASEAN countries as well
as China have seen stable economic growth since that time, the middle
class can safely be assumed to have expanded robustly.

Rising Intraregional Trade Ratio and Production Networks of Japanese Companies

In East Asia (ASEAN+6), intraregional trade is expanding. The
intraregional trade ratio (total of exports and imports) increased from
33.0 per cent in 1990 to 43.1 per cent in 2007. Although this ratio was
below the European Union's (27 countries) 65.8 per cent, it was above
NAFTA's 41.0 per cent. While the European Union's intraregional trade
ratio is high, it has remained at almost same level since 1990. NAFTA's
intraregional trade ratio meanwhile is declining after peaking around
1999 (see Figure 4.1). Meanwhile, East Asia's ratio is expected to rise
further with many FTAs being put into practice as described later.[3]

The activities of foreign companies in the East Asia region, especially
Japanese companies, are thought to have significantly contributed to
this expansion of intraregional trade. According to the basic survey
on overseas business activities conducted annually by the Ministry of
Economy, Trade and Industry (METI) of Japan, the number of local
subsidiaries of Japanese companies with overseas bases was 16,370
worldwide as of March 2007. Of these, 9,671 entities (about 60 per

FIGURE 4.1
Trend of Intraregional Trade Ratio in East Asia

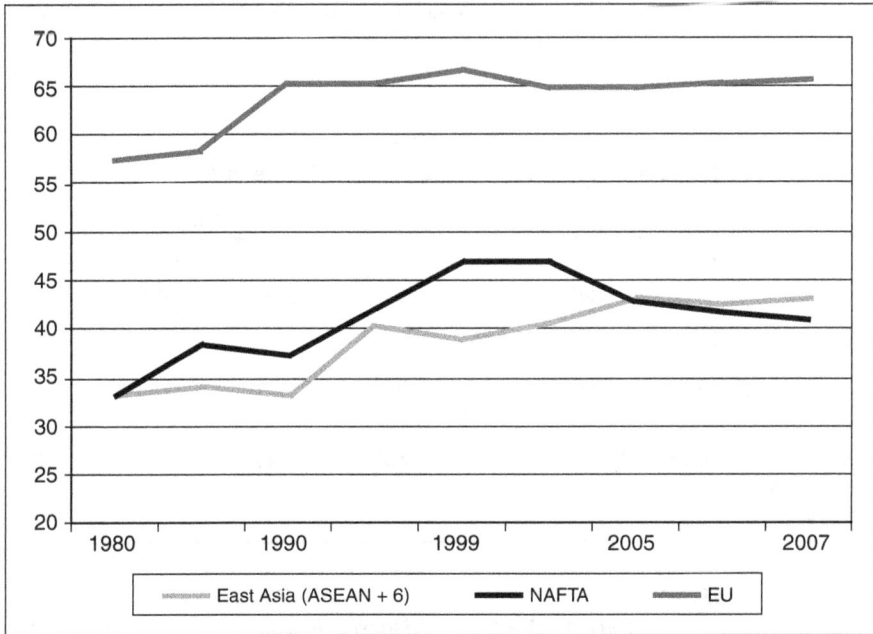

Source: Japan External Trade Organization (2008b) (original source: *Direction of Trade Statistics,*
    IMF, etc.).

cent) are in the Asia region. While the breakdown by country reveals China's dominant position with 3,520 subsidiaries, there are more local subsidiaries (3,828) in the six major ASEAN countries (Thailand, Malaysia, Indonesia, the Philippines, Singapore, and Vietnam) combined. The Asia region, as the world's factory, is characterized by the entry of many manufacturing companies. Looking only at the manufacturing industry, we find that Asian local subsidiaries account for about 70 per cent (5,700 subsidiaries) of Japanese companies' overseas subsidiaries across the world. A more detailed breakdown by sector shows that transportation equipment (automobile, motorcycle, etc.) companies have the largest number of Asian local subsidiaries (863), followed by information and communications equipment (IT) companies (851), chemical companies (713), general machinery companies (562), and electrical machinery companies (502). As described here, Japanese companies, led by the machinery industry, have deployed local subsidiaries over a wide area across the Asia region, forming supply chain networks (see Table 4.2).

TABLE 4.2
Number of Japanese Companies with Bases in Asia

(Unit: No. of companies)

	World Total	Asia Total	China	Hong Kong	Taiwan	South Korea	India
Total	16,370	9,671	3,520	898	714	500	151
Manufacturing industry	8,287	5,700	2,376	305	371	285	96
Non-manufacturing industry	8,083	3,971	1,144	593	343	215	55

	ASEAN 6	Thailand	Malaysia	Indonesia	The Philippines	Singapore	Vietnam
Total	3,828	1,205	601	574	373	845	230
Manufacturing industry	2,238	762	393	400	228	291	164
Non-manufacturing industry	1,590	443	208	174	145	554	66

Note: "Asia Total" includes other Asian countries.
Source: "Basic Survey on Overseas Business Activities" (As of March 2007), METI, published in June 2008.

According to the survey, Japanese companies' local subsidiaries (manufacturing industry) in Asia have an export ratio of 48.1 per cent with an export value of US$173.5 billion.[4] Out of this, the value of exports bound for Asia, including Japan, accounts for more than 80 per cent or US$143.6 billion.

Note that the intraregional trade value by item in East Asia (in 2005) indicates that the proportions of IT parts and electronic parts are as high as 27.9 per cent and 14.3 per cent respectively, together accounting for more than 40 per cent of the total intraregional trade value. For both items, the ratios of intraregional export to total export are very high — 71.2 per cent for IT parts, and 80.6 per cent for electronics parts (Ikegami and Onishi 2007, chapter 1).

III. ENVIRONMENTAL CHANGES CAUSED BY FTAS

Formation of an FTA Network with ASEAN as Its Hub

In the Asia region, once called an FTA vacuum, a number of FTAs have come into effect especially in the last five years, which significantly alter the trade and investment environment. The number of FTAs already effective within East Asia (ASEAN+6) reached nineteen by 2008 (see Table 4.3).

As many Japanese companies have entered the ASEAN region and established manufacturing networks as described above, FTAs using the ASEAN framework are gaining particular attention. As an FTA within the ASEAN region, the *ASEAN Free Trade Area* (AFTA) came into effect in 1993, and FTAs between ASEAN and China and South Korea were implemented in 2005 and 2007 respectively. In addition, the *ASEAN-Japan Comprehensive Economic Partnership* (AJCEP) became effective on 1 December 2008. The FTA with Australia/New Zealand as well as that with India also became effective in January 2010. The so-called five "ASEAN+1" FTA networks have been completed with ASEAN serving as their hub. These networks are important since they are considered to be the basis for a broader FTA among East Asian countries (RCEP: Regional Comprehensive Economics Partnership), on which the working group for trade and investment liberalization is to be set up in 2012.

Another development that deserves special mention is the successive implementation of Japan's bilateral FTAs with ASEAN member countries. Japan's FTAs with Singapore, Malaysia, Thailand, Indonesia, Brunei, and the Philippines are already effective and the FTA with ASEAN as

TABLE 4.3
FTAs Already Effective within East Asia (ASEAN+6) Region

FTAs	Effective Year/Status
Australia–New Zealand	January 1983
Lao PDR–Thailand	June 1991
ASEAN Free Trade Area (AFTA)	January 1992 and January 1993 (started tariff reduction)
Singapore–New Zealand	January 2001
Japan–Singapore	November 2002
Singapore–Australia	July 2003
ASEAN–China	July 2003
	January 2004 (EH targeting agricultural and fishery products)
	July 2005 (started tariff reduction in the goods sector)
Thailand–India	September 2004 (started Early Harvest program)
Thailand–Australia	January 2005
Thailand–New Zealand	July 2005
Singapore–India	August 2005
Singapore–South Korea	March 2006
Japan–Malaysia	July 2006
ASEAN–South Korea	June 2007
Japan–Thailand	November 2007
Japan–Indonesia	July 2008
Japan–Brunei	July 2008
ASEAN–Japan	December 2008 (Japan, Vietnam, Laos, Myanmar and Singapore)
Japan–Philippines	December 2008

Source: Japan External Trade Organization (2008*b*).

a whole has been effective since December 2008 as described above. Japan's FTA with Vietnam also became effective in October 2009. In quite a short period of time, the trade and investment environment surrounding Japan and the ASEAN member countries has been significantly altered. Furthermore, the Japan-India FTA has entered into force in August 2011 and Japan-Australia FTA is now in the process of negotiation. Japan's FTA network is expanding beyond ASEAN to reach the East Asia region. Now that Japan has reached a certain level in its efforts for FTAs with ASEAN member countries, the progress of FTAs involving Japan, China, and South Korea will attract further attention.

The Impact of FTAs on Trade

a) Accelerated Reorganization of Japanese Companies in ASEAN Affected by AFTA

To what extent are FTAs practically utilized in East Asia after so many have been successively implemented? First, let's look at the utilization status of AFTA, the most advanced FTA in the region. The tariff reduction under AFTA began in 1993 as mentioned above, according to the Common Effective Preferential Tariff (CEPT) agreement. Under CEPT, the intraregional tariff rates on all manufactured goods for the ASEAN original members (Thailand, Malaysia, Indonesia, the Philippines, Singapore, and Brunei) came down to, or below, 5 per cent as of 2003, its tenth year, except for some items. The reduction of tariffs continued until they were eliminated (0 per cent) in 2010.

For example, Thailand's exports under CEPT accounted for 22.6 per cent of the total exports to the ASEAN region in 2007, and this ratio is rising year after year (see Table 4.4). By destination, the ratio for exports to Indonesia is especially high at 50.7 per cent, followed by Vietnam and the Philippines, at 45.1 per cent and 40.9 per cent, respectively. In ASEAN member countries, tariff exemption programmes for the import of parts and raw materials have been widespread, including those for export processing zones; therefore, the utilization of CEPT is not necessary for many import transactions. Given this fact, it can be assumed that CEPT is utilized to a considerable extent in business transactions.

TABLE 4.4
**Trend of Thailand's Ratio of Exports under CEPT to Total Exports to the ASEAN
Region**

(%)

Destination	2001	2002	2003	2004	2005	2006	2007
Indonesia	24.9	23.8	32.1	41.5	45.9	50.6	50.7
Cambodia	0.0	0.1	0.0	0.0	0.0	0.0	0.0
Singapore	0.4	0.9	1.8	2.7	2.7	2.5	2.5
The Philippines	20.2	24.3	31.6	40.4	41.8	37.6	40.9
Brunei	1.4	2.3	2.1	3.2	3.9	8.2	9.3
Vietnam	8.2	13.8	31.2	33.8	41.5	39.9	45.1
Malaysia	15.5	20.4	20.7	22.1	22.4	20.5	22.1
Myanmar	0.0	0.0	0.2	0.2	0.2	0.4	0.9
Lao PDR	0.0	0.0	0.9	3.1	2.8	2.3	2.1
Total	8.6	10.8	15.5	19.3	21.5	20.2	22.5
(Excl. Singapore)	14.6	17.7	23.0	27.5	30.0	28.2	30.9

Source: Prepared by JETRO, based on the World Trade Atlas and materials from the Department of
Foreign Trade, Ministry of Commerce, Thailand.

The industries that have seen notable developments associated with
the utilization of CEPT include the home appliance, automobile, and
motorcycle industries. The home appliance industry, which manufactures
TVs, washing machines, refrigerators, and others, started in the ASEAN
region as an industry dependent on domestic demand. During 1960s
and 1970s, major Japanese manufacturers established small factories
in each ASEAN country to meet domestic demand, regarding the
ASEAN region as a group of markets separated by high tariffs. After
the creation of AFTA brought down the intraregional tariffs, some
manufacturers have integrated production bases that had been set
up in parallel in each country to benefit from economy of scale. For
example, although there were twelve TV factories in the Philippines
in 2001, only three remained in 2004 after companies closed down
one factory after another in those three years. This trend is confirmed
by trade statistics. Table 4.5 shows the trend of TV imports in the
Philippines by exporting country. This table indicates that from 2003,
imports from Thailand and Malaysia, where Japanese companies have
TV factories, have been rapidly increasing. At the same time, imports

from Japan and South Korea decreased, implying that imports from these countries were replaced with imports from neighbouring ASEAN member countries.

TABLE 4.5
Trend of TV Imports (HS 8528) in the Philippines by Exporting Country

(million dollars)

Exporting	2002	2003	2004	2005	2006	2007
Thailand	0.9	7.1	14.8	19.6	20.4	28.9
Malaysia	6.4	21.0	30.4	25.6	28.3	20.6
Indonesia	5.9	12.8	17.0	9.2	9.0	11.9
Singapore	1.7	2.6	2.7	3.4	3.4	8.0
China	3.2	2.6	4.6	6.1	4.4	4.6
Vietnam	0.0	0.0	0.5	1.7	1.8	4.3
Japan	4.9	4.1	5.7	5.6	9.3	3.8
Taiwan	0.2	1.0	0.6	0.7	0.6	2.7
Hong Kong	1.8	1.3	1.3	1.6	2.1	2.6
South Korea	6.9	3.2	5.8	3.1	2.9	0.6
Total	32.9	56.7	84.8	78.9	83.5	88.7

Source: World Trade Atlas.

The automobile industry was also heavily protected with tariff barriers as high as, or much higher than, those for the home appliance industry. Major manufacturers, including Japanese ones, established assembly plants in each country to meet domestic demand. However, since 1 January 2003, when most of the ASEAN original member countries completed bringing down tariffs on finished vehicles to, or below, 5 per cent, intraregional exports of automobiles under CEPT have been gaining momentum. Making the most of the parts supply network within the ASEAN region, some companies make Thailand their base for exporting passenger cars to the ASEAN region and pickup trucks to the world, while other companies make Indonesia their base for exporting minivans to the ASEAN region.

In the bilateral trade between Thailand and Indonesia, in 2002, Thailand's exports of passenger cars to Indonesia amounted to US$19.5 million, with car exports ranked only twentieth of all items

(4-digit HS code) — in 2003, when CEPT tariffs rates were brought down to 5 per cent, the export value rapidly increased to US$180.4 million (9.3 times YoY) and US$371.6 million in 2004 (2.1 times YoY), surging to the top of all items in a short period of time.

b) Utilization of the Thailand-Australia FTA and the Thailand-India FTA

Significant effects of FTAs are also apparent in the trade between Thailand and Australia. The Thailand-Australia bilateral FTA came into effect in January 2005. Calculations using data such as statistics from the Ministry of Commerce of Thailand show that in 2007, 66.2 per cent of Thailand's exports to Australia used preferential tariff rates under the FTA. On an item basis, exports of automobiles from Thailand by Japanese car makers, including Toyota and Honda, are again noticeable here. In 2004, before the implementation of the FTA, Thailand's exports to Australia of passenger cars and commercial vehicles such as pickup trucks amount to be at US$1.1 million and US$25.3 million, respectively. In 2005, when the FTA was implemented, its export of passengers and commercial vehicles rapidly increased to US$2.2 million (up 100 per cent YoY) and US$38.1 million (up 50.6 per cent YoY), respectively (see Table 4.6).

Similarly, in the Thailand-India FTA, which started in September 2004 (only the 82-item Early Harvest programme), almost all (98.1 per cent) of Thailand's exports are under the FTA. Japanese companies in particular actively utilize the FTA. This has resulted in an apparent increase in the trade statistics of Thailand's exports. For example, while its exports of polycarbonate (plastic resin) to India came up to US$17 million in 2004, the trade expanded 6.6 times year-on-year to US$112 million in 2005. Similarly, its exports of air conditioners and cathode-ray tubes for TVs rapidly increased from US$8 million and US$5 million respectively to US$16 million and US$21 million, respectively. In the opposite direction, India's exports of gear boxes to Thailand jumped from US$4 million in 2004 to US$30 million in 2005. However, since Thailand's total exports increased more steeply than its total imports in its bilateral trade with India, the trade balance between them was reversed from Thailand's deficit of US$233 million in 2004, to Thailand's surplus of US$244 million in 2005 (see Table 4.7).

TABLE 4.6
Trend of Imports of Passenger Cars and Commercial Vehicles in Australia

(million dollars, %)

		2004	2005	2006	2007	Share increase from 2004
Passenger cars	Total import value	8,141	9,268	9,482	11,651	—
	Share Japan	58.9	55.1	49.6	45.3	−13.6
	Germany	13.4	10.5	10.3	10.6	−2.8
	South Korea	5.9	7.5	10.0	9.8	3.9
	Thailand	1.1	2.2	4.8	8.5	7.4
Commercial vehicles	Total import value	2,556	3,040	3,343	4,596	—
	Share Thailand	25.3	38.1	32.0	36.3	10.9
	Japan	43.8	29.9	28.3	27.6	−16.2
	United States	15.0	13.1	21.3	14.1	−0.9

Source: Japan External Trade Organization (2008b) (original source: Australia's trade statistics).

TABLE 4.7
Thailand's Trade with India in Major Items on a Trade Value Basis among the Thailand-India Early Harvest List

(million dollars, %)

	Items	2003	2004	2005	2006	2007	Avg. growth rate from 04 to 07
Export	Polycarbonate	11	17	112	52	115	90.6
	Air conditioner	9	8	16	28	37	69.4
	Cathode-ray tube for TV	0	5	21	32	32	88.9
	Epoxy resin	3	5	11	16	27	73.5
	Total export value	639	905	1,519	1,815	2,853	46.6
Import	Gear box	0	4	30	40	36	103.0
	Total import value	877	1,138	1,275	1,625	2,236	25.2
Trade balance		−239	−233	244	190	617	—

Note: While the HS 2002 code for gear boxes was originally 8708.40 until 2006, part of 8797.99 was incorporated into 8708.40 in 2007.

Source: Japan External Trade Organization (2008b) (original source: Thailand's trade statistics).

c) Further Expansion of Intraregional Trade

In addition to these FTAs, the ASEAN-China FTA has been in effect since July 2005. However, the utilization ratios in 2007 were as low as 11.1 per cent for Thailand's exports to China, and 10.5 per cent for Malaysia's exports. The utilization ratios of the ASEAN-South Korea FTA are also low, with only 11.1 per cent of Malaysia's exports to South Korea using the FTA. However, from 2009 onward, given that the efforts for tariff reductions will be intensified with tariff rates expected to be lowered to or below 5 per cent except for certain items, and then eliminated (to 0 per cent) in 2010, a rapid increase in FTA utilization can be assumed. As described above, with FTAs actively utilized especially by multinational companies, including Japanese companies with local bases, the intraregional trade in East Asia is expected to expand robustly.

For individual companies, the elimination of tariff barriers represents an expansion of opportunities for market share growth. But it also represents tougher competition. The point to be considered regarding the effects of FTAs is that even products out of FTA coverage can be indirectly affected by FTAs. For example, if a customer of a parts supplier that is an assembly manufacturer is forced to reduce production through competition with imported products under FTAs, the parts supplier would be affected. Conversely, if the customer company expands production utilizing FTAs, the supplier would benefit from the positive effect. Companies exporting goods will need to examine carefully aspects such as which countries the destination country has entered or will enter FTAs with, and what changes those FTAs will cause to the competitor in the market of the destination country.

Challenges to Be Met

a) Trade Facilitation Gaining Importance

Many challenges need to be addressed in order to make economic integration in East Asia more effective. In particular, to make the effects of the economic integration more apparent on lower tariff rates under FTAs, efforts for trade facilitation are gaining importance. This is evident in AFTA where tariff elimination has already been implemented to a considerable extent. Although the ten ASEAN member countries comprise a market with a total population of over 500 million, they are still far from constituting a "single market". While ASEAN aims at becoming an economic community, a blueprint for a customs union along the lines of the European Union has not emerged so far. Therefore, in spite of the smooth progress in lowering intraregional tariff rates, customs clearance is required at every border in the region. In addition, to benefit from preferential tariff rates under AFTA, an exporter has to obtain a Certificate of Origin (Form D). Furthermore, in some cases, certificates for codes and standards in the destination country are also required. Ideally, an environment where goods flow freely in the ASEAN region as if they were traded in a single country should be realized.

b) More Prompt Customs Clearance Expected with the ASEAN Single Window

Customs clearance issues attract much attention from Japanese companies in ASEAN as these directly affect their daily operations. In the inquiry survey targeting Japanese companies in ASEAN and India conducted by JETRO from October to December of 2007, the largest number of respondents (39.9 per cent) answered "Customs clearance is too complicated" as the problem with the trade system, followed by "Customs clearance takes much time" (39.1 per cent) and "Efforts to familiarize the regulation changes are insufficient" (38.9 per cent).

Regarding customs clearance, ASEAN is now putting into place the ASEAN Single Window (ASW) among member countries, an effort that has attracted much attention. Single Window is a scheme where a company has to submit only a single electronic application form for applications and permissions concerning exports or imports to multiple administrative bodies. It can be called a one-stop service for customs clearance.

The ASW will be integrated to enable data exchange among the single windows of each ASEAN member countries, while their declaration forms for customs clearance are standardized in line with international regulations adopted by bodies such as the World Customs Organization (WCO) and the WTO. By doing so, data for export procedures can be also used for import procedures in the importing country, making customs clearance simpler and more prompt.

Regarding the establishment of ASW, the agreement concerning its implementation was signed at the ASEAN economic ministers' meeting in December 2005[5] and the deadline for the ASW introduction was set at 2010. Differences in development status of member countries, however, mean that while the six original members were scheduled to implement the ASW by 2008 at the latest, new members (Cambodia, Lao PDR, Myanmar, and Vietnam) are slated to implement it by 2012. A pilot model for ASW has already been completed and experimental data exchange for the Certificate of Origin (Form D) and the export/ import declaration form to be submitted for preferential tariff rates under AFTA was implemented between the Philippines and Thailand in 2006. The Certificate of Origin required at customs is also included in the Single Window. The Single Window scheme is expected to contribute significantly to making customs clearance more prompt and also transparent.

c) Issues Concerning the Rules of Origin and Certificate of Origin

In the East Asia region, new FTAs have been coming into effect one after another. To utilize the preferential tariff rates under an FTA, a company needs to comply with the Rules of Origin for the goods to qualify as made in an FTA-party country and obtain the Certificate of Origin from the governmental body of the country or the certification organization.[6] Issues concerning the Rules of Origin for companies can be summarized in two points: (1) the issue concerning standards, that is, the Rules of Origin must be met; and (2) the issue concerning procedures, that is, the Certificates of Origin must be obtained in daily operations.

(1) Issues of Rules of Origin

The trouble with the Rules of Origin is that the rules may vary depending on the FTA. For example, while the Rules of Origin for AFTA is "40 per cent or more ASEAN cumulative value added", under the Thailand-India FTA (Early Harvest program), not only the value added standard of "40 per cent or more", but also the tariff line change standard of "change on a four-digit or six-digit base", must be met at the same time.

A situation where multiple FTAs become entangled, thereby causing confusion about the Rules of Origin among companies and preventing the smooth utilization of the FTAs, is referred to as the "spaghetti bowl phenomenon". But in practical terms, either of the value addition standard or the tariff line change standard is applied for the Rules of Origin in most cases, and other standards are seldom used. As a result, confusion has not occurred on the front line so far.[7] This said, when multiple FTAs are available and their schedules for tariff elimination vary, efforts to grasp accurate information are required to utilize the most advantageous FTA. In the actual field, tariff reduction schemes other than FTAs may exist, requiring comparative examination of multiple schemes.

Additionally, the treatment of intermediary trade sometimes becomes an issue associated with the Rules of Origin. Intermediary trade is a transaction pattern with separate commercial and logistical flows. Specifically, while goods are directly transferred between the FTA party countries, the buy/sell transaction is conducted via a third-party country. The exporter issues the invoice for the intermediary in the third party country, and the importer receives a new invoice issued by the intermediary called a "re-invoice". Although this trade pattern is common among multinational companies, it is not explicitly allowed in some FTAs, thus preventing active utilization of those FTAs. An advantages of intermediary trade is that by integrating the financial function into a specific country, such as Japan or Singapore, settlement operations can be made more efficient and the exchange risk can be managed.

For example, in AFTA (CEPT) and FTAs signed by Japan, intermediary trade (re-invoice) is explicitly specified and allowed in the agreement. In contrast, the ASEAN-China FTA and Thailand-India FTA do not have specific provisions, and the utilization of an FTA is sometimes ruled out at customs in some countries.

(2) Issues of Procedures for Obtaining the Certificate of Origin

When it comes to procedures for obtaining the Certificate of Origin, efforts have been made to simplify them and, like for the ASW, an electronic application has been made available also in Japan. However, especially for the value added standard, documentation that proves the origin of each part of the product needs to be prepared, requiring much work that entails collecting certification documents from suppliers of products with many parts, such as automobiles and consumer electronics products. Even after the application, the relevant documents need to be kept and managed, and companies incur the issuance fee. Therefore, the advantages of the preferential tariffs must be comparatively examined against these disadvantages from expenses and work for clerical procedures.

d) Land Transportation Attracting Attention as a New Transportation Mode

In the European Union, logistics mainly depends on land transportation. Meanwhile, sea transportation has been mainly used for the intraregional trade within the ASEAN region so far, but in some cases, including trade between Thailand, Malaysia, and Singapore, land transportation has been used to a considerable extent for the past few years. Along the East-West Economic Corridor between Vietnam and Thailand, land transportation is seldom used for routine business regardless of much interest shown by Japanese companies.

According to the survey by JETRO, land transportation between Bangkok and Hanoi takes seventy-four hours, which is about a third of the time required for sea transportation (213 hours). However, land transportation costs US$5,300 (per 40-foot container), which is almost double the cost for sea transportation (US$2,660). The largest obstacle to the introduction of land transportation at present is freight imbalance as more goods go from Thailand to Vietnam than the other way around. Resolving this problem will lower the cost and enable the utilization of land transportation.

The actual run survey conducted by JETRO in 2007 revealed that much time is consumed in waiting for customs offices to open, especially in Lao PDR, a transit country. By eliminating this waiting time, the transportation time between Bangkok and Hanoi can be shortened to forty-eight hours. This reduces the time difference between air and land transportation to only one day. Given the cost difference, the utilization of the land transportation would rapidly increase (Japan External Trade Organization 2008a, pp. 112–15). To eliminate the waiting time, measures such as the following should be taken: (1) make the customs office temporarily open when the freight arrives; or (2) establish a transportation system to ensure the freight arrives when the customs office is open.

Many would also like more prompt customs clearance. In the inquiry survey conducted by the Japanese Chamber of Commerce in Bangkok in November 2006, the response most selected to the item on the "Challenges to be met to make the East-West Economic Corridor more effective" was "More prompt clerical procedures for customs, inspection, etc." (78 per cent, multiple selections allowed) (*JETRO Business News*, 6 February 2007). According to the actual run survey described above, the time required for customs clearance was around one hour in most cases, so the processing time itself was not deemed to be a problem. However, it is doubtful whether an increase in freight could be handled as efficiently as this, and a speedy and stable customs system needs to be established when realizing single-stop customs and promoting computerization.

Besides the East-West Economic Corridor between Thailand and Vietnam, the need for developing efficient logistical routes between the ASEAN region and India is expected to increase in the near future. The trade value between ASEAN and India has been rapidly expanding year after year. In 2002, it was US$9.054 billion (in both directions). Just five years later, in 2007, it had increased nearly fourfold to US$34.952 billion.

For example, from Laem Chabang Port, the main port in Thailand (where many Japanese manufacturing companies operate), to Chennai Port in southern India, transportation currently takes at least twelve to fourteen days via Singapore. Given this situation, the route which links Ranong Port on the Indian Sea in southern Thailand to Chennai is likely to attract attention. The sea transportation time between Ranong and Chennai is about four days. Even after the land transportation time from Bangkok to Ranong (about 650 kilometres, thirteen hours) is added to this, significant time saving can be achieved. An Indian logistics company already started providing services for this route in September 2008. Attention will be paid to how often this route will be used in Thailand-India trade.

Liberalization of Investment and Migration

Although the term FTA is associated with the elimination of tariffs on goods, most of the FTAs signed in recent years cover the liberalization of investment and services, as well as trade in goods, cooperation, etc. The FTAs signed or negotiated by Japan are called Economic Partnership Agreements (EPAs), which aim at the abolition of various regulations, coordination of economic systems, and other measures to liberalize and facilitate the flow of people, goods, and money between the counterparts of such agreements.

As for investment, while many Asian countries allow 100-per cent foreign ownership for foreign direct investment in the manufacturing industry, many prohibit majority foreign ownership in the services industry. However under the Japan-Thailand EPA (JTEPA), foreign ownership of over 50 per cent is allowed in certain services sectors:: up to 100 per cent for consulting services, up to 51 per cent for logistics, up to 60 per cent for repair and maintenance conducted by manufacturers or group companies of goods made in Thailand or Japan, and up to 60 per cent for hotels and restaurants. The examples above show that the liberalization of investment, especially in the field of services, has not been developed as extensively as the liberalization of trade in goods. Regardless of their sensitive aspect, services assume a crucial role in establishing an integrated supply chain in each country, so further liberalization is expected.

Most EPAs that Japan has already signed with ASEAN member countries also cover migration. In particular, labour migration to Japan has been one of the items on the agenda in many FTA negotiations. For labour-exporting countries, this is expected to have economic effects through remittances by workers. The EPAs with Indonesia and the Philippines include provisions for Japan's acceptance of human resources in the nursing and care field. In this system, Japan accepts prospective nurses and caregivers and allows them to work as part of preparatory activities to obtain official qualifications in Japan. From Indonesia, whose EPA with Japan has come into effect, 204 Indonesian nurses and caregivers had already come to Japan as of August 2008.

In Japan's ageing society, there is already a shortage of nurses and caregivers, and a more severe shortage is likely to develop in the future. Therefore, accepting nurses and caregivers from Asian countries is an inevitable choice for Japan, and a positive attitude towards this issue is required. Additionally, there is also a severe shortage of engineers in Japan. Since the need for developing embedded software has been rapidly expanding as more and more electronic control functions are used in automobiles and home electronics products, it is likely the shortage of engineers will become increasingly severe. Japan has to establish win-win relationships with other Asian countries and utilize their human resources.

IV. JAPAN'S STRATEGY

Japanese Companies and Asia

Since 2005 the population of Japan has been on the decline. Down the road, the ageing of Japan's society, combined with its declining birthrate, will accelerate and Japan is likely to face depopulation. Therefore, considerable expansion of the domestic market cannot be expected and the workforce is also likely to dwindle. According to estimates by the Japan Institute for Labour Policy and Training, Japan's workforce of 66.57 million as of 2006 will fall by about 4.40 million to 62.17 million by 2017, and by about 10.70 million to 55.84 million by 2030 (Ministry of Health, Labour and Welfare 2008, p. 47). A shortage of business successors is also a serious concern. It is estimated that out of about 290,000 companies that are closed down each year (average from 2001 to 2004), about 70,000 companies went out of business because they could find "no successors" (Small and Medium Enterprise Agency 2006).

Against this background, the foreign production ratio has been rising year after year. According to the basic survey on overseas business activities annually conducted by METI, the rising trend in the foreign production ratio of Japanese manufactures has been apparent since around FY2000, and the ratio of 11.8 per cent in FY2000 is assumed to have jumped to 18.3 per cent in FY2007. The ratios are especially high in sectors such as transportation equipment (37.8 per cent) and information and communications equipment (34.0 per cent). As for production sites, the percentage of these in Asian countries has been increasing, almost doubling from 4.2 per cent in FY2000 to 8.1 per cent in 2007, exceeding North America in FY2004.

The foreign earnings of Japanese listed companies also show that the foreign divisions, especially those in the Asia region, have gained importance (see Table 4.8). According to the aggregate calculation by

TABLE 4.8
Overseas Earnings of Japanese Listed Companies

Fiscal Year (No. of companies surveyed)	Sales Breakdown by Region (%)						Operating Profit Breakdown by Region (%)					
	Domestic	Overseas	Americas	Europe	Asia/ Pacific	Others	Domestic	Overseas	Americas	Europe	Asia/ Pacific	Others
FY1997 (582)	71.4	28.6	11.3	5.4	5.8	6.1	76.6	23.4	9.8	3.4	4.8	5.3
FY1998 (593)	71.1	28.9	13.4	6.0	4.9	4.6	73.4	26.6	13.8	4.8	4.4	3.6
FY1999 (643)	72.5	27.5	12.4	5.4	5.5	4.2	75.0	25.0	14.1	2.1	5.0	3.7
FY2000 (668)	71.9	28.1	12.6	5.2	6.4	3.9	79.9	20.1	10.4	0.7	6.0	3.0
FY2001 (715)	69.7	30.3	13.7	5.5	6.7	4.4	76.0	24.0	12.4	0.6	6.7	4.2
FY2002 (728)	68.0	32.0	13.7	6.0	7.8	4.6	72.9	27.1	13.0	2.8	7.2	4.1
FY2003 (738)	67.9	32.1	12.9	6.1	8.2	4.9	73.3	26.7	11.1	4.3	7.5	3.7
FY2004 (774)	67.3	32.7	12.2	6.4	8.8	5.3	71.8	28.2	10.9	4.7	8.6	4.0
FY2005 (804)	66.1	33.9	12.5	6.3	10.1	5.0	70.8	29.2	10.8	4.7	10.0	3.7
FY2006 (832)	66.2	33.8	12.6	6.9	10.3	4.1	73.5	26.5	9.1	4.1	8.3	5.1
FY2007 (866)	63.1	36.9	13.0	8.5	12.0	3.5	67.1	32.9	8.7	6.8	12.2	5.2

Note: 1. Listed companies (excluding banks and insurers) that close accounts during the period from December to March, and give descriptions on segment information by location were surveyed.

2. For FY2007, only companies that published earnings reports by May 31, 2008 were surveyed.

3. Sales include intersegment sales.

4. As some listed subsidiaries are also surveyed, some overlapping sales and profit are included.

5. "Others" includes the adding item for multiple regions ("Europe" and "Overseas").

Source: Japan External Trade Organization (2008b) (original source: "Kaisha Zaimu Karute CD-ROM" (to FY2005), Toyo Keizai, and companies' earnings reports and securities reports (for FY2006 and FY2007).

JETRO, the foreign ratio to total operating profit of listed companies rose from 23.4 per cent in FY1997, to 32.9 per cent in FY2007. In terms of region, the share of Asia (including the Pacific region) increased significantly from 4.8 per cent to 12.2 per cent. In FY2007, it exceeded the share of the Americas for the first time and the Asian region became the largest source of profit. It can be said that Asia is becoming more and more important for Japanese companies.

Note that with the expansion of overseas operations, the income balance surplus in the balance of payment has been rapidly increasing due to remittance received from overseas subsidiaries. Since 2005 the income balance surplus has been larger than the trade balance surplus and the difference has been increasing year after year. In 2007, while the trade surplus was US$104.7 billion, the income surplus reached US$138.6 billion (see Figure 4.2).

FIGURE 4.2
Trends of Japan's Trade Balance and Income Balance
(million dollars)

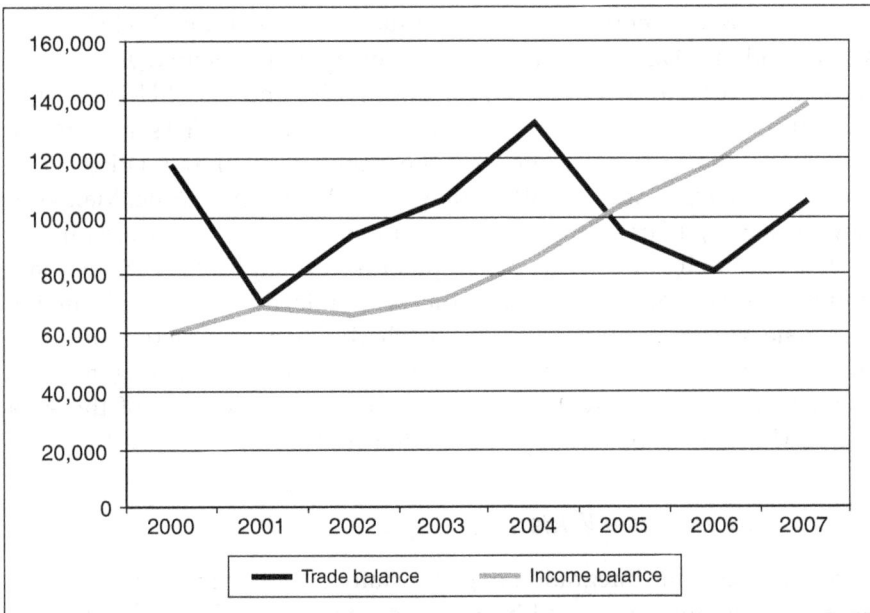

Source: Ministry of Finance, Balance of Payments Statistics (converted into dollars by JETRO).

Strategies Japan Should Adopt

a) Towards the East Asia FTA

Given the current situation of the Japanese economy and companies described above, it is obvious that Japan's course of action to achieve sustainable growth is to contribute to the growth of Asia while *utilizing the resources* in the region, and to aim to grow together with Asia as one community. To do so, a number of FTAs and EPAs in the Asia region that are now being rapidly put into practice should be bundled together to realize broader economic integration in East Asia. In these efforts, given the development of the supply chain of Japanese companies in Asia, the near-term goal should be the realization of the Regional Comprehensive Economic Partnership (RCEP) by ASEAN+6 (Japan, China, South Korea, India, Australia, and New Zealand).

However, economic integration in East Asia also needs to be open to external regions. A look at the history of East Asia, which has been developing through exports to European and U.S. markets, shows this argument to be obviously right. Indeed, cross-regional FTAs are simultaneously emerging rapidly with the U.S.-Singapore, the EU-South Korea, and the U.S.-South Korea FTAs being implemented in January 2004, July 2011 and March 2012 respectively, and the EU-India, the EU-India, the EU-Singapore, and the EU-Malaysia FTAs are in the process of negotiations. Moreover, the negotiation of the TPP (Trans-Pacific Partnership agreement) among Australia, Brunei, Chile, Malaysia, New Zealand, Peru, Singapore, the United States, and Vietnam has started in March 2010. These developments (seeking FTAs with external countries while proceeding with the economic integration within the East Asia region) can be said to match the current practice of trade and investment in Asian countries. In the medium and long term, it is hoped these efforts will evolve into the Free Trade Area of the Asia Pacific (FTAAP) proposed by the United States.

b) Dealing with the Widening Gaps

To realize economic integration that is sustainable in the medium and long term, the widening gaps within the region need to be dealt with. For the European Union, in terms of GDP per capita, the region's highest income area of Luxemburg (US$103,125) is about twenty times as high as the region's lowest income area of Bulgaria (US$5,186). For East Asia, meanwhile, the region's highest income area of Singapore (US$35,163) is more than 150 times higher than the region's lowest income area of Myanmar (US$234).[8] This wide economic gap within the region can become an obstacle in the road to deeper integration. For all the countries in the region to enjoy the advantages of the liberalization through economic integration, political support to strengthen the competitiveness of developing nations in the region is essential. Without these efforts, people might have no incentive for liberalization, and may even block the development of economic integration. Specifically, developed nations in the region such as Japan need to support developing nations actively through the nurturing of human resources, development of industries, and cooperation for supporting small and medium enterprises, among other things.

c) Aiming at Reinforcing Regional Cooperation

Economic integration in East Asia will contribute to economic development across the region. Removing trade barriers within the region generates trade and pushes up the GDP. According to the estimation conducted by JETRO using the GTAP model, if the FTA by ASEAN+6 is realized, the total GDP will increase 1.3 per cent (Japan External Trade Organization 2008*b*, p. 53). Economic integration will reinforce the complementary relationships among countries with different development stages through liberalized business activities within the region, and enhance the economic growth rate of each country. Furthermore, economic integration in East Asia needs not to be limited to the liberalization of trade and investment. Rather, regional cooperation in a broad field should be included. The number of issues to be dealt with across borders at the regional level has significantly increased, such as environmental issues, food and energy issues, epidemics such as bird flu, terrorism, international crime, pirates, and disaster management.

As for issues in the economic field, the Economic Research Institute for ASEAN and East Asia (ERIA) was established in June 2008 as an international organization to propose policies to participant countries. ERIA has initiated research and studies with three themes "deepening economic integration", "narrowing gaps of economic development", and "sustainable economic growth" — as its pillars, and much is expected of its future activities as a practical policy recommendation organization.

d) Regional Financial Cooperation through Efforts Such as the Nurturing of the Asian Bond Market

Among East Asian countries, which experienced the Asian currency crisis, the most developed form of regional cooperation can be seen in the field of financial cooperation. A framework for cooperation, called the Chiang Mai Initiative, has already been completed. This is a network established under the bilateral currency swap agreement adopted at the ASEAN+3 financial ministers' meeting (held in Chiang Mai) in May 2000 to serve as a safety net when a foreign currency liquidity crisis occurs. A network with a total scale of US$36.5 billion was established at the end of 2003 (Umada and Kimura 2008, chapter 5).

In addition, the Asian currency crisis has motivated efforts to nurture bond markets in Asia. The intention is to correct a situation where much of the excess money in Asia flows into the U.S. financial markets while only short-term speculative money that is converted into dollars returns to Asia, and establish a structure to help Asia's money circulate in the Asia region. The bond market in Asia is still immature, so companies depend excessively on banks. To correct the situation, two main cooperation measures are being promoted: (1) initiatives for nurturing the Asian bond market; and (2) the Asian Bond Fund (ABF).

As part of the initiative for nurturing the Asian bond market, the following four agendas are being discussed in the framework of the ASEAN+3 financial ministers' meeting: the development of new bonds utilizing securitization; a system for credit guarantee that enables Asian companies with low credit ratings to issue bonds; a bond settlement system desirable for Asia, and the enhancement of competency of local credit rating agencies in Asia. The specific results of this initiative were the issuance of local currency-denominated bonds by international development financial institutions such as the World Bank and the Asian Development Bank and government agencies; the guarantee and insurance grant for issuance of bonds by companies such as Isuzu Thailand, and other projects (Umada and Kimura 2008, chapter 5).

Meanwhile, the Asian Bond Fund was established in June 2003 as part of cooperation efforts among central banks under the Executives' Meeting of East Asia Pacific Central Banks (EMEAP).[9] This fund intends to provide stable money management vehicles in the Asia region. In

December 2004, ABF2, whose investment targets are sovereign bonds and quasi-sovereign bonds denominated in the local currencies of the countries in the region, was founded. While ABF1 limited the participants to central banks of the EMEAP member countries, ABF2 is open to investors in the private sector.[10]

e) Huge Demand for Infrastructure in Asia

In the joint study conducted by the Japan Bank for International Cooperation (JBIC), the Asian Development Bank (ADB), and the World Bank, it is estimated that there is demand for infrastructure construction worth over US$1 trillion for the five years from 2006 to 2010 in East Asia.[11]

In the inquiry survey targeting Japanese companies in ASEAN and India conducted by JETRO from October to December 2007, the most selected response to the question regarding problems in the investment environment was "Infrastructures are insufficient" (42.4 per cent, multiple selections allowed), followed by "Overly complicated administrative procedures" (35.8 per cent) and "Unclear policy management by the government of that country" (33.9 per cent).

Since it is impossible to raise the huge amount of money necessary for infrastructure development only from the public sector, including ODA, private money should be utilized. In East Asia, while the savings ratio is high, the investment ratio has been generally on the decline since the Asian currency crisis, except for China (see Figures 4.3 and 4.4). Therefore, more Asian money can be circulated within the region. The nurturing of the Asian bond market described above is part of the efforts to help ensure that money stays in the region.

In India, the "Delhi-Mumbai Industrial Corridor Project" is being developed through cooperation between the Japanese and Indian governments. This project is entirely new in that development and improvement of both hardware and software infrastructures will be simultaneously implemented utilizing private money. At the ASEAN+6 economic ministers' meeting held in August 2008, the East Asia Industrial Corridor Project, the extensive version of the Indian model to be implemented across East Asia, was proposed by the Japanese Government and gained support from participant countries.

FIGURE 4.3
Savings Ratios of Major Asian Countries

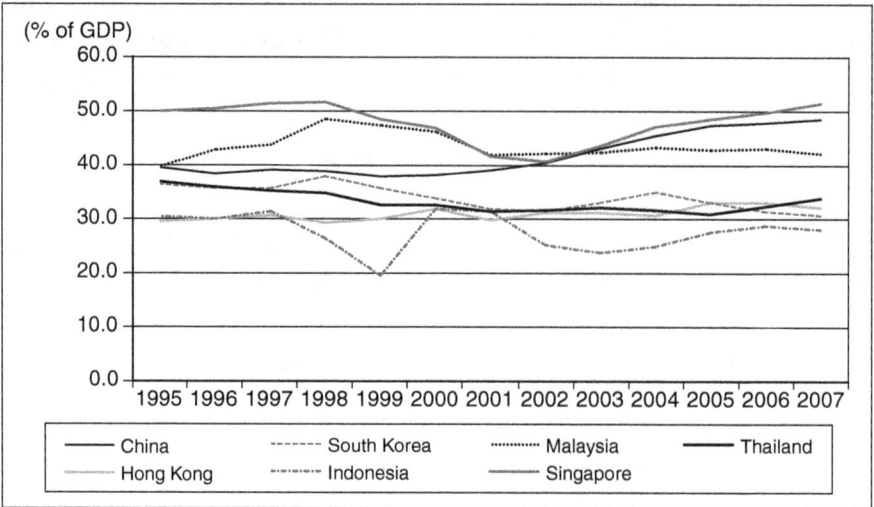

Source: Key Indicators for Asia and the Pacific 2008, ADB.

FIGURE 4.4
Investment Ratios of Major Asian Countries

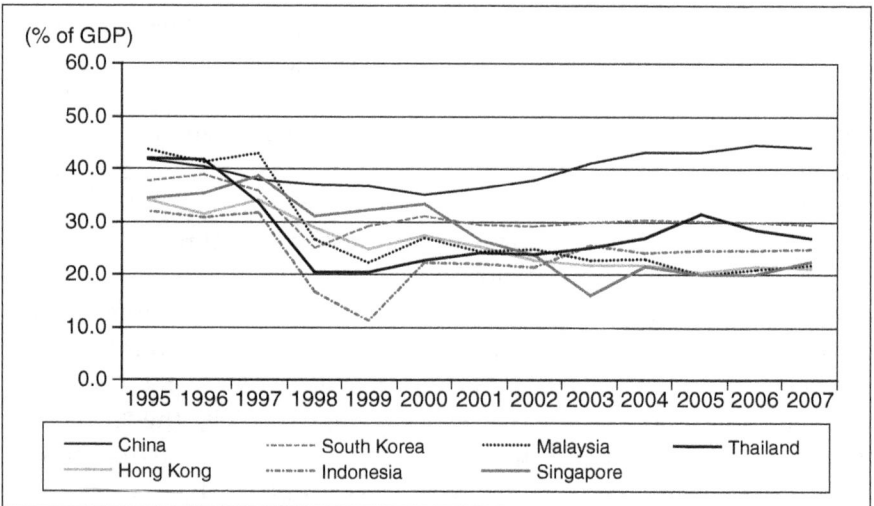

Source: Key Indicators for Asia and the Pacific 2008, ADB.

f) *Asia as a Leading Force of the Global Economy*

As stated in the introduction, after the outbreak of the U.S. financial crisis, the global economy experienced the worst recession since the Great Depression in 1929. Much of the blame for the financial crisis lies in the global imbalance of international payments: the income balance surplus (excessive savings) of Asian and Middle Eastern countries flowed into the United States, causing stable, low long-term interest rates and the expansion of the mortgage market. As a result, U.S. consumption expanded and became a powerful absorber of the world supply, propping up the rapid growth of the global economy from the early 2000s. The collapse of the U.S. real estate market triggered the subprime loan crisis in 2007 and developed into this financial crisis. Given the magnitude of the impact of the U.S. financial crisis, the past U.S.-dependent model of economic growth is no longer viable, at least for the time being. The East Asian economy, as the world's growth centre, should play a role in leading the global economy from the demand side. The stable development of the global economy depends on the expansion of demand through investment in infrastructure and consumption in the East Asia region.

Notes

1. ASEAN-5 includes Thailand, Malaysia, Indonesia, the Philippines, and Vietnam.
2. IMF press release, 22 April 2009.
3. In this chapter, "FTA" is used in a broad sense and covers agreements such as economic partnership agreements (EPAs) that Japan has signed with other countries.
4. Figures for FY 2006 (April 2006 to March 2007). For the exchange rate, 117.76 yen/dollar, the average rate (FRB) for 2007, is used.
5. For the original text of the agreement, see <http://www.aseansec.org/18005.htm>.
6. Some FTAs adopt a self-certification system which does not require the submittal of the Certificates of Origin (e.g. the U.S.-Singapore FTA). However, preparation of documentation that proves compliance with the Rules of Origin is required even in the self-certification system.
7. For textile products, the processing standard that requires specific processing procedures is often applied.

8. IMF, *World Economic Outlook Database 2008*. As of 2007, for both the European Union and ASEAN. Japan's GDP per capita that year was US$34,296 and lower than Singapore's.
9. The EMEAP members are the central banks and monetary authorities of the following eleven countries/region: Australia, China, Hong Kong, Indonesia, Japan, South Korea, Malaysia, New Zealand, the Philippines, Singapore, and Thailand.
10. Official website of the Bank of Japan.
11. JBIC press release, 8 July 2005.

References

Ikegami, Hiroshi, and Yasuo Onishi. *New Era of Logistics in East Asia – Response to Globalization and Challenges*. Chiba: Institute of Developing Economies, JETRO, 2007.

Japan External Trade Organization. *2003 JETRO White Paper on International Trade and Foreign Direct Investment*. Tokyo: JETRO, 2003.

———. *ASEAN Logistics Network Map 2008*. Tokyo: JETRO, 2008a.

———. *2008 JETRO White Paper on International Trade and Foreign Direct Investment*. Tokyo: JETRO, 2008b.

Ministry of Health, Labour and Welfare. *Annual Report on Health, Labour and Welfare 2007–2008*. Tokyo, 2008.

Small and Medium Enterprise Agency. *2006 White Paper on Small and Medium Enterprises in Japan*. Tokyo, 2006.

Umada, Keiichi, and Fukunari Kimura. *Corroboration of East Asian Regionalism and Japan*. Tokyo: Bunshindo, 2008.

5

The Nature of East Asian Integration and Australia's Engagement

Jiro Okamoto

This chapter focuses on states' involvement in the institutional integration processes in East Asia. "Institutional integration" here means formal agreements between states, such as free trade agreements (FTAs), as well as their participation in regional cooperation frameworks, such as ASEAN and ASEAN+3 (ten ASEAN members and Japan, China, and South Korea).

The outbreak of the Asian financial crisis in 1997 gave direct momentum to the creation of the concept of "East Asia" as a region and political and economic integration in the region. Since then, the integration processes in East Asia have developed in various aspects and forms: from separate bilateral currency swap agreements to the Chiang Mai Initiative, from bilateral FTAs to ASEAN+1 FTAs, and from ASEAN cooperation to ASEAN+3 and ASEAN+6 (ASEAN+3 plus Australia, New Zealand, and India) initiatives, among others. During these processes several characteristics of East Asian integration processes have emerged. The main aim of this chapter is to identify these characteristics and try to explain the factors behind such characteristics.

First, this chapter points out that integration processes in East Asia are generally sector- and function-based, and bilateral, subregional, and multilateral frameworks coexist in the same sectors. It also shows that "extra-regional" states are participating in many of these bilateral and multilateral frameworks. Then, the chapter considers the factors behind these characteristics. It assumes that individual East Asian states are seeking practical and concrete benefits from the processes and they are not tying themselves to any particular method, or geographical area, to achieve the benefits.

Second, it argues that East Asian engagement policies of Australia — whose place in "East Asia" remains ambiguous — illustrate the characteristics of East Asian integration in the last twenty years. Australia changed its foreign policy approach significantly at the turn of the century. The chapter explains the change in some detail, and argues that the nature of East Asian integration can be explained in sharp relief by examining the differences in intentions and results of Australia's Asian engagement policies in the 1990s and 2000s.

The chapter concludes with some implications, drawn from the overall argument, on the future of East Asian integration.

I. THE NATURE OF EAST ASIAN INTEGRATION PROCESSES

Characteristics

Tables 5.1 and 5.2 demonstrate how institutional integration processes have been developing in East Asia.

Table 5.1 indicates the proliferation of FTAs, or Economic Partnership Agreements (EPAs). Over the last decade, FTAs seem to have become almost synonymous with the concept of institutional economic integration in East Asia. In Table 5.1, AFTA (ASEAN Free Trade Area) is quite notable. The intraregional trade liberalization process within ASEAN, which marked the beginning of institutional economic integration in East Asia, had commenced in 1993. By 2003, five original members (Indonesia, Malaysia, the Philippines, Singapore, and Thailand) and Brunei had all achieved intraregional tariffs of five per cent or less, with a small number of exceptions. These members eliminated all regional tariffs by 2010 and others (Cambodia, Lao PDR, Myanmar, and Vietnam) are to do the same by 2015. The development of FTAs between ASEAN members and Japan is also noticeable. Starting with Singapore, Japan has negotiated FTAs with seven out of ten ASEAN members. The number of China's and Korea's bilateral FTAs with ASEAN members is small compared with Japan because they preferred to negotiate FTAs with ASEAN as a whole. As a result, the FTAs between China and ASEAN, and between Korea and ASEAN, have come into effect earlier than that between Japan and ASEAN. Another point that should be mentioned is that most East Asian states are looking for "extraregional" FTA partners as well as "intraregional" ones.

Table 5.2 shows major multilateral cooperation frameworks in and around East Asia. ASEAN, ADPS, APEC, ARF, and ASEM already existed before the Asian financial crisis, but other frameworks have emerged over the last decade. The ASEAN+3 framework was created in the midst of the financial crisis for the purpose of financial cooperation first, but the areas for cooperation have been extended significantly since. BIMSTEC is mainly a Thai and Indian initiative for economic cooperation across the Bay of Bengal. The members of BIMSTEC are also negotiating their own FTA. Australia, India, and South Africa lead the IOC-ARC framework, which focuses on cooperation in trade liberalization and facilitation, investment, science and technology, and tourism, among others. The SCO has started as a security cooperation framework among members, especially between China and Russia, and remains primarily so, but it also intends to expand efforts to economic cooperation areas. While the EAS is an economic cooperation framework for the wider "East Asian" region (includes ASEAN+3 plus Australia, New Zealand, and India), ACMECS focuses on cooperation in part of Southeast Asia, which is a subregion of East Asia.

Even from these simple observations on what have been happening in and around East Asia, some characteristics of East Asian integration processes can be pointed out.

First, institutional integration or cooperation processes in East Asia are sector- and function-based. For instance, the FTAs and EPAs in Table 5.1 are typical function-based integration. Yet the contents of the FTAs differ, reflecting the policy preferences of each FTA party. APEC also works on trade and investment liberalization and facilitation, economic and technical cooperation, and economic structural reform as is the case

TABLE 5.1
FTAs/EPAs of East Asian States/Regions
(as of November 2010)

	Japan	China	(Hong Kong)	(Macau)	South Korea	Taiwan	Mongolia	Indonesia	Malaysia	Philippines	Singapore	Thailand	Brunei	Cambodia	Laos	Myanmar	Vietnam	ASEAN	India	Bangladesh	Sri Lanka	Nepal	Bhutan	Pakistan
Japan	–	● ●†			△ ●†		△	☆	☆ ◇∗	☆	☆ ◇∗	☆	☆ ◇∗				☆ ◇∗	☆	○					
China	● ●†	–	☆	☆	●† ◎	◎#	●				☆	☆			◎			☆	● ◎	◎	◎			☆
(Hong Kong)	☆	–																						
(Macau)	☆		–																					
South Korea	△ ●†	●† ◎			–						☆	△			◎			☆	☆ ◎	◎	◎			
Taiwan		◎#				–					▲													
Mongolia	△	●																						
Indonesia	☆							–	∗	∗	∗	∗	∗	∗	∗	∗	∗	–	●					
Malaysia	☆ ◇∗							∗	–	∗	∗ ◇∗	∗	∗ ◇∗	∗	∗	∗	∗ ◇∗	–	△					☆
The Philippines	☆							∗	∗	–	∗	∗	∗	∗	∗	∗	∗	–						
Singapore	☆ ◇∗	☆			☆	▲		∗	∗ ◇∗	∗	–	∗	∗ ◇	∗	∗	∗	∗ ◇∗	–	☆					△
Thailand	☆	☆						∗	∗	∗	∗	–	∗	∗	∗	∗ ◇	∗	–	☆ □	□	□	□	□	●
Brunei	☆ ◇∗							∗	∗ ◇∗	∗	∗ ◇∗	∗	–	∗	∗	∗	∗ ◇∗	–						
Cambodia								∗	∗	∗	∗	∗	∗	–	∗	∗	∗	–						
Lao PDR		◎			◎			∗	∗	∗	∗	∗	∗	∗	–	∗	∗	–	◎	◎	◎			
Myanmar								∗	∗	∗	∗	∗ ◇	∗	∗	∗	–	∗	–	□	□	□	□	□	
Vietnam	☆ ◇∗							∗	∗ ◇∗	∗	∗ ◇∗	∗	∗ ◇∗	∗	∗	∗	–	–						
ASEAN	☆	☆			☆			–	–	–	–	–	–	–	–	–	–	–	☆					

☆ = in effect, ◎ = signed, ○ = agreed, △ = under negotiation/agreed to start negotiations,
● = under feasibility studies/completed feasibility studies, ▲ = proposed, ⊙ = Asia-Pacific Trade Agreement
(APTA [formerly known as Bangkok Agreement], in effect since 1975. China joined in 2001), ∗ = AFTA,
◇ = Trans-Pacific Strategic Economic Partnership Agreement (TPP, in effect since 2006. ∗ Australia, Malaysia,
Peru, the United States, and Vietnam started accession negotiations in 2010, and Japan has shown its interest in
joining in 2010), □ = BIMSTEC FTA (agreed in July 2009), # = China–Taiwan Economic Cooperation Framework
Agreement (ECFA: signed in June 2010), † = China–Japan–Korea FTA feasibility study

United Sates	Canada	Mexico	Honduras	El Salvador	Guatemala	Nicaragua	Costa Rica	Dominican Republic	Panama	Colombia	Chile	Peru	Australia	New Zealand	South Africa	SACU	Egypt	Jordan	Bahrain	GCC	Israel	Turkey	Ukraine	Switzerland	Norway	Iceland	Russia	EFTA	EU
◇*		☆									☆ ◇*	△ ◇*	△ ◇*	▲ ◇*	▲						△			☆					△
							◎				☆	☆	△	◎	△						△			●	△	△			
													◎																
◎	△	△								△	☆	◎	△	△	▲	●					△	●	△				●	☆	◎
			☆	☆	☆	☆		△	☆					▲															
▲											▲		△								▲								
△ ◇*											◎ ◇*	◇*	△ ◇*	☆ ◇*									△						
▲											●																		
☆ ◇*	△	△							◎	☆	◇	☆ ◇*	☆ ◇*	☆ ◇	△	△	☆			◎			△						☆
△											●	◎	☆	☆	▲			☆											△
▲ ◇*											◇	◇*	◇*	◇															
◇*											◇	◇*	◇*	◇															
▲														☆															△

Other multilateral FTA initiatives include:
East Asian Free Trade Agreement (EAFTA: 10 ASEAN members, China, Japan, and Korea) = under feasibility study
Comprehensive Economic Partnership in East Asia (CEPEA: 10 ASEAN members, China, Japan, Korea, Australia, India, New Zealand) = under feasibility study
Free Trade Area of the Asia Pacific (FTAAP: 21 APEC members) = APEC is exploring possible pathways

TABLE 5.2
Multilateral Cooperation Frameworks Involving East Asia
(as of November 2010)

| | East Asia | | | | | | | | | | | | | | | | | | |
| | Northeast Asia | | | | | | | Southeast Asia | | | | | | | | | | | |
	Japan	China	(Hong Kong)	South Korea	North Korea	Taiwan	Mongolia	Indonesia	Malaysia	The Philippines	Singapore	Thailand	Brunei	Cambodia	Lao PDR	Myanmar	Vietnam	PNG	Timor Leste
ASEAN (1967–)								☆	☆	☆	☆	☆	☆	☆	☆	☆	☆	○	○
ADPS (1972–)	☆	☆		☆				☆	☆	☆	☆	☆	☆	☆	☆	☆	☆	○	○
APEC (1989–)	☆	☆	☆	☆		☆		☆	☆	☆	☆	☆	☆					☆	☆
GMS (1992–)		☆										☆		☆	☆	☆	☆		
ARF (1994–)	☆	☆		☆	☆		☆	☆	☆	☆	☆	☆	☆	☆	☆	☆	☆	☆	☆
ASEM (1996–)	☆	☆		☆			☆	☆	☆	☆	☆	☆	☆	☆	☆	☆	☆		
ASEAN+3 (1997–)	☆	☆		☆				☆	☆	☆	☆	☆	☆	☆	☆	☆	☆		
BIMSTEC (1997–)												☆				☆			
IOR-ARC (1997–)	○	○						☆	☆		☆	☆							
CAREC (1997–)		☆					☆												
SCO (2001–)		☆					○												
ACD (2002–)	☆	☆		☆				☆	☆	☆	☆	☆	☆	☆	☆	☆	☆		
ACMECS (2003–)												☆		☆	☆	☆	☆		
EAS (2005–)	☆	☆		☆				☆	☆	☆	☆	☆	☆	☆	☆	☆	☆		

☆ = members/signatories,   ○ = observers/dialogue partners

ASEAN (Association of Southeast Asian Nations), **ADPS** (ASEAN Dialogue Partners System), **APEC** (Asia-Pacific Economic Cooperation), **GMS** (Greater Mekong Subregion), **ARF** (ASEAN Regional Forum), **ASEM** (Asia-Europe Meeting), **BIMSTEC** (Bay of Bengal Initiative for Multi-Sectoral Technical and Economic Cooperation), **IOR-ARC** (Indian Ocean Rim Association for Regional Cooperation),

	South Asia						Central Asia						Americas — North America			Americas — South America		Oceania		Russia
	India	Bangladesh	Sri Lanka	Nepal	Bhutan	Pakistan	Azerbaijan	Kazakhstan	Kyrgyzstan	Tajikistan	Turkmenistan	Uzbekistan	United States	Canada	Mexico	Chile	Peru	Australia	New Zealand	Russia
ASEAN (1967–)																				
ADPS (1972–)	☆					☆							☆	☆				☆	☆	☆
APEC (1989–)													☆	☆	☆	☆	☆	☆	☆	☆
GMS (1992–)																				
ARF (1994–)	☆	☆	☆			☆							☆	☆				☆	☆	☆
ASEM (1996–)	☆					☆												☆	☆	☆
ASEAN+3 (1997–)																				
BIMSTEC (1997–)	☆	☆	☆	☆	☆															
IOR-ARC (1997–)	☆	☆	☆															☆		
CAREC (1997–)						☆	☆	☆	☆	☆	☆	☆								
SCO (2001–)	○		○			○		☆	☆	☆		☆								☆
ACD (2002–)	☆	☆	☆		☆	☆		☆	☆	☆		☆								☆
ACMECS (2003–)																				
EAS (2005–)	☆												☆					☆	☆	☆

CAREC (Central Asia Regional Economic Cooperation), **SCO** (Shanghai Cooperation Organization), **ACD** (Asian Cooperation Dialogue), **ACMECS** (Ayeyawady–Chao Phraya–Mekong Economic Cooperation Strategy), **EAS** (East Asian Summit: Russia and the United States joined in 2011)

TABLE 5.2
(Con'd)

	Middle East									Africa						Europe		
	Afghanistan	Iran	Bahrain	Kuwait	Oman	Qatar	Saudi Arabia	UAE	Yemen	Kenya	Madagascar	Mauritius	Mozambique	South Africa	Tanzania	France	United Kingdom	EU
ASEAN (1967–)																		
ADPS (1972–)																		☆
APEC (1989–)																		
GMS (1992–)																		
ARF (1994–)																		☆
ASEM (1996–)																☆	☆	☆
ASEAN+3 (1997–)																		
BIMSTEC (1997–)																		
IOR-ARC (1997–)		☆			☆			☆	☆	☆	☆	☆	☆	☆	☆	○	○	
CAREC (1997–)	☆																	
SCO (2001–)		○																
ACD (2002–)		☆	☆	☆	☆	☆	☆	☆										
ACMECS (2003–)																		
EAS (2005–)																		

with FTAs in recent years, but it is a multilateral consultation forum without the ability to bind members' activities. The ARF and SCO are multilateral cooperation frameworks mainly on security issues.

Second, bilateral and multilateral processes coexist in functional integration in the same sector. This characteristic is illustrated by FTAs involving Southeast Asia. ASEAN members' foreign economic policies are based on AFTA, which is a regional FTA, but individual members have been seeking FTAs with non-ASEAN states at the same time. Furthermore, ASEAN as a whole has negotiated FTAs as well, resulting in the emergence of ASEAN+1 FTAs with China, Korea, Japan, India, and Australia/New Zealand. The basis of security cooperation in East Asia lies in the network of bilateral alliance relations, but, with division of roles, multilateral frameworks such as the ARF are also in operation.

Third, it is not uncommon that extraregional states participate in East Asian integration processes. In Table 5.1 and 5.2, East Asia is tentatively placed within the thick-line frame. It is quite obvious that many "outsiders" have been involved in function-based integration. Some of the most active "intruders" are Australia, Chile, India, New Zealand, Peru, and the United States, among others.

In sum, East Asian integration processes have a flexible, inclusive, and multi-layered nature. They are flexible because they are sector- and function-based. They allow some integration/cooperation efforts to make progress faster than others, even in the same sector. They are inclusive as they involve "extraregional" states not as exceptions, but rather as rules. They are multilayered because bilateral and multilateral frameworks coexist in the processes. It seems that the nature of East Asian integration is better understood when the processes are seen as a whole, and the focus is not on specific frameworks as separate entities.

Factors

Why then has East Asian integration as a whole shown a flexible, inclusive, and multilayered nature? Several factors can be assumed.

First, East Asian states seem to be searching for practical benefits from integration processes. In other words, they are seeking concrete political benefits and economic gains from the combination of bilateral and multilateral integration/cooperation frameworks.

Second, in achieving such concrete benefits and gains, it seems that East Asian states are not tying themselves to any geographical areas. As long as they can expect such benefits, the stage for integration/cooperation activities can be "subregional" (i.e. Southeast Asia), "regional" (i.e. East Asia), or "cross-regional" (i.e. the Asia Pacific).

Third, East Asian states, especially ASEAN members, seem to be concerned about any specific state's influence to dominate the integration processes. "Influence" here implies not only the traditional concept of "power", but also institutions and rules; in other words the way of doing things. East Asian states are trying to balance influences and, at the same time, are aiming to reflect their individual institutions and rules in the integration processes. To balance influences, it seems that they are not only concerned about relations between East Asian states, but are also utilizing extraregional states' involvement.

II. EXPLAINING THE NATURE OF EAST ASIAN INTEGRATION BY AUSTRALIA'S ASIAN ENGAGEMENT

The nature of East Asian integration and factors behind it can be explained in sharp relief through an examination of Australia's foreign policy and Asian engagement policy over the last twenty years.

Australia's foreign economic policy orientation changed at the turn of the century. The Australian Labor Party (ALP) Government (1983–96), led by Bob Hawke and Paul Keating, tried to transform the domestic economy from one that was inward-looking, inflexible, and specializing in the export of primary products to an open, market-responsive economy, with a more diverse pattern of exports by substantial liberalization and deregulation of the domestic trade and investment regime (Garnaut 1994, p. 51). In doing so, the government gave clear priority to unilateral and multilateral liberalization on an MFN basis. After the election victory in March 1996, the new Liberal/National Parties Government, led by John Howard, embarked on the change in Australia's foreign policy approach. It was a relative but distinctive shift towards greater emphasis on bilateral relations on the basis of a liberalized domestic economic regime. The bilateral approaches of the Howard Government were to provide reciprocal preferential treatment to particular trade partners and, on the other side of the coin, to discriminate against outsiders.

Asian Engagement through Multilateral Approaches

a) Backgrounds

(1) Efforts for Structural Reform of the Domestic Economy

The international economic structure changed dramatically after the first oil crisis. The end of the long primary commodities "boom" after World War II and the beginning of globalization of national economies were associated with a slide in Australia's terms of trade from the mid-1970s well into the 1990s. The Australian economy had plunged into lingering recession since the mid-1970s.

The Hawke Government, which won the 1983 general election, became the first Australian Government to implement fundamental economic reform policies. In the same year that it was elected, the government floated the exchange rate and surrendered most official controls over exchange dealings. The government removed restrictions on foreign ownership of merchant banks in 1984, allowed fifteen foreign banks to commence operations in 1985, and removed interest rate controls on trading banks in 1986. By the end of 1988, the exchange rate had depreciated by 24 per cent to the level prevailing at the beginning of the decade (Keating and Dixon 1989).

At the same time as implementing liberalisation and deregulation in the financial sector at a relatively fast pace, the government also introduced active promotion policies to certain industries such as steel, automobiles, textile, clothing and footwear, shipbuilding, pharmaceuticals, and information technology. A series of individual industry policies was collectively referred to as the "Button Plan" after the name of the Minister for Industry and Commerce who played a central role in its making. The government successfully and consistently involved the trade union movement in the policy process as well. The *Accord*, a social contract on wages and prices between the government and the Australian Council of Trade Unions (ACTU), stood out as an example. The *Accord*, which was renewed seven times between 1983 and 1996, was basically a deal between the government and trade unions to solve economic problems as far as possible to the mutual benefit of the two parties (Gruen and Grattan 1993, p. 111).

The depreciation of the currency and the introduction of industrial and export promotion policies were expected to result in an increase in exports, and a decrease in the current account deficit and foreign debt, but it did not have this effect immediately. In fact, the economic situation worsened after a brief recovery in 1984. The current account deficit rose to about 4.5 per cent of GDP in 1986, and foreign debt was also still increasing.

Low productivity, and thus less competitiveness against foreign products, was perceived to be the major obstacle to a comprehensive reduction of the current account deficit. Despite the government's efforts to liberalize the financial sector, it did not have an immediate impact on improvement of productivity of the sector. The increase in productivity of the manufacturing sector over the 1980s was consistent, thanks partly to the *Accord*, but was very slow.[1]

The government reaffirmed the urgency of structural reform. To increase productivity and competitiveness in manufacturing industries, the government finally decided to expose them to competition in the domestic and world markets by phasing out the protection they, and the trade unions, had long enjoyed. In October 1987, the government confirmed that all quantitative import restrictions would be gradually abolished. The Economic Statement of May 1988 announced a general programme of phased reductions in protection for all manufacturing industries. Furthermore, the Industry Policy Statement of March 1991 declared the continuation of the programme, stating that tariffs of most imports were to be phased down to five per cent by 1996.

(2) Deepening Economic Relations with East Asia

Under the GATT regime, economic interdependence among the economies in the Asia Pacific region had developed steadily since the 1960s. For Australia, the trend was illustrated by a significant increase in trade with East Asian economies.[2] Australia's exports to Japan started to increase rapidly in the mid-1960s and Japan became its largest single export destination in the latter half of the 1960s. Exports to Asian Newly Industrializing Economies (Hong Kong, South Korea, and Taiwan) and ASEAN (Indonesia, Malaysia, the Philippines, Singapore, and Thailand) started to grow quickly in the mid-1970s. From 1980 to 1995, the fastest growing export destination was NIEs, with a more than a fourfold increase over the period, followed by ASEAN, with a more than threefold increase. Imports from East Asian economies also steadily increased from the 1970s. Imports from Japan started to grow earlier than those from other East Asian economies. The fastest growing import sources over the period from 1980 to 1995 were NIEs, with an increase of more than fourfold, then New Zealand, with an almost threefold increase, followed closely by ASEAN, with a just under threefold increase.

The growing importance of East Asian economies for Australia's trade was reflected in the significant increase in their share in Australia's exports and imports. In 1948, Japan's share in total Australian exports and imports was negligible, but by 1965 it had increased to 17 per cent in exports, and nine per cent in imports. The figures reached almost 30 per cent in exports and 25 per cent in imports in the mid-1980s. The growth in the share of NIEs and ASEAN was also considerable. Collectively they accounted for only three per cent of Australia's total exports, and just a little more than one per cent of its imports in 1948. By 1995, their shares reached 32 per cent and 17 per cent respectively, due to the rapid economic growth of NIEs, and ASEAN over the period. If the figures for Japan, NIEs and ASEAN are combined, East Asia accounted for 55 per cent of Australia's total exports, and 32 per cent of its imports in 1995, compared with just 4 per cent and 1 per cent respectively in 1948.

The change in the economic environment in the Asia Pacific region was distinguished by the rapid development of East Asian economies, which was later called the "East Asian miracle". The economic climates of East Asia and Australia were quite contrasting. Among policy actors in Australia, there was a growing conception that Australia should build closer economic relations with East Asia to take advantage of their dynamic economic development in order to pull out of a lingering recession.[3]

(3) A Liberal World View

Under this domestic and international environment, leaders of the government generally had a "liberal" view of the world. People such as Hawke, Keating, and Gareth Evans (Minister for Foreign Affairs, 1988–96), saw international relations *not* as "zero-sum games" among states competing for national interests. Keating observed in 1996 that: "the drag out/knock down approach to trade negotiations has surely reached the end of its useful life in an environment where every country in the world, rather than just a handful of industrialised countries, has a stake in global trade" (Keating 1996, pp. 19–20). They also believed that multilateral cooperation was not only possible, but also necessary even without a hegemonic power. Furthermore, they believed that Australia, which they defined as a "middle power", could make an impact on international society if it chose the appropriate method and timing.

b) Policies and Results

(1) The Cairns Group Initiative: Creating the Third Force in Multilateral Negotiations

Against this background, Australia's foreign policy in general came to have a distinctive multilateralist characteristic. Because the government's liberalization and deregulation measures were introduced unilaterally, it needed to underpin these domestic efforts by attention to strengthening international economic regimes, especially the General Agreement on Tariffs and Trade (GATT).

Just a month before the formal launch of the Uruguay Round in August 1986, the government invited representatives from fourteen agricultural exporting countries to Cairns and led the formation of a coalition to become a "third force" in international negotiations alongside with the European Commission and the United States (Evans and Grant 1995, p. 37). The members of the new international coalition, the Cairns Group, came from various parts of the world: North America (Canada), Latin America (Argentina, Brazil, Chile, Colombia, and Uruguay), Eastern Europe (Hungary), Southeast Asia (Indonesia, Malaysia, the Philippines and Thailand), and Oceania (Australia, Fiji, and New Zealand).

The establishment of the Cairns Group made an immediate impact on international trade negotiations. Mainly through the pressure from the Group, the government could settle the full inclusion of agriculture in multilateral negotiations for the first time in GATT's history. Australia continued to lead the Cairns Group to the conclusion of the Uruguay Round negotiations. The end results of the Uruguay Round on agriculture, however, turned out to be less than what the Cairns Group had hoped for, mainly because of strong resistance from the European Union during the final weeks of negotiations. Nonetheless, the fact that the agreement that extended all the rules and disciplines of GATT to agricultural trade had been reached for the first time in GATT's history was significant.

(2) The APEC Initiative: Seeking Multilateral Liberalization through Regional Cooperation

The international trade regime, nevertheless, was fragile in the late 1980s and early 1990s. When the Uruguay Round was deadlocked, the United States prioritized its bilateralist policies. It opted for the creation of an FTA with Canada, in effect from January 1989, and subsequently extended this to Mexico as NAFTA, from January 1994. It also suggested that other bilateral and regional arrangements could follow. The European Commission advanced its programme of creating a single market by 1993 through the *Single European Act* of 1987. The *Treaty on European Union* (the Maastricht Treaty) in 1992 led to the creation of the European Union the following year, and advanced political and economic union issues. These economic groupings involving economic powers such as the United States and the European Union made outsiders, including Australia, very cautious.

The Hawke government reacted to the United States and the European Union moves by setting on a policy course to promote global free trade and investment using cooperation in the Asia Pacific region as its springboard. Working together with Japan, the Hawke government called for cooperation for freer trade and investment in the Asia Pacific region. In the short term, if a new regional forum at the ministerial level was created, it could put pressure on the Uruguay Round participants in other regions to move more quickly towards a successful conclusion. In the longer term, the activities of the forum for policy cooperation and coordination in areas such as trade, investment, industrial development, financial and other services and food and energy security, would significantly increase regional interdependence, which would lead to improved economic performances of potential members of the forum, including Australia. Furthermore, increased economic interdependence in the region was expected to encourage a more stable and cohesive political environment (Harris 1989, p. 17).

The Australian Government's intensive lobbying in 1989 culminated in the first ministerial meeting of APEC in November that year, in which foreign and trade ministers representing twelve states in the region (Australia, Canada, Japan, Korea, New Zealand, the United States, and six ASEAN members) participated. From its inception, APEC consistently argued the importance of the successful conclusion of the Uruguay Round. It was widely acknowledged that APEC's pressure contributed to the positive conclusion of the Round.[4]

(3) Aiming for Political, Economic, and Social Integration with East Asia

On top of its aspiration for closer economic relations with East Asia, the government's Asian engagement policy was based on the recognition that Australia should be integrated politically and socially with the region. Evans stated in 1989 that:

> Australia and Australians should see the region not as something external ... but as a common neighbourhood of extraordinary diversity and significant economic potential. It is where *we must find a place and role* if we are to develop our full potential as a nation. So it is an area ... on which *we need to concentrate our resources of diplomacy and defence, political management and economic energy.*
>
> (Evans 1989, p. 9, italics added)

After succeeding Hawke as Prime Minister at the end of 1991, Keating articulated a strong personal commitment to this conception of Australia's interests, and drove the argument forward. He later said:

> My ... conviction was that Asia was where Australia's future substantially lay and that we needed to engage with it at a level and with an intensity we had never come close to doing in the past. ... *all* our national interests – political, economic, strategic and cultural — coalesced so strongly in the one place as they did now.
>
> (Keating 2000, p. 17)

Evans' and Keating's Asian engagement, in fact, demanded a change in national identity as well. Keating reasserted his view by stating that "we can and should aim to be a country which is deeply integrated into the region around us" and this integration would be achieved by Australia having a national culture that "is shaped by, and helps to shape, the cultures around us" (Kelly 2006, p. 26). For Keating, engagement with Asia was not just a policy for closer economic relations, but also one of the measures to renovate Australia politically and socially, along with his inclination towards establishing an Australian republic.

(4) Comprehensive Engagement with Southeast Asia

Foreign policies based on multilateral approaches and the aspiration for integration with East Asia were gradually introduced in the 1980s under the Hawke government and more decisively in the first half of the 1990s under the Keating government. In this process, ASEAN became a regional focus of Australia's foreign policy because of ASEAN members' sustained rapid economic development and the organization's increasing tendency towards a regionalist approach.[5]

The government emphasized the need to consolidate multifaceted relations with ASEAN and its members as a basis of its foreign policy towards East Asia. Minister for Foreign Affairs Gareth Evans made a statement on "comprehensive engagement" with Southeast Asia in 1989 that read:

- building a more diverse and substantive array of linkages with the countries of Southeast Asia, so that they have an important national interest in the maintenance of a positive relationship with Australia;
- continuing to support the major existing regional association, ASEAN, and working with the countries of the region to shape additional regional organisations or arrangements, such as APEC, which can contribute to the social and economic evolution of the region;
- participating actively in the gradual development of a regional security community based on a sense of shared security interests.

(Evans and Grant 1995, pp. 195–96).

However, the Australian Government's intention to engage with Southeast Asia comprehensively met with mixed responses.

In 1989, the government initiated its renewed efforts to resolve the Cambodian problem by proposing a peace plan that emphasized the comprehensive involvement of the United Nations in a transitional authority. A detailed Australian proposal was released as the "Red Book" in February 1990 and widely circulated among the concerned parties (Evans and Grant 1995, pp. 225–27). Along with some other countries such as Indonesia, Japan, and the United States, Australia's diplomatic efforts leading to the *Agreement on the Comprehensive Political Settlement of the Cambodian Conflict* signed in October 1991, and its role played in the United Nations Transitional Authority in Cambodia between 1992 and 1993, were critical for the eventual settlement of the external aspect of the Cambodian problem.

As Evans' comprehensive engagement statement in 1989 foreshadowed, the government sought to create a new regional security community. At the ASEAN Post-Ministerial Conference (PMC) in July 1990, Evans suggested the establishment of a security dialogue forum, which could gradually develop into something like the Conference (since 1995, Organization) on Security and Cooperation in Europe, a regional security organization that has brought most European states, the United States, and Canada together. Evans' proposal initially met with sceptical responses from ASEAN and the United States, but the ASEAN Summit in 1992 decided to use its PMC process to cover the security issues. Subsequently, ASEAN initiated the creation of the ARF in 1994. The United States, under the new Clinton Administration, also agreed to participate.

The East Asian Economic Group (EAEG) proposal from Malaysian Prime Minister Mahathir bin Mohamad in 1990 was primarily a reaction to the moves in North America and Europe to form or deepen regional economic blocs, but it assumed as potential members only East Asian states, excluding Australia. The United States vocally opposed the EAEG concept and petitioned Japan and Korea to reject the proposal. Australia was as outspoken as the United States in opposing the proposal. For the Hawke government, the EAEG concept appeared to mean the negation of Australian efforts to engage more closely with the region (Ravenhill 1998, p. 281).

The AFTA initiative, ASEAN's response to the changing international and regional economic environment with an increasingly regionalist approach, was also potentially problematic for Australia. As AFTA aimed for liberalization of intraregional trade, it could diversify trade flows away from Australia. The Australian Government was quick to study the potential effects of AFTA on Australia's trade and investment, and published a report in 1994. The report concluded that the negative effects of AFTA on Australian industries via a trade diversion effect would be minimal, but argued that the Australian Government should encourage ASEAN to regard AFTA as a "building block" that should contribute to increased liberalization of trade in the region (EAAU/DFAT 1994, pp. 101–13).

The government attempted to overcome this challenge through an economic cooperation dialogue process with ASEAN, both at government and private business levels. The process started in 1995 and came to be called the "AFTA–CER linkage dialogue", involving all ASEAN members and CER states (Australia and New Zealand). Although the objective and the modality of the dialogue were both configured reasonably well, concrete results did not follow as the government had hoped.

In sum, Australia's intention of comprehensive engagement was not fully accepted in East Asia, especially by ASEAN members.

Asian Engagement through Bilateral Approaches

a) Backgrounds

(1) Public Fatigue and Uneasiness

Between the mid 1980s and the mid-1990s, there was broad bipartisan support for a policy strategy that sought unilateral and MFN-based multilateral trade liberalization focused on initiatives in the Asia Pacific region to underpin domestic economic reform and structural change. By the mid-1990s, however, this policy strategy was associated with developments that caused growing public disquiet. The decade-long implementation of economic reform led to reform fatigue and an ideological attack on "economic rationalism".[6] Public disquiet about the "Asianisation of Australia" (Cotton and Ravenhill 1997, pp. 12–13; Milner 1997, pp. 35–36) had grown to a level where it could no longer be ignored politically (Cotton and Ravenhill 2001, pp. 6–7; Milner 2001, p. 35). This was part of the background to the demise of the Keating government and the rise of the Liberal and National Party opposition under the leadership of John Howard in the March 1996 general election.

(2) The Initiative of the New Government

The new Howard government initiated a review of the foreign policy of previous governments. The government brought a more "realist" understanding of the international society to foreign policy than previous governments. The government attached paramount importance to individual states as actors and prioritized bilateral relations between states over international organizations such as the United Nations (UN) and the World Trade Organization (WTO), and multilateral cooperation. In other words, it saw that Australia's national interest would be best served through good bilateral relations with shared interests and mutual respect. And for the Howard government, "shared interests" meant practical and concrete political and economic interests, and what should be respected mutually were traditions, values, beliefs, and identity which naturally varied between states (Wesley 2007, p. 42, pp. 52–55).

The government was inclined to push Australia's "national interest" through bilateral means, including FTAs that sought reciprocal liberalization and short-term, concrete economic benefits, rather than through multilateral negotiations. With the completion of its review of foreign policy, the government published Australia's first ever White Paper on foreign and trade policy (Commonwealth of Australia 1997). The White Paper stated that "a central feature of the Government's approach ... is the importance it attaches to strengthening bilateral relationships" (Commonwealth of Australia 1997, p. 53). On FTAs, it argued that:

> Australia will keep an open mind about new approaches, including preferential free trade arrangements. Compared with global negotiations, they are perceived as being able to go further faster, and are more likely to include "new issues" arising from the globalisation of economic activity.
>
> (Commonwealth of Australia 1997, p. 42)

Australia's bilateral economic relations under successive governments after World War II sought to secure and extend mutual MFN treatment under the GATT regime. Although governments until 1970s were generally sceptical of multilateral liberalization, the direction of the policy strategy was to extend mutual MFN status to growing partners. In contrast, the bilateral approaches that the Howard government asserted was a clear departure from the traditional strategy in the sense that they mutually provide preferential treatment on the one hand, and discriminate against third states on the other.

(3) The Asian Financial Crisis and the Emergence of East Asian Regionalism

The Howard government's clear indication of its readiness to adopt new bilateral approaches in foreign policy coincided with the outbreak of the Asian financial crisis. After the crisis, East Asian states found renewed motives for building their own economic cooperation framework. Of the emergency loan package for Thailand worth US$17 billion, for instance, the IMF provided less than 25 per cent, but enforced strict "conditionalities". The United States and European Union members did not participate in the package. These circumstances led East Asian states, especially Japan, to realize that a future currency crisis in any East Asian economy, which would be highly transmissible to others, had to be dealt with primarily within the region. Sharing this view, the heads of governments of ASEAN members, China, Japan, and Korea held a meeting in November 1997 to discuss regional financial and economic cooperation.

After the inaugural summit, this East Asian regional cooperation (ASEAN+3) process began to evolve. In 2000, the ASEAN+3 process saw agreement on the "Chiang Mai Initiative", which was a network of bilateral currency swap agreements among East Asian states, and the establishment of a working group to study the feasibility of an East Asian FTA. To accommodate these increasing activities, the ASEAN+3 institution has been expanded. By 2003, in addition to the annual summit, the frameworks for Economic, Foreign, Labour, Health, Tourism, and Agricultural Ministers Meetings had been established.

b) Policies and Results

(1) The Legacy of Multilateral Approaches

The bilateralist approaches, nevertheless, were not readily digested among policy actors. There were several reasons for that. First, Australia's export performance in the latter half of the 1990s had been good compared with other economies in the region. Considering that most East Asian economies, which usually absorb more than half of Australia's exports, were facing extreme economic hardship following the financial crisis and Japan was struggling to overcome the lingering recession, Australia's export performance in this period was outstanding. From the trade policy point of view, the government did not have to rely on bilateral arrangements to promote the "national interest" in this difficult regional economic environment.

Second, during this period of strong export growth, there were good reasons for policy actors to prefer multilateral approaches to reducing trade barriers. As mentioned earlier, the Hawke and Keating govern-ments actively involved themselves in the Uruguay Round with success, particularly in agricultural trade. After the completion of prolonged negotiations at the end of 1993, domestic industries in Australia, especially agriculture, wanted to secure the steady implementation of the Uruguay Round results by trade partners and did not want bilateral or regional FTAs to interrupt the process. In addition, it was already agreed at the completion of the Uruguay Round that new negotiations on liberalization in the agricultural and services sectors were to start in 2000 as a "built-in agenda". These legacies of the Uruguay Round did not change just because of the change of government.

Furthermore, there was a series of multilateral and regional develop-ments, such as the Early Voluntary Sectoral Liberalization (EVSL) initiative of APEC and the anticipated launch of the first round of trade negotiations under the WTO, which was often referred to then as the "Millennium Round", from which Australia could expect significant benefits. In this period, most society actors, including business and industry organizations, clearly preferred these multilateral approaches over bilateral ones (ACCI 2000, pp. 5–10) and did not encourage the government to pursue specific bilateral FTAs until 2000.

(2) The Failure of Multilateral Initiatives and the Implementation of Bilateral Approaches

Yet all these multilateral initiatives failed by 2000. The APEC EVSL initiative was effectively discarded due mainly to the different understanding of the concept of "voluntary" liberalization among the members. While the APEC Leaders and Ministerial Meetings in September 1999 managed to support the launch of a new round in principle, the WTO Ministerial Conference in Seattle two months later virtually collapsed and failed to launch a new round.

In 1998 as the EVSL initiative was heading towards failure, some states in the Asia Pacific region began to move towards bilateral FTAs. In September, New Zealand commenced formal FTA negotiations with Singapore. In December, Japan and Korea, the states that traditionally favoured multilateralism in trade liberalization and had not been involved in any FTAs before, agreed to start a joint study on a bilateral FTA at semi-governmental level. Japan also began similar studies with

Mexico and Singapore early in 1999 and early in 2000 respectively. The United States' intention to create the Free Trade Area of the Americas (FTAA) was clearly stated at the inaugural summit of the Americas in December 1994. The U.S. drive for the FTAA intensified after the second summit in Santiago in April 1998.

What appeared at this very time was an ASEAN proposal to study the feasibility of an FTA between ASEAN and CER members (Agreement Closer Economic Relations, between Australia and New Zealand). In October 1999, ASEAN proposed to set up a task force to study the feasibility of establishing an ASEAN–CER FTA by 2010. The Howard government welcomed the proposal. The Task Force submitted a report titled, *The Angkor Agenda*, to the meeting of Economic Ministers Meeting from ASEAN, Australia, and New Zealand in October 2000. Ultimately, the report resolved that:

> Establishing a free trade area between AFTA and CER is *not only feasible but also advisable.* [The Task Force members] strongly suggest ... undertak[ing] the necessary steps toward the establishment of the proposed AFTA–CER FTA *at the earliest possible time.*
>
> (High-Level Task Force 2000, italics added)

Despite the task force's strong recommendation to start negotiations for the FTA immediately, the responses from the ASEAN side were indecisive. Singapore and Thailand were in favour of the ASEAN–CER FTA, but opposition was raised mainly by Indonesia and Malaysia. ASEAN could not reach a consensus on this issue. In reality, the Ministerial Meeting effectively shelved the ASEAN–CER FTA indefinitely.

The setback of the ASEAN–CER FTA worked as the final blow to the legacies of multilateral approaches. At this stage, the government decided to take the first step towards bilateral FTAs. In November 2000, Howard made a joint announcement with Singapore Prime Minister Goh Chok Tong that the two governments would start negotiations for a bilateral FTA. By the end of the year, the government began considering negotiating an FTA with the incoming George W. Bush Administration in the United States (Ravenhill 2001, p. 285). Growth of support for the bilateralist policy ideas from social actors became more obvious when negotiations for an FTA with the United States became a possibility in 2001. By 2004 most social actors, including major business and industry organizations, had shown their support for bilateral FTAs as an effective trade policy strategy.[7]

(3) Engaging with Asia with Confidence

The Howard government's Asian engagement policy began to reflect its "realist" world view and bilateralist intentions more clearly. It contrasted with that of the Keating-Evans era which demanded the alteration of national identity from the public. Howard stated:

> I think one of the mistakes we made for a while in our relationship with Asia was to fret too much about where we stood. Whether we were Asian, or part of Asia, enmeshed with Asia, or in Asia — forget that. We should really be as we are, and that is Australia, not denying for a moment our past associations or seeking to adjust them in order to please.
>
> (quoted in Kelly 2001, p. 250)

On the premise of "differences" between Australia and Asian countries, bilateral reconciliation of interests became the central feature of the Howard government's Asian engagement.

From the Asian financial crisis experience, the government had also gained confidence in Australia's economic management — during the crisis, the Australian economy was virtually unaffected and grew strongly — and a self-image that Australia could be a good example of economic reforms to crisis-hit economies (Wesley 2001, pp. 310–11). In addition, the East Timor experience and active participation in the war against terrorism worked to strengthen the government's belief in Australian values, identity and institutions. This confidence was manifested in the second foreign and trade policy White Paper published in 2003, which in part sounded so triumphant:

- Australia's identity is strong. We have developed our own distinctive culture and sense of confidence (p. viii).
- Our economic underpinnings are strong and dynamic. We have responded well to the challenges of deeper integration into the global economy, including by successful management of the economy during the East Asian financial crisis (p. 128).
- Our security capabilities are sound as we showed by our contribution to East Timor's transition to independence and our participation in the war against terrorism. Our diplomacy has been effective. We have a proud humanitarian record. We are well educated. Few

countries of Australia's size can point to such a record of contemporary accomplishment (p. 129).

(Commonwealth of Australia 2003)

The Howard government considered that Australia was "well placed to make a distinctive contribution" to other states' efforts to improve their political and economic governance (Commonwealth of Australia 2003, pp. 114–15). The government also asserted that Australia should go out to the region "not as a supplicant but as a partner" seeking to work with neighbours for mutual benefit (Commonwealth of Australia 2003, p. 85).

Since embarking on the shift in foreign policy orientation, the Howard government's approach towards East Asia has brought mixed results, especially in the early stage. From the beginning of the Asian financial crisis, the government involved itself in IMF rescue packages for Indonesia, Thailand, and Korea. Australia became one of only two states (along with Japan) to contribute to all three packages. When the negotiations between Indonesia and the IMF on loan conditions intensified in early 1998, the government was sympathetic to Indonesia and tried to play a mediating role. Australia's contribution to the IMF packages and other activities were appreciated by the recipients. Alexander Downer, Minister for Foreign Affairs, claimed that by "proving we are a partner and a neighbour for the long haul", Australia's image in the region had changed decisively "from something close to regional mendicant to a regional mate" (quoted in Pitty 2003, p. 42). Yet these activities did not culminate in acceptance from the Asian side of Australia's membership in the Asia–Europe Meeting (ASEM) process (Wesley 2001, p. 317).

The government's active involvement in East Timor's independence process in 1999, particularly the central role it played in the UN peacekeeping operation, was praised domestically and by the United Nations, but it provoked resentment in Indonesia. Amid the political confusion and violent conflict in East Timor, the four-year old *Australia–Indonesia Agreement on Maintaining Security* was abrogated by the Indonesian Government in September 1999. A journal interview with Howard appeared on 28 September on the so-called "Howard Doctrine". Featuring the catch phrase of Australia playing the role of "deputy sheriff" to the United States in the region, it increased Asian anger further not only in Southeast Asia, but also in Japan and Korea (Milner 2001, pp. 41–45).

Since the September 11 terrorist attacks in the United States in 2001, the Howard government worked closely with ASEAN members in an effort to contain terrorism in the region (DFAT 2004, pp. 15–16). However, after the Bali bombings on 12 October 2002, which killed or injured more than 200 people, including 88 Australians, Howard's statement about the possibility that Australia could launch "pre-emptive military strikes" against terrorists operating in neighbouring countries caused yet another wave of resentment in the region. Partly as a result, ASEAN effectively rejected Australia's proposal to hold an annual ASEAN–Australia Summit.

By the end of 2005, however, the government signed a bilateral Memoranda of Understanding on Counter-Terrorism with all original ASEAN members (Indonesia, Malaysia, the Philippines, Singapore, and Thailand). Furthermore, a bilateral security agreement, which was once abrogated by Indonesia in 1999, was revived as a new *Indonesia–Australia Security Cooperation Framework Agreement*. This agreement, which covers cooperation in non-traditional security areas such as people smuggling and trafficking of persons, trafficking in narcotics drugs, money laundering, anti-terrorism, corruption, and natural disaster, was signed in November 2006 and came into effect in February 2008.

In the area of economic relations, Australia had completed bilateral FTAs with Singapore and Thailand, and had commenced negotiations with Malaysia and China by 2005. In 2007, the government was also in FTA negotiations with Japan and conducting joint feasibility studies with Korea, Indonesia, and India in the area of security cooperation.

"Unexpected" Results of Bilateral Approaches

a) Resurgence of the ASEAN–CER FTA and Australia's Participation in the East Asia Summit

When the Howard government decided to negotiate an FTA with the United States, some academics and ALP members were alarmed that the FTA would enhance perceptions in Asia that Australia saw its interests mainly outside the region and that would disadvantage

Australia in its engagement with Asia.[8] This concern has not been realized in practice. Rather, it has been notable that, through driving its bilateral approaches, the Howard government not only secured bilateral FTAs with East Asian states, but also achieved the unexpected result of promoting multilateral economic relations with ASEAN as a whole, and East Asia as a whole.

The ASEAN Economic Ministers Meeting in April 2004 decided to invite Howard and New Zealand Prime Minister Helen Clark to attend the ASEAN Summit later in the year and revive the ASEAN–CER FTA initiative. The summit held in November declared that ASEAN members, Australia, and New Zealand would start negotiations for an FTA in early 2005, to be completed in two years (ASEAN–Australia–New Zealand Summit 2005). The negotiations were concluded in August 2008.

While the ASEAN+3 process has further evolved to aim explicitly at the establishment of an East Asian FTA and an East Asian community (APT Summit 2005a), Howard, along with his Indian and New Zealand counterparts, was invited to attend the inaugural East Asia Summit to discuss the development of regional cooperation with ASEAN+3 leaders in December 2005. Howard stated that he saw the East Asia Summit as an expression of a reality in the region from which Australia — a modern, sophisticated western country with an economy that was performing well — could not, should not, and would not be excluded (Howard 2006).

All these developments appeared to justify the effectiveness of the Howard government's bilateral foreign policy approaches towards East Asia in general and ASEAN in particular. In a sense, what could not be achieved by multilateral approaches in the 1990s was achieved in the 2000s by bilateral approaches.

b) Regional Factors behind the Success of Bilateral Approaches

The Howard government's successful engagement with East Asia through bilateral approaches, however, should also be seen from the perspective of the individual situation of East Asian states at the time, and the delicate and sometimes unstable relations among them.

The lesson learnt by East Asian governments, especially those of ASEAN, from the experience of the financial crisis was that, it was crucial to restore and maintain market confidence to realize stable management of the national economy. In addition, the fact that the Southeast Asian region was increasingly seen as one of the main areas for international terrorists' operation after the 9/11 attacks has become a factor for the governments of ASEAN members to recognize the urgent need to enhance their political and economic governance capabilities and demonstrate them to the world (Wesley 2007, pp. 101–02). ASEAN governments sought opportunities to rebuild their reputations for strong governance and to ensure stable investment conditions. Singapore's, Thailand's, and Malaysia's agreements with Australia to negotiate bilateral FTAs, and the signing of a Memoranda of Understanding on Counter-Terrorism with Australia by all five original ASEAN members between 2001 and 2005 were among their attempts towards this end.

Howard was invited to the inaugural East Asian Summit not exclusively because Australia and its economy were important for the region. Since the realization of an East Asian "community" appeared on the ASEAN+3 agenda in 2001 as a long-term goal, China, Malaysia, Myanmar, and some others who wanted to avert external influences on the community building process, argued that membership should be limited to the participants in the ASEAN+3 process (ASEAN members, China, Japan, and Korea). Japan, on the other hand, maintained that East Asian cooperation should be expanded to include Australia and New Zealand, which had been dialogue partners of ASEAN since the mid-1970s and had substantial political and economic relations with East Asia. Japan did this partly because it wished to allay the impression of an exclusive community, taking into account the U.S. response to its formation.

More importantly, though, it was also because Japan was concerned with the possible domination of the community building process by China with which it did not share basic values such as democracy, rule of law, human rights, and market economy. As Japan sees such values, along with "openness" and "inclusiveness", as the principles for community building in East Asia (MOFA 2006, p. 61), it wished Australia and New Zealand, who shared these values more than other East Asian countries, to be involved in the regional community building process. In varying degrees, Indonesia, Singapore, Vietnam, and some others shared the Japanese concern about Chinese influence. The end result of extending invitations to Australia, New Zealand, and India — but not to Russia and the United States — to the East Asian Summit was a compromise between these two groups.

Similarly, ASEAN's decision to negotiate an FTA with Australia and New Zealand needs to be interpreted not only from the Australian perspective, but also from the perspective of ASEAN's intention to maintain its relevance as the core element in the architecture of East Asia. As it was in the APEC process, ASEAN as a whole is concerned about the marginalization of the organization in the process of East Asian cooperation, integration, and community building. While it was reiterated at the ASEAN+3 and East Asia Summits in 2005 that "ASEAN integration and the ASEAN Community" were the important basis of an East Asian community (APT Summit 2005*b*; East Asia Summit 2005), ASEAN has been trying to balance the influence of powers in the region, namely China and Japan, in the ASEAN+3 process. This has been expressed in its efforts not only to establish FTAs with China, Japan, and Korea concurrently, but also to negotiate FTAs with extraregional states such as India, Australia, and New Zealand. ASEAN has also expressed its intention to negotiate FTAs with the European Union and the United States in the near future.

III. CONCLUDING REMARKS

East Asian integration processes in recent years have a flexible, inclusive, and multilayered nature. This chapter explained that Australia's Asian engagement policies and their results over the last twenty years illustrate the nature of East Asian integration processes.

Australia's policy towards East Asia in the 1990s, which was based on multilateral approaches and comprehensive engagement, brought some distinctive successes. Among them, initiatives for the Cairns Group, APEC, the resolution of the Cambodian Problem, and the creation of the ARF are notable. Yet Australia was excluded from the EAEG proposal, the AFTA–CER linkage dialogue did not produce immediate results, and the ASEAN–CER FTA initiative was effectively shelved.

Australia's new foreign policy orientation since the turn of the century, which is marked by realistic and bilateral approaches, has also produced mixed results. Nevertheless, it is notable that its Asian engagement policies, on the premise of political, economic, and cultural differences between Australia and Asian countries, have gradually produced regional and multilateral outcomes in the form of the restoration of the once discarded ASEAN–CER FTA and participation in the East Asia Summit.

The analysis and arguments in this chapter reveal several implications for the current prospects of East Asian integration processes.

First, East Asian integration will continue to have practical and realistic focuses. Rather than designing a "big picture" for the future of East Asia and moving towards the realization of that big picture, it is more likely that integration processes will be the accumulation of many cooperation frameworks that are perceived to realize individual, concrete benefits. Second, the content of such benefits and the method to realize them must be acceptable for East Asian states. This sounds a matter of course, but whether the contents and methods are acceptable for ASEAN members and ASEAN as a whole will remain crucial. Third, because foreign policy and foreign economic policy preferences among East Asian countries are likely to remain diversified, the existence of multiple integration/cooperation frameworks in the same sector are also likely to remain. Fourth, extraregional states' participation in such multiple frameworks will not be denied as long as the realization of concrete and mutual benefits for both parties is realistically expected. Lastly, if integration processes proceed in the above mentioned nature, which is more likely than not, the geographical concept of "East Asia" would become increasingly vague. Regions are created by politics (see Chapter 2). In other words, they are created by power and purpose. Yet the nature of East Asian integration suggests a lack of coherent direction of power and purpose in this "region". As it does now, East Asia will continue to mean different concepts in different situations and to the different people who discuss it.

Notes

1. The Productivity Commission's website at <http://www.pc.gov.au/ commission/work/productivity/performance/productivityestimates0304/ industry2004.xls>.

2. The trade data used in this section are from: International Monetary Fund, *Direction of Trade Statistics Yearbook*, various issues.
3. See, for example, Garnaut (1989).
4. Petri (1999, p. 15) pointed out that APEC played an effective "cheerleading role" encouraging and supporting the Uruguay Round negotiations.
5. Richard Woolcott, a former Secretary of Department of Foreign Affairs and Trade (1988–92), stated in 1995 that "every regional initiative Australia has taken in recent years has depended for its success or failure on ASEAN's reaction" (quoted in Ravenhill 1998, p. 268).
6. In early 1996, an opinion poll showed that 59 per cent of respondents either "strongly agreed" or "agreed" with the proposition that "Australia should use tariffs to protect its industry" (Ravenhill 2001, p. 290).
7. See, for instance, ACCI (2004).
8. See, for instance, Garnaut (2002, p. 135).

References

ACCI (Australian Chamber of Commerce and Industry). *Australia's Relationship with the World Trade Organization*. ACCI Submission to the Joint Standing Committee on Treaties, Parliament of Australia, August 2000.

——. *The Australia–United States Free Trade Agreement*, April 2004. Available at <http://www.acci.asn.au/text_files/issues_papers/Trade/Australia-Unite d%20State%20Free%20Trade%20Agreement%20_April%202004_.pdf>.

APT Summit (ASEAN Plus Three Summit). *Chairman's Statement of the Ninth ASEAN Plus Three Summit*. Kuala Lumpur, 12 December 2005a. At <http:// www.aseansec.org/18042.htm>.

——. *Kuala Lumpur Declaration on the ASEAN Plus Three Summit*. Kuala Lumpur, 12 December 2005b. At <http://www.aseansec.org/18037.htm>.

ASEAN–Australia–New Zealand Summit. *Joint Declaration of the Leaders at the ASEAN–Australia and New Zealand Commemorative Summit*. November 2005. At <http://www.aseansec.org/16796.htm>

Commonwealth of Australia. *In the National Interest: Australia's Foreign and Trade Policy White Paper*. DFAT, August 1997.

——. *Advancing the National Interest: Australia's Foreign and Trade Policy White Paper*. DFAT, February 2003. At <http://www.dfat.gov.au/ani/dfat_white_ paper.pdf>.

Cotton, James, and John Ravenhill. "Australia's 'Engagement with Asia'". In *Seeking Asian Engagement: Australia in World Affairs, 1991–95*, edited by James Cotton and John Ravenhill. Melbourne: Oxford University Press, in association with the Australian Institute of International Affairs, 1997.

————. "Australia in World Affairs 1996–2000". In *The National Interest in a Global Era: Australia in World Affairs 1996–2000*, edited by James Cotton and John Ravenhill. Melbourne: Oxford University Press, in association with the Australian Institute of International Affairs, 2001.

DFAT (Department of Foreign Affairs and Trade). *ASEAN and Australia: Celebrating 30 Years*. 2004. At <http://www.dfat.gov.au/publications/asean30/ASEAN30.pdf>.

EAAU/DFAT (East Asia Analytical Unit/DFAT). *ASEAN Free Trade Area: Trading Bloc or Building Block?*. Canberra: Australian Government Publishing Service, 1994.

East Asia Summit. *Kuala Lumpur Declaration on the East Asia Summit*. Kuala Lumpur, 14 December 2005. At <http://www.aseansec.org/18098.htm>.

Evans, Gareth. "Australian Foreign Policy: Priorities in a Changed World". *Australian Outlook*, Vol. 43, No. 2 (August 1989): 1–15.

Evans, Gareth, and Bruce Grant. *Australia's Foreign Relations: In the World of the 1990s* (second edition). Melbourne: Melbourne University Press, 1995.

Garnaut, Ross. *Australia and the Northeast Asian Ascendancy*, Canberra: Australian Government Publishing Service, 1989.

————. "Australia". In *The Political Economy of Policy Reform*, edited by John Williamson. Washington, D.C.: Institute for International Economics, 1994.

————. "An Australia-United States Free Trade Agreement". *Australian Journal of International Affairs*, Vol. 56, No. 1 (2002): 123–41.

Gruen, Fred, and Michelle Grattan. *Managing Government: Labor's Achievements & Failures*, Melbourne: Longman Cheshire, 1993.

Harris, Stuart. "Regional Economic Cooperation, Trading Blocs and Australian Interests". *Australian Outlook*, Vol. 43, No. 2 (August 1989): 16–24.

High-Level Task Force (on the AFTA-CER Free Trade Area). *The Angkor Agenda: Report of the High-Level Task Force on the AFTA-CER Free Trade Area*. Presented to the Fifth Informal Consultations between ASEAN Economic Ministers and the Ministers from the CER Countries, Chiang Mai, 6 October 2000. At <http://www.dfat.gov.au/cer_afta/angkor.pdf>.

Howard, John. *Joint Press Conference with the Prime Minister of New Zealand Helen Clark*. Transcript of Prime Minister John Howard, MP, Canberra, 8 February 2006. At <http://www.pm.gov.au/news/interviews/Interview1767.html>.

Keating, Michael S., and Geoff Dixson. *Making Economic Policy in Australia 1983-1988*. Melbourne: Longman Cheshire, 1989.

Keating, Paul. *Australia, Asia and the New Regionalism*. Singapore Lecture 1996. Singapore: Institute of Southeast Asian Studies, 1996.

————. *Engagement: Australia Faces the Asia-Pacific*. Sydney: Pan Macmillan Australia, 2000.

Kelly, Paul. *100 Years: The Australian Story*. Crows Nest: Allen & Unwin, 2001.

———. "Howard's Decade: An Australian Foreign Policy Reappraisal". *Lowy Institute Paper*, No. 15. 2006. At <http://www.lowyinstitute.org/Publication Get.asp?i=522>.

Milner, Anthony. "The Rhetoric of Asia". In *Seeking Asian Engagement: Australia in World Affairs, 1991–95*, edited by James Cotton and John Ravenhill. Melbourne: Oxford University Press, in association with the Australian Institute of International Affairs, 1997.

———. "Balancing 'Asia' against Australian Values". In *The National Interest in a Global Era: Australia in World Affairs 1996–2000*, edited by James Cotton and John Ravenhill. Melbourne: Oxford University Press, in association with the Australian Institute of International Affairs, 2001.

MOFA (Ministry of Foreign Affairs, Japan). *Diplomatic Blue Book 2006*. April 2006.

Petri, Peter A. "APEC and the Millennium Round". Paper presented to the twenty-fifth PAFTAD conference on "APEC: Its Challenges and Tasks in the 21st Century". Osaka, 16–18 June 1999.

Pitty, Roderic. "Regional Economic Co-operation". In *Facing North: A Century of Australian Engagement with Asia, Volume 2: 1970s to 2000*, edited by Peter Edwards and David Goldsworthy. Melbourne: Melbourne University Press/ Department of Foreign Affairs and Trade, 2003.

Ravenhill, John. "Adjusting to the ASEAN Way: Thirty Years of Australia's Relations with ASEAN". *Pacific Review*, Vol. 11, No. 2 (1988): 267–89.

———. "Australia and the Global Economy". In *The National Interest in a Global Era: Australia in World Affairs 1996–2000*, edited by James Cotton and John Ravenhill. Melbourne: Oxford University Press, in association with the Australian Institute of International Affairs, 2001.

Wesley, Michael. "Australia and the Asian Economic Crisis". In *The National Interest in a Global Era: Australia in World Affairs 1996–2000*, edited by James Cotton and John Ravenhill. Melbourne: Oxford University Press, in association with the Australian Institute of International Affairs, 2001.

———. *The Howard Paradox: Australian Diplomacy in Asia, 1996–2006*. Sydney: ABC Books, 2007.

6

The Migration of Professionals in an Integrating East Asia

Manolo Abella
Geoffrey Ducanes

Asian professionals have been going to the United States, Canada, Australia, the United Kingdom, and other western European countries over much of the contemporary history of migration.[1] This is partly a legacy of a long history of colonial relationship, especially in the case of the Philippines and the United States, Malaysia, Hong Kong, Singapore and the United Kingdom, and Indonesia and The Netherlands, and also due to strong trade and investment links between them which occasion movements of traders, managers, and technicians, including intracompany transfers. The desire of many young Asians to acquire advanced degrees from western educational institutions has reinforced these trends, while shortages of skills and talents in western industrial countries have prompted the adoption of welcoming immigration policies. Compared with other destinations these countries also offer easier access to certain niches of their labour market because of language and early steps taken to recognize professional degrees and qualifications acquired in foreign countries.

The rise of East Asian economies has deflected some of these flows towards destinations within the region and there are signs that the flows are accelerating, albeit from a low base. Expatriate Japanese managers have for some time been ubiquitous in the region's capitals from Seoul to Jakarta, but today one also finds among their ranks Koreans, Taiwanese, Filipinos, Malaysians, and Thais. They manage factories in China and Thailand, run banks in Lao PDR and Cambodia, staff hospitals in Singapore and Brunei, and pilot passenger airlines from Hong Kong and Malaysia. The numbers engaged in these movements are difficult to ascertain, but they have clearly grown over the past decade and are likely to continue into the future in spite of the global economic crisis. Intracorporate transferees and the movements of professional managers and engineers are bound to grow with the extension of supply chains among East Asian economies as evidenced by the growth in the volume of intraregional trade in intermediate goods and commodities, related services, and direct foreign investments.

I. INTEGRATION OF EAST ASIA

According to the Asian Development Bank (ADB) intraregional trade in East Asia has grown from less than 35 per cent of total trade in 1980 to 54 per cent in 2003. This is a lower proportion than in the European Union, but higher than NAFTA's, which is around 46 per cent (Kuroda 2005). The growth of intraregional trade, according to ADB, reflects intra-industry trade in parts, components, semi-finished products, and finished goods as multinational companies diversify their operations and create production networks across the region. These have led to a rapid growth of foreign direct investment flows within the region. Nearly half of total foreign direct investments in China and in the ASEAN countries are said to come from companies in Singapore, Hong Kong, and Taipei (China) and almost half of the value of recent bond issues by East Asian economies have been purchased by East Asian banks.

More than 60 per cent of the tourists in ASEAN countries are from East Asia. This growing regionalization is also manifest in the increased labour mobility across countries in the region. It is estimated that there are more than five million cross-border migrant workers within East Asia. Thailand has an estimated 1.8 million migrant workers, more than three-quarters of whom are estimated to come from Myanmar, and most of the rest from Cambodia and Lao PDR. Malaysia hosts 1.4 million registered migrant workers from other Southeast Asian countries, 80 per cent of whom are from Indonesia, 9 per cent from Myanmar, and others from Vietnam, the Philippines, Thailand, and Cambodia. There are about 400 thousand migrants in Japan from Thailand, Singapore, the Philippines, and Malaysia collectively. Over 640,000 in Singapore's labour force are foreign nationals, the largest majority of them from Asia. The Republic of Korea, Hong Kong, and Taiwan have been importing hundreds of thousands of workers from nearby countries every year mostly for blue-collar work, while China has drawn technical workers and managers from Hong Kong, Taiwan, and the Republic of Korea.

The integration of the East Asian economies reflected in these indicators prompt the following questions:

- Is there a redirection of flows of professional migration towards destinations in East Asia?
- Are immigration policies likely to induce significant redirection of flows?
- How rapidly are East Asian countries producing highly educated workers?

These are relevant questions to raise in view of the obvious importance of skilled human resources in the transformation of the region's economies. The common trajectory taken by the more successful East Asian economies is to gain initial success at low-end manufacturing, and then move eventually to higher-end manufacturing and service industries. Such a move, particularly if occurring rapidly, requires the employment of a greater number of higher skilled workers than the countries themselves could supply. Since supply has tended to be outpaced by demand, most countries have started to open their doors wider to highly skilled workers, offering them incentives that are typically denied the more abundant lower skilled workers. Their relative scarcity means that mobile higher skilled workers are among the largest gainers in the emerging global economy. Many are able to earn in another country a multiple of what they would have earned at home.

II. ASIAN PROFESSIONALS IN THE OECD COUNTRIES

The Organization for Economic Cooperation and Development (OECD) has developed a database that permits a closer examination of these issues. Its recently constructed database on skilled migration for the year 2000 provides a count of tertiary educated migrants in each OECD country and the means to trace their countries of origin.[2] Pertinent data on Asians with tertiary education who migrated to the OECD countries have been extracted and shown in table 6.1. They include Japanese and Koreans who emigrated to other OECD countries. Of the two OECD Asian member states, only Japan, however, has reported data on the population of foreign professionals.

At the turn of the century there were about 3.7 million people from East Asia with tertiary education who were residing in OECD countries. The most striking feature is their heavy concentration (over 77 per cent) in North America, with eight out of every ten of them in the United States. Japan has less than 5 per cent of the total for all OECD countries.

In terms of origin, the largest numbers in OECD countries were from China (including those from Hong Kong and Taiwan), with more than 1.2 million tertiary educated migrants. The Philippines follows next with 891,000 tertiary educated migrants, also heavily concentrated in the United States, but with substantial numbers in Canada, Australia, and Japan. Vietnam has 347,000 tertiary educated migrants in OECD countries, mostly in the United States, but also in Canada, France, and Australia.[3]

Korea and Japan, themselves in need of, and are admitting, skilled workers, have substantial numbers of professionals in other OECD countries. Japan has some 277,000 tertiary educated professionals abroad, largely in the United States (77 per cent). Korea has 425,000 tertiary educated migrants in OECD countries, mainly in the United States, Japan, and Canada.

East Asian professionals who have been admitted to Japan numbered some 184,000, nearly half of whom are Koreans and the rest are mostly Chinese and Filipinos. Unfortunately no data are available on the Republic of Korea as a destination country.

What kind of work are these professionals doing in foreign countries? Not all of these highly educated migrants were employed. Some are accompanying spouses and other family members. In the United States, employed migrants from East Asia numbered some 1.7 million. They were spread out in a variety of occupations the more prominent of which were health care and technical occupations, management, office and administrative support, and computer and mathematical occupations (see Table 6.2).

TABLE 6.1
Migrants with Tertiary Education from East Asia to OECD Countries

Country of birth	Country of Destination										
	United States	Canada	Australia	Japan	United Kingdom	France	Netherlands	New Zealand	Italy	Others	Total
Brunei	322	1,395	692	0	849	20	0	48	2	30	3,373
China	508,333	127,260	45,405	62,863	19,943	7,851	0	8,703	2,051	17,425	807,169
Hong Kong	0	99,480	21,628	0	22,273	468	0	2,421	0	845	147,354
Indonesia	34,572	5,260	15,232	2,284	2,683	1,190	51,247	1,134	263	3,007	118,948
Japan	211,275	14,395	8,883	0	17,299	8,745	0	1,389	2,927	11,908	281,565
Cambodia	19,642	3,140	2,092	89	257	10,413	0	273	20	528	36,861
South Korea	351,119	38,530	11,359	90,309	6,117	5,534	0	2,424	1,425	9,477	520,875
Lao PDR	25,854	2,725	1,422	88	164	6,781	0	66	7	362	37,764
Myanmar	15,264	1,765	3,065	1,293	2,986	219	0	207	41	170	25,103
Malaysia	24,449	10,525	34,852	1,118	24,330	502	0	4,242	79	1,895	102,719
The Philippines	659,852	123,070	36,195	21,608	17,952	1,751	0	3,681	7,053	15,491	891,343
Singapore	11,862	4,785	12,787	463	13,719	351	0	1,284	89	976	46,805
Thailand	53,295	1,740	5,960	3,120	4,387	1,340	0	675	294	3,608	76,926
Timor-Leste	0	0	904	0	0	0	0	0	12	452	1,368
Taiwan, China	213,037	33,460	6,970	0	4,085	1,642	0	2,214	221	1,457	263,914
Vietnam	237,142	34,560	24,856	1,159	4,163	30,343	0	435	338	9,748	347,249
Total	2,366,018	502,090	232,302	184,394	141,207	77,150	51,247	29,196	14,822	77,379	3,709,336
India	662,121	124,855	42,510	2,589	132,812	5,416	0	7,089	2,736	16,685	996,813

Source: OECD Database

TABLE 6.2
Distribution of Employed Tertiary Educated Migrants from East Asia to the U.S. by Occupations (%)

Occupation	Brunei	China	Indonesia	Japan	Cambodia	South Korea	Lao PDR	Myanmar	Malaysia	The Philippines	Singapore	Thailand	Taiwan, China	Vietnam	Total East Asia	India
1 Management occupations	24.8	11.1	12.5	19.9	7.1	12.9	5.5	9.5	14.8	6.7	17.2	11.3	16.1	7.1	10.8	11.3
2 Business and financial operations occupations	8.3	8.8	10.1	7.9	8.7	6.87.1	9.0	8.4	8.7	11.3	6.8	9.9	8.7	8.5	6.4	
3 Computer and mathematical science occupations	12.0	17.6	11.2	5.5	9.9	5.7	7.0	7.5	15.0	4.6	13.6	6.9	16.8	13.2	10.0	26.3
4 Architecture and engineering occupations	14.5	9.9	8.8	5.7	8.7	4.2	7.4	9.2	10.8	4.2	8.1	5.5	9.6	13.5	7.3	7.8
5 Life, physical, and social science occupations	0.0	10.4	3.3	4.5	1.8	3.1	1.7	3.6	4.1	1.6	4.6	2.3	4.6	2.4	4.4	4.2
6 Community and social services occupations	0.0	0.9	1.3	1.7	3.8	3.3	5.0	0.8	1.6	1.1	1.6	1.2	1.0	1.7	1.5	0.7
7 Legal occupations	0.0	0.8	0.7	1.5	0.6	1.5	0.7	0.3	0.9	0.7	1.5	1.1	1.0	1.0	1.0	0.5
8 Education, training, and library occupations	0.0	9.5	5.9	9.7	5.8	7.3	7.1	3.7	7.4	3.0	8.3	6.5	6.6	3.6	6.2	6.1
9 Arts, design, entertainment, sports, and media occupations	4.1	2.3	3.1	5.6	2.6	4.0	1.8	1.6	3.0	1.4	3.9	3.1	2.8	2.3	2.6	1.0
10 Health care practitioner and technical occupations	10.3	6.7	8.9	6.0	8.2	10.1	5.7	16.4	10.1	26.2	5.8	11.8	7.8	9.4	13.4	13.7
11 Health care support occupations	0.0	0.6	1.5	0.6	1.4	0.7	1.4	1.6	0.5	3.9	0.7	1.0	0.4	1.2	1.7	0.7
12 Protective serviced occupations	4.1	0.2	0.4	0.9	0.5	0.5	1.2	0.3	0.5	0.9	0.2	0.4	0.2	0.6	0.6	0.3
13 Food preparation and servicing related occupations	0.0	1.9	3.8	2.2	1.9	2.5	1.9	2.7	3.4	1.6	1.4	9.2	1.2	1.5	2.0	0.8
14 Building and grounds cleaning and maintenance occupations	0.0	0.4	0.8	0.6	1.1	0.8	1.1	0.6	0.7	1.4	0.5	1.2	0.2	0.7	0.8	0.2
15 Personal care and service occupations	0.0	0.9	1.4	2.1	2.0	2.1	1.5	1.0	1.1	2.1	0.9	1.8	0.8	2.9	1.7	0.5
16 Sales and related occupations	3.3	6.0	8.2	9.5	7.8	16.4	7.2	7.7	6.5	6.2	8.8	9.0	9.1	7.0	8.3	7.4
17 Office and administrative support occupations	18.6	7.8	10.7	10.9	12.6	8.7	13.9	12.9	7.9	16.4	8.0	12.0	8.8	10.3	11.3	6.8
18 Farming, fishing, and forestry occupations	0.0	0.0	0.0	0.1	0.0	0.1	0.2	0.0	0.0	0.1	0.0	0.0	0.0	0.1	0.1	0.0
19 Construction and extraction occupations	0.0	0.3	0.9	0.7	1.1	1.0	1.1	0.5	0.3	0.7	0.0	0.6	0.2	0.7	0.6	0.2
20 Installation, maintenance, and repair occupations	0.0	0.9	1.3	1.1	3.2	1.2	3.8	2.7	0.8	1.9	0.9	1.6	0.8	3.2	1.6	0.6
21 Production occupations	0.0	2.3	3.2	2.1	9.5	5.8	15.2	7.0	1.5	4.7	1.2	5.0	1.7	7.74	.3	3.0
22 Transportation and material moving occupations	0.0	0.6	1.7	1.1	1.6	1.1	2.3	1.2	0.6	1.6	0.8	1.7	0.5	1.1	1.1	1.2
23 Military specific	0.0	0.0	0.1	0.3	0.1	0.2	0.3	0.0	0.0	0.2	0.4	0.2	0.1	0.1	0.2	0.0
Total (#)	242	362,312	22,410	142,865	14,671	229,359	19,136	11,222	18,873	486,051	8,465	36,264	149,446	180,138	1,681,454	488,848

Source: OECD Database

The Japanese were largely in management occupations, running subsidiaries and branches of Japanese companies in the United States. Some 63,700 Chinese (from Hong Kong, Taiwan, China) were in computer and mathematical science occupations, and another 40,000 in management. Filipinos were more likely to be in health care and technical occupations and administrative occupations; South Koreans were probably mostly with Korean companies in sales and related occupations, but there were also many health practitioners.

East Asian professionals work in Japan in a number of occupational categories. The Koreans, however, tend to be more concentrated in white collar jobs, performing professional, managerial and sales functions. One in every three Chinese is in IT or another technical job. Tertiary educated Filipinos are found in a variety of occupations, but one in every two is in a blue-collar production job (see Tables 6.3a and 6.3b).

III. HAS THERE BEEN A SHIFT TO DESTINATIONS WITHIN THE REGION?

There are no comparable statistics on the population of tertiary educated migrants residing in non-OECD countries that would allow us to have a full global picture of where most are going. Moreover, the OECD database is only for the year 2000 or thereabouts, so we cannot say what has changed over time. To answer the question, we need to look at other data bases and individual country sources. A study by Docquier and Marfouk (2006), which incorporated data for 1990, makes it possible to compare change over ten years to 2000.[4] This study of migrants to OECD countries shows that those with tertiary education rose in number from twelve to twenty million (see Table 6.4). Among them Asian migrants rose by 83 per cent. Those who migrated to North America almost doubled in number from some 2.6 million to 5.1 million but the number who were reported as residents in other Asian countries hardly increased, edging from 295,000 to 296,000. Intraregion migration of East Asians thus appears to be bucking overall trends.

We next look at more recent statistics from immigration authorities of destination countries and from regulatory bodies in origin countries. The number of tertiary educated migrants who reported being admitted into another East Asian country or leaving from one for another appears to have grown somewhat in the first half of the current decade, but

TABLE 6.3a
Employed Tertiary Educated Migrants from East Asia to Japan by Occupation

Occupation	China	Indonesia	Cambodia	Korea	Lao PDR	Myanmar	Malaysia	The Philippines	Singapore	Thailand	Vietnam	Total East Asia	India
1 Agricultural, forestry and fisheries workers	189	29	0	115	2	2	4	179	0	29	5	554	4
2 Clerical and related workers	6,282	114	2	12,600	9	65	149	663	80	151	43	20,158	231
3 Managers and officials	1,297	4	0	4,925	0	4	25	41	17	18	9	6,340	113
4 Production process workers and labourers	9,165	895	25	9,008	26	213	172	5,990	32	788	510	26,824	269
5 Professional and technical workers	14,052	244	18	15,091	11	76	232	1,291	97	224	146	31,482	761
6 Protective service workers	21	5	0	114	0	2	1	7	0	3	1	154	2
7 Sales workers	5,109	60	2	12,751	2	65	103	583	34	126	54	18,889	296
8 Service workers	4,141	80	4	7,545	4	552	52	2,491	10	270	33	15,182	124
9 Workers in transport and communications	171	4	2	905	1	1	6	92	2	5	6	1,195	4
10 Workers not classified by occupation	1,477	44	7	1,736	4	72	14	467	8	116	31	3,976	53
Total	41,904	1,479	60	64,790	59	1,052	758	11,804	280	1,730	838	124,754	1,857

Source: OECD Database

TABLE 6.3b

Distribution of Employed Tertiary Educated Migrants from East Asia to Japan by Occupation (%)

Occupation	China	Indonesia	Cambodia	Korea	Lao PDR	Myanmar	Malaysia	Philippines	Singapore	Thailand	Vietnam	Total East Asia	India
1 Agricultural, forestry and fisheries workers	0.5	2.0	0.0	0.2	3.4	0.2	0.5	1.5	0.0	1.7	0.6	0.4	0.2
2 Clerical and related workers	15.0	7.7	3.3	19.4	15.3	6.2	19.7	5.6	28.6	8.7	5.1	16.2	12.4
3 Managers and officials	3.1	0.3	0.0	7.6	0.0	0.4	3.3	0.3	6.1	1.0	1.1	5.1	6.1
4 Production process workers and labourers	21.9	60.5	41.7	13.9	44.1	20.2	22.7	50.7	11.4	45.5	60.9	21.5	14.5
5 Professional and technical workers	33.5	16.5	30.0	23.3	18.6	7.2	30.6	10.9	34.6	12.9	17.4	25.2	41.0
6 Protective service workers	0.1	0.3	0.0	0.2	0.0	0.2	0.1	0.1	0.0	0.2	0.1	0.1	0.1
7 Sales workers	12.2	4.1	3.3	19.7	3.4	6.2	13.6	4.9	12.1	7.3	6.4	15.1	15.9
8 Service workers	9.9	5.4	6.7	11.6	6.8	52.5	6.9	21.1	3.6	15.6	3.9	12.2	6.7
9 Workers in transport and communications	0.4	0.3	3.3	1.4	1.7	0.1	0.8	0.8	0.7	0.3	0.7	1.0	0.2
10 Workers not classified by occupation	3.5	3.0	11.7	2.7	6.8	6.8	1.8	4.0	2.9	6.7	3.7	3.2	2.9
Total (#)	41,904	1,479	60	64,790	59	1,052	758	11,804	280	1,730	838	124,754	1,857

Source: OECD Database

TABLE 6.4
Regional Distribution of All Adult Migrants with a Tertiary Education by Source and Receiving Region (%)

Source Area	Receiving Area					Table Total	Number of residents
	Europe	Northern America	Latin America and the Carribean	Asia	Oceania		
2000							
Total	23.6	64.8	0.7	2.4	8.5	100	20,082,686
Europe	36.7	49.9	0.6	1.6	11.3	100	6,686,361
Northern America	24.9	62.1	4.6	2.3	6.1	100	947,801
Latin America and the Carribean	8	88.3	1.3	1.4	1	100	3,655,136
Asia	14.5	73.1	0.1	4.2	8	100	7,041,367
Oceania	22.4	27.2	0.1	0.7	49.6	100	364,055
Africa	47.8	44.5	0.1	0.1	7.6	100	1,387,966
1990							
Total	20.3	64.9	1	3.2	10.7	100	12,086,508
Europe	27.2	57.2	0.8	0.9	13.9	100	4,803,501
Northern America	19.1	67.2	4.8	2.9	6	100	722,634
Latin America and the Carribean	7.9	87.3	2.2	1.2	1.5	100	1,856,287
Asia	13.5	69	0.2	7.7	9.6	100	3,836,581
Oceania	15.3	28.5	0.1	0.8	55.3	100	215,591
Africa	46.8	43.2	0.1	0.1	9.8	100	651,916

Source: Lowell (2007).

TABLE 6.5
Japan's Stock of Foreign Workers by Admission Category, 2002–06

Status of Residence	2002	2003	2004	2005	2006
Professor	7,751	8,037	8,153	8,404	8525
Artist	397	386	401	448	462
Religious Activity	4,858	4,732	4,699	4588	4654
Journalist	351	294	292	280	273
Investor/Manager	5,956	6,135	6,396	6743	7,342
Legal/accountant Service	111	122	125	126	141
Medical Service	114	110	117	146	138
Researcher	3,369	2,770	2,548	2494	2,232
Instructor	9,715	9,390	9,393	9449	9511
Engineer	20,717	20,807	23,210	29,004	35,135
Specialist in Humanities	44,496	44,943	47,682	55276	57,323
Intracorporate Transferee	10,923	10,605	10,993	11,977	14,014
Entertainer	58,359	64,642	64,742	36374	21053
Skilled Labour	12,522	12,583	13,373	15112	17,869
Subtotal *	179,639	185,556	192,124	180,465	178,781
Designated activities	121,280	120,914	127,382	144,091	157,728
	47,706	55,048	63,310	87,326	97,476
Part-time work of students	59,435	98,006	106,406	96,959	103,595
Worker of Japanese descendant	220,844	239,744	231,393	239,259	241,325
Overstayers	224,067	220,552	193,745	207,299	193,745
Non-designated activities	—	—	—	—	—
Total	710,000	80,000	800,000 +α	+	80,000+
Ordinary permanent residents	39,154	86,942	101,904	113,899	128,441
Grand total	750,000 +α	870,000 +α	900,000 +α	920,000 +α	930,000 +α

Source: Iguchi (2008)

from a very low base. The total number of foreign professional and skilled workers[5] residing in Japan (from all sources) rose from 121,000 at the end of 2002 to 158,000 at the end of 2006 (see Table 6.5). The largest number came from "specialists in humanities" (36 per cent), but there was also a very notable increase in the number of intracorporate transferees. Recent flow data indicate a more rapid increase in the number of professionals and skilled workers. Japan's Immigration Bureau reports that the number of foreign engineers admitted from all countries (but very largely from Asia, especially China and Korea) rose from 16,500 in 2000 to 23,200 in 2004.

In Singapore the government reported that the admissions of unskilled foreign workers outnumbered the skilled ones by about 4.5 to 1 between 1999 and 2004. Work permit holders (issued for unskilled workers) rose in number by 3.5 per cent a year, from some 450,000 to 540,000. On the other hand, holders of employment passes (for skilled and professional workers) from all origin countries has fluctuated between 70,000 and 100,000, revealing no particular rising trend in spite of Singapore's well known policy of attracting the best talents in arts and sciences. In the Republic of Korea there was a very significant growth in the number of foreign workers admitted, which rose almost ten times from 30,500 in 1994, to 297,000 in 2004. Most of them were admitted as unskilled foreign worker trainees. From 2004 to 2007, the number of professionals and skilled workers (with employment visa E1 to E7) grew 16 per cent a year to reach 32,000 in 2007, from 20,000 in 2004 (see Table 6.6).

TABLE 6.6
Republic of Korea: Stock of Foreign Professionals, 2004–07

Profession	2004	2005	2006	2007
Foreign Language Instructor	11,072	12,296	14,806	17,615
Special Occupation	3,432	4,412	5,527	6,753
Arts & Performances	2,821	3,268	3,189	3,038
Researchers	1,569	1,738	2,076	2,291
Others	1412	1563	1652	1915
Total	20,306	23,277	27,250	31,612

Source: Hur and Lee (2008).

Growth has been especially strong among foreign language instructors,[6] research professionals, and those under "special occupations". However, in contrast to the earlier trend, the number of non-professional foreign workers barely changed over the same period.

In Taiwan, China, as of 2006, there were an estimated 15,000 foreign professionals with employment permits. Of these, 60 per cent were from East Asia, mainly Japan. The preponderant proportion of foreign workers, however, were blue-collar workers from East Asia employed in manufacturing and services. In Hong Kong the annual admission of professional and managerial workers from all origin countries rose steadily, but slowly from 16,500 in 1997 to 19,200 in 2004.

Thailand and Malaysia have the largest populations of foreign workers in East Asia. Most of their foreign workers, however, are in low-skill occupations in plantations, petty trading, manufacturing, and services. Those in Thailand are mainly from neighbouring Myanmar, Lao PDR, and Cambodia, while in Malaysia they come from Indonesia, Myanmar, the Philippines, and South Asia (especially Bangladesh and Nepal). Malaysia has actively sought out foreign professionals to work in its high priority industries, but the numbers have remained insignificant compared with the admissions of unskilled or low-skilled migrant workers. In 2008, some 11,000 foreigners from all countries of origin were registered under the "expatriates" or professional category.

The circular cross-border movements of professionals are not well tracked by immigration statistics since they are able to move about more easily than others and are often admitted under temporary visit categories. This is especially true of those belonging to one of the countries of ASEAN, which has an agreement for visa-free travel for nationals of member states (with some exceptions such as Myanmar). There are a few growth poles for migration in East Asia, but these do not represent the overall trend. It has been estimated by some observers, for example, that Shanghai alone already has half a million professionals, managers, and technical workers, mostly from Hong Kong and Taiwan, but admissions into Japan, Singapore, and Hong Kong have not been impressive in volume and have fluctuated in recent years.

Trends in the temporary migration of professionals from the Philippines offer a glimpse of the phenomenon from an origin country. The data in Table 6.7 come from the Philippine Overseas Employment

Administration which regulates recruitment and registers Filipino contract workers leaving for employment abroad.[7] Its records show an initial upward trend in the emigration of professional, technical, and managerial workers from the Philippines from 65,000 in 1993, to slightly over 100,000 in 2002, but the trend was reversed and numbers were down to 44,000 by 2007.

The available data thus permit only a few guarded conclusions. The OECD database indicates that the United States and Canada are hosting a large population of professionals from East Asia, notably China (including Hong Kong and Taiwan), Japan, Republic of Korea, the Philippines, and Vietnam. We know from other sources that many

TABLE 6.7
The Philippines: New-hired Filipino Professional, Technical, and Managerial Workers by Sex

Year	Male	%	Female	%	Total
1993	48,617	74.6	16,539	25.4	65,156
1994	57,716	78.0	16,324	22.0	74,040
1995	30,908	70.3	13,067	29.7	43,975
1996	24,302	66.8	12,058	33.2	36,360
1997	37,306	71.8	14,647	28.2	51,953
1998	41,720	74.7	14,121	25.3	55,841
1999	50,736	80.7	12,097	19.3	62,833
2000	67,530	85.5	11,439	14.5	78,969
2001	83,161	85.0	14,672	15.0	97,833
2002	84,967	84.9	15,095	15.1	100,062
2003	67,439	85.0	11,904	15.0	79,343
2004	80,637	85.1	14,075	14.9	94,712
2005	52,097	80.9	12,334	19.1	64,431
2006	24,335	57.8	17,740	42.2	42,075
2007	22,185	50.0	22,179	50.0	44,364

Source: POEA

of them arrived only recently.[8] In East Asia individual country statistics on recent admissions of professionals do not follow a uniform pattern — some show rapid increases while others show fluctuations, but in all cases the numbers are much smaller than those reported as residing in the western countries. In other words, from the distribution of professionals among the OECD countries in year 2000 and from data on recent admissions into individual countries in the East Asian region, we find nothing to suggest that a significant shift has occurred in the direction of highly skilled migration flows. We had hypothesized that because of the rapid integration of the East Asian economies, there should have been a shift away from traditional destinations in the west towards East Asia, but this is not supported by the evidence available.

IV. PREDICTING THE ABSORPTION OF FOREIGN WORKERS

To what extent do countries "depend" on foreign sources for their professional workforce? We know that countries in early stages of development tend to import managers and technical workers to start their industries, as well as their public services. Their education institutions are not yet well developed, hence they are not in a position to send skilled or educated workers abroad. As countries advance, their need to rely on foreign sources for skills will rise just as their capabilities to develop those skills at home improve. They then enter a stage when they experience rising immigration as well as emigration of educated workers. Net migration may be positive or negative, depending on circumstances. Eventually they become more or less self-sufficient, and much later even become net "exporters" of skills as their economic interests spread beyond their borders. The driving force is not higher wages abroad, but the need to trade or develop subsidiaries or branches abroad. The demographic changes that accompany rising affluence, however, often lead to declining fertility rates, and eventually a shrinking and ageing workforce. This brings in a new era of progressive dependence on foreign sources of labour, first for the unskilled and low skilled, and eventually for the skilled and professional workers as well.

This highly simplified paradigm does not take into account a host of other factors, most notably, a country's geography and history, which may have stronger impacts on the patterns of migration than simply demographics. For example, Canada's proximity to the United States and close political relations have led to a virtually integrated labour market for the two countries. Canada loses a good proportion of its talents (that is, athletes, artists, medical graduates) to the United States in spite of very similar standards of living.

In this section we do not attempt to explore the evidence on the experience of countries at different stages of development. Such an exercise demands data that are not readily available. Instead we confine ourselves to exploiting available data from OECD in order to see if dependence on foreign sources of skilled labour can be predicted by looking at possible determinants.

From the OECD database we are able see the degree to which the rich countries have absorbed foreign professionals into their workforces. In Figure 6.1, we compare the proportion of local and foreign-born among skilled workers in major destination countries — Australia, Canada, the United States, Germany, and Japan. Among them Australia has the largest proportion (30 per cent) of foreign-born among her skilled workforce. Canada follows with 24 per cent, and the United States with 13 per cent. By contrast, only 1 per cent of Japan's skilled workforce are foreigners. Indeed Japan accounts for an insignificant proportion of the total tertiary educated migrants in the OECD countries.

From Figure 6.1, it appears that Japan, among the world's richest economies, is an outlier in terms of its use of foreign labour. How much of an outlier is it?

Since there is no "norm" on which to base an answer to the question, we have to develop a model to estimate, on the basis of past experience of many countries, how much foreign labour will be needed given certain conditions. These conditions are largely economic and relate to the labour market. Excess demand for foreign labour depends, on the one hand, on how fast an economy is growing and how dependent that growth is on skilled labour, and on the other, on the size and growth of its own native workforce, among other factors. This "prediction model", indicates what would be the likely degree of dependence on foreign labour should certain conditions exist. This

FIGURE 6.1
Proportion of Local and Foreign-born Skilled Workers in Major Destination Countries

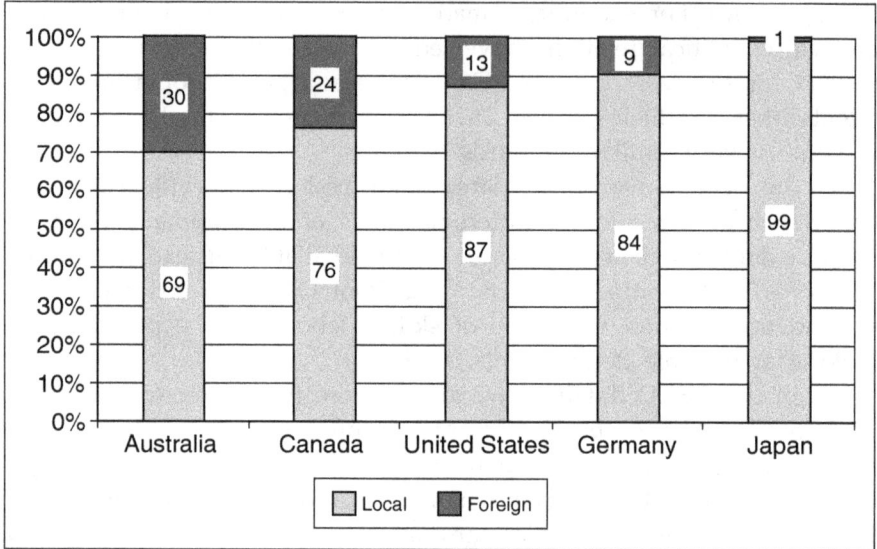

Source: OECD.

likely degree of dependence can thus be treated as a norm with which the actual degree of dependence can be compared. We combine data from the OECD, the World Bank's Word Development Indicators, and the United Nations' World PopulationProjections to estimate the model parameters.

Prediction Model

We hypothesize that the proportion of foreigners in a country's stock of total and of skilled workers is a function of several factors:

- *per capita income level* and *growth*,
- *economic* structure (share of GDP, growth rate)
- *demographic structures* (percentage of population aged 15–64, to total population)
- *labour market tightness* (average unemployment, *2001–2005*)

a) Percentage of Foreign Workers' Share to Total Numbers of Workers

The first model makes no distinction by skill between foreign and local workers.

Proportion of foreign workers to total number of workers in OECD countries = f (per capita GDP level and growth, economic structure, demographic structure, labour market tightness).[9]

After eliminating insignificant variables, the regression analysis yields the following final model (Table 6.8).

The variables that emerged as significant predictors of the proportion of foreign workers are the level of per capita GDP, the share of services in total output, the growth rate of industry, the percentage of the working-age population to total population, and the unemployment rate. The share of services in output is taken as a measure of the "knowledge economy", or how far an economy has advanced technologically. The signs of the coefficients are as expected — the more affluent a country, the more advanced its economy, the faster the growth of the relatively more labour-dependent industrial sector, the tighter the labour market; and the smaller the share of the working age population, the higher

TABLE 6.8
Prediction Model: Foreign Workers Share

fwrkr_sh	Coef.	Robust Std. Err.	t	P>|t|	[95% Conf. Interval]	
lnpcgdp_us	8.217883	3.396933	2.42	0.028	1.016708	15.41906
ser_sh	0.8571361	.2877927	2.98	0.009	0.2470429	1.467229
ind_gr	2.360702	1.055975	2.24	0.040	0.1221357	4.599269
pop_1564	2.690094	1.022545	2.63	0.018	0.5223954	4.857793
unemp	−1.109055	0.4492474	−2.47	0.025	−2.061417	−0.1566932
_cons	−305.776	99.99992	−3.06	0.008	−517.7664	−93.78568

Linear regression

Number of obs = 22
$F(5, 16)$ = 6.39
Prob > F = 0.0019
R-squared = 0.7118
Root MSE = 6.0243

the expected share of foreign workers in the total workforce. Note the model is highly significant and the R^2 is high at 0.71.

Table 6.9 below compares the predicted percentages with actual percentages of foreign workers in the labour force around the year 2000 for OECD countries. Most of the countries have an actual share which is close to what is predicted by the model. The most notable

TABLE 6.9
Actual vs Predicted Proportion of Foreign Workers to Total Number of Workers

Country	Actual	Predicted	Mean Absolute Proportional Error
Australia	24.5	19.1	0.2
Austria	13.8	17.7	0.3
Belgium	9.7	9.3	0.0
Canada	20.5	15.8	0.2
Czech Republic	4	5.7	0.4
France	10.8	10.8	0.0
Germany	12.3	7.6	0.4
Greece	13.6	13.5	0.0
Hungary	2.9	7.7	1.7
Ireland	12.1	—	—
Italy	5	4.1	0.2
Japan	**1.1**	**11.8**	**9.7**
Luxembourg	42.6	35.9	0.2
Mexico	0.4	—	—
Netherlands	9.8	—	—
New Zealand	19.8	12.3	0.4
Norway	7.5	4.5	0.4
Poland	0.9	−4.4	5.8
Portugal	8.5	3.7	0.6
Slovak Republic	2.6	6.5	1.5
Spain	6.8	12.2	0.8
Sweden	10.9	16.8	0.5
Switzerland	25.3	20.2	0.2
Turkey	1.8	—	—
United Kingdom	8.8	12.8	0.4
United States	13.6	21.9	0.6

Note: No predicted value indicates missing value for at least one explanatory variable.

exception is Japan (1.1 vs. 11.8) where the actual share of foreign workers is less than a tenth of what is predicted, given its economic structure and growth, the tightness of its labour market, and its demographic structure.

b) Percentage of Foreign Skilled Workers' in Total Force of Skilled Workers

The second model looks only at skilled workers, foreign and local. We postulate the same determinants as above for the share of foreigners in the total skilled workforce of each country.

After eliminating insignificant variables, the regressions yielded the following final model.

> Regression Model: Share of foreign skilled workers in total force skilled workers in OECD countries = f (per capita GDP level and growth, economic structure, demographic structure, labour market tightness)

The variables that emerged as significant predictors of the share of foreign skilled workers to total force of skilled workers are the share of services in total output, the share of the working-age population in total population, and the unemployment rate. As a measure of the level of advancement in an economy, it is assumed that the higher the share of services to total output the greater its need for higher skilled

TABLE 6.10
Prediction Model: Foreign Skilled Workers Share

fprof_sh	Coef.	Robust Std. Err.	t	P>|t|	[95% Conf. Interval]	
ser_sh	1.139978	0.4683799	2.43	0.025	0.1596477	2.120308
pop_1564	3.137316	1.334729	2.35	0.030	0.343695	5.930936
unemp	−2.01448	0.5046765	−3.99	0.001	−3.07078	−0.9581802
_cons	−261.9402	111.9845	−2.34	0.030	−496.3264	−27.55407

Linear regression

Number of obs = 23
F(3, 19)   = 6.17
Prob > F   = 0.0041
R-squared   = 0.5462
Root MSE   = 7.9219

workers. The signs of the coefficients are as expected. Note the model is highly significant and the R^2 is still relatively high at 0.55.

Table 6.11 below compares the predicted percentages with actual percentages of foreign skilled workers to total skilled workers. Most of the countries have an actual share which is reasonably close to what

TABLE 6.11
Actual vs Predicted Proportion of Foreign Skilled Workers to Total Number of Skilled Workers

Country	Actual	Predicted	Mean Absolute Proportional Error
Australia	30.0	18.3	0.4
Austria	12.5	19.2	0.5
Belgium	9.6	12.3	0.3
Canada	23.8	15.9	0.3
Czech Republic	5.9	13.6	1.3
France	11.0	11.2	0.0
Germany	9.6	9.0	0.1
Greece	11.0	11.5	0.0
Hungary	5.1	17.0	2.3
Ireland	17.0	11.2	0.3
Italy	5.5	8.1	0.5
Japan	**1.0**	**13.3**	**12.3**
Luxembourg	49.1	35.3	0.3
Mexico	0.9	—	—
Netherlands	10.0	—	—
New Zealand	22.6	12.2	0.5
Norway	7.4	1.0	0.9
Poland	1.5	−3.8	3.5
Portugal	15.5	17.0	0.1
Slovak Republic	3.5	2.4	0.3
Spain	6.0	10.5	0.8
Sweden	11.3	11.8	0.0
Switzerland	25.6	22.1	0.1
Turkey	3.9	—	—
United Kingdom	14.6	18.8	0.3
United States	13.0	24.3	0.9

Note: No predicted value indicates missing value for at least one explanatory variable.

is predicted by the model. Once again, the most notable exception is Japan (1.0 vs. 13.3) where the actual share of foreign workers is less than a thirteenth of what is predicted given its economic structure, the tightness of its labour market, and its demographic structure.

Unfortunately, Korea, a more recent OECD member, is not part of the database. But were it part of the database, it would likely also show the country to be an outlier because of its relatively much lower admission of foreign workers in general, and high-skilled workers in particular. Based on the record of foreign professional and technical workers residing in Korea in 2000, we see that they probably account for a mere 0.03 per cent of the total number residing in all OECD countries (Lowell 2007).

V. DEMOGRAPHIC OUTLOOK ON THE SUPPLY OF WORKERS

The relatively insignificant proportion of foreigners in the workforces of Japan and Korea is likely to change in the coming decades. An important factor likely to lead to a relaxation of immigration policies is fertility decline and ageing of the workforce, which will also be felt by other East Asian countries, such as Singapore and Thailand.

The younger cohorts of the population of the region's most economically advanced countries have started to shrink. Figure 6.2 shows the decline from 2005 to 2050 of the combined young population (defined as those from fifteen to thirty-nine years of age) of Japan, Singapore, Hong Kong, and the Republic of Korea. Their young workforces are projected to decline rapidly by nine million from 2010 to 2020.

Given its fertility decline, Japan is already facing a gradual decline in labour force for the next twenty years, and a more rapid decline almost twenty years later. Iguchi estimated that the decline of the labour force in Japan is around 200,000, rising gradually to 300,000 persons per year until 2020. By 2030 the decline will be much higher at more than 400,000 a year, rising further to 500,000 by 2040. These predictions assume that people are able to work up to seventy years of age and that women workers will have no problems between child-bearing and pursuing their occupational careers (Iguchi 2005).

FIGURE 6.2

Projected Population of Those Aged 15–39 in Developed East Asian Economies (Hong Kong, Singapore, Korea, Japan) in Millions

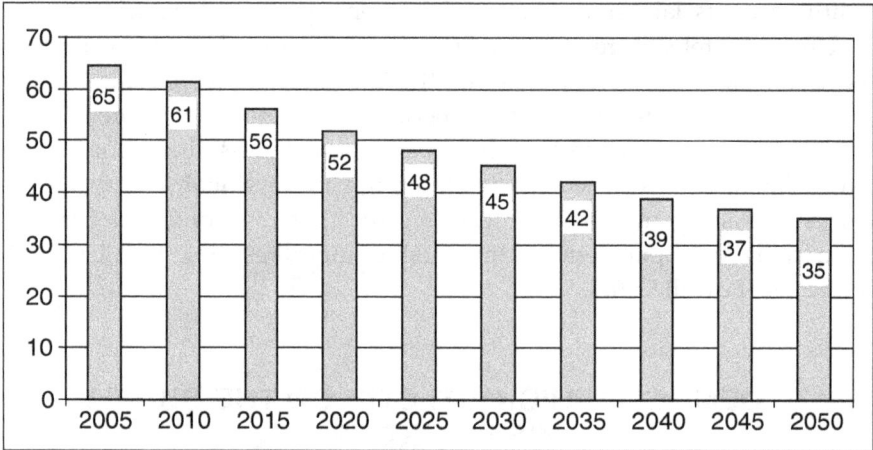

Projections of population change in selected countries by the UN Population Division, after taking into account fertility decline, shows that Japan will experience a sharp drop of 21.7 million people over the half century between 2000 and 2050 if zero immigration is assumed. The share of those aged sixty-five years and above in the total population will rise from 17 per cent to 32 per cent, making it only next to Italy as the most aged population among the OECD countries. By comparison the United States will still see an increase in its population by 71 million, and its aged population representing 22 per cent of the total by 2050 (UNDESA 2001). Whether or not a decision will be made to open immigration doors more widely to slow down the population ageing process remains to be seen. For societies not used to facing the challenges posed by multi-ethnicity, the social adjustments required cannot be underestimated. However, continuation of the present policy of restricting low-skill immigration is likely to entail a heavy cost in terms of foregone incomes and welfare as the most productive segments of the workforce shrinks, and those employed are made to bear the burden of supporting a third of the population that retires.

We have already seen some policy shifts in the region. Despite an avowed earlier policy to reduce dependence on foreign workers, especially through industrial restructuring and technology upgrading, Singapore was forced to open its borders even more widely because of declining birth rates and an ageing population. Today a third of its workforce are non-Singaporeans. Even with annual additions of 50,000 permanent immigrants over the next thirty years, economists and demographers project that the annual growth rate of the resident labour force will drop from about 2 per cent in 2004, to less than 1 per cent from 2020. According to Hui (2004), this means that increases in the labour force will drop to about 28,000 from 2020, making it difficult for Singapore to meet its own long-term economic growth targets.

By contrast, the young populations in the more populous developing countries of East Asia are expected to continue rising up to 2020. Figure 6.3 shows the combined young populations of Indonesia, the Philippines, and Vietnam from 2005 to 2050. Growth of their young populations is expected to continue until their combined numbers reach

FIGURE 6.3
**Projected Population of Those Aged 15–39 in Developing East Asian Economies
(Indonesia, the Philippines, Vietnam) in Millions**

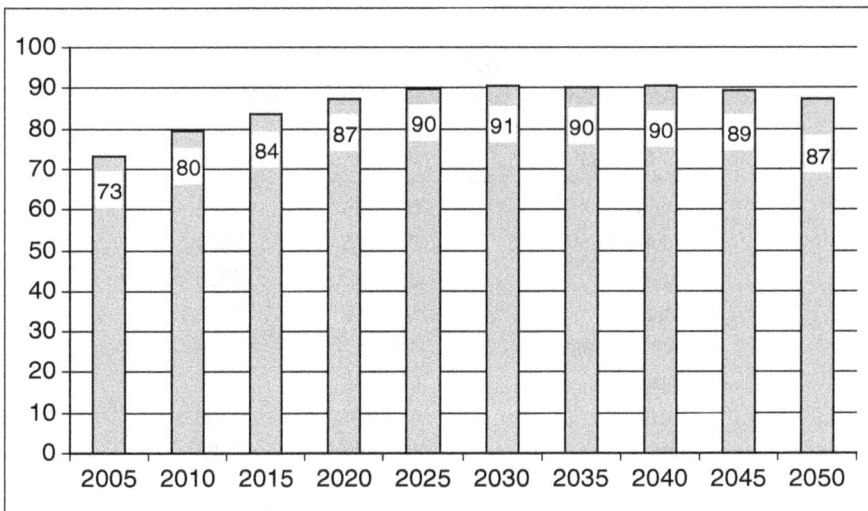

90 million in about 2025, after which their numbers will stabilize. A decline is not expected until after 2045.

Of the three countries, Vietnam is closest geographically, culturally, and linguistically to Japan, Korea, and Taiwan. Pressures for integration of its labour markets with those of the latter are likely to become strong in the coming decades, especially if reinforced by integration of their markets for goods and capital. In fact the flows of unskilled Vietnamese workers to Korea and Taiwan have been accelerating in recent years, but supply scarcities in Vietnam for skilled and educated workers have restrained their movements.

East Asian countries have invested heavily in education which, at first glance, may be seen to explain the relatively small proportion of foreigners among their skilled workforces. Japan still produces over a million tertiary education graduates each year, while Korea produces another 605,000. The East Asian region as a whole produces more than nine million tertiary graduates every year. China alone accounts for about 5.6 million tertiary graduates or slightly over 60 per cent of the total for the region. Four ASEAN countries — Indonesia, the Philippines, Thailand and Malaysia account for another 1.7 million. Table 6.12 below provides the country breakdown.

In some countries there are signs of an excess supply of workers with tertiary degrees relative to demand. Filipino college graduates are,

TABLE 6.12
Annual Tertiary Graduates, Most Recent Year

Country	Number	Year
China	5,622,795	2006
Indonesia	612,975	2004
Japan	1,067,939	2006
Malaysia	183,940	2005
The Philippines	410,067	2006
Korea	605,160	2006
Thailand	483,924	2006
Vietnam	182,489	2005

Source: UNESCO.

for example, twice as likely to be unemployed as elementary school graduates. The existence of a growing pool of unemployed tertiary education graduates explains the pressures to seek employment in foreign countries. Indeed some governments have adopted foreign employment programmes because of the problem of soaring numbers of the educated unemployed. Over the past five years, more and more Filipino professionals have left for Europe and North America for employment. Paradoxically, their employment in East Asian countries has been on a decline.

The high unemployment among the educated may not, however, be simply because of an excess supply of skills. Recent studies of the ILO and a survey by the Economist Intelligence Unit reveal that many countries in the region, in fact, face severe skill shortages. These indicate a problem with mismatches between skills demanded and skills supplied (ILO 2008). The ILO conducted Workplace Practices Surveys in China, India, and Malaysia in 2007, and in the Republic of Korea in 2008. These surveys focused on fast growing industries in each country and within these, the leading domestic companies. The surveys revealed that more than 70 per cent of surveyed employers in Malaysia and China reported difficulty in recruiting suitable employees.[10] The biggest shortages noticed were in managerial, technical, and professional occupations.

The EIU conducted two "Asia Business Outlook Surveys", one at the end of 2006 and another at the end of 2007, among the members of its corporate network in the region.[11] The findings are consistent with those of the ILO surveys in that companies found a lack of qualified workers, especially middle level managers, as a serious constraint to growth. The most affected sectors were ICT and professional services, and electronics and engineering.

Various other studies have shown that there is a need to improve the quality of education in the region to provide the cognitive and professional skills necessary for raising productivity and competitiveness. These skills appear to be unevenly developed in the region, with some Southeast Asian countries faring poorly in comparison with member countries of the OECD. For example, Indonesia and Thailand participated in the Programme for International Student Assessment (PISA) surveys to assess the extent to which fifteen-year old students have acquired key competencies and cognitive skills for work and daily life as an adult. The Indonesian and Thai students who tested in math, sciences, and reading, scored below the average for twenty-eight middle-income economies, and significantly below the OECD average in all three subject areas.[12]

VI. COMPARING ATTRACTIVENESS OF IMMIGRATION POLICIES

Do the East Asian countries have immigration policies which welcome the highly educated? How do their policies compare with those in the western countries?

By and large, one can say that from the standpoint of immigration policy that East Asian countries are less attractive destinations for migrant professionals than their western counterparts. A country that offers the possibility of permanent settlement (and thus also the possibility of economic and social integration) will, *ceteris paribus*, be a more attractive destination than those that do not. Those admitted for limited periods of stay generally enjoy fewer rights and entitlements under national laws than those admitted for settlement. In East Asia however, almost all countries offer only temporary admission to foreign nationals, regardless of skill,[13] and admission programmes sometimes restrict them to certain nationalities.

While there are also no equivalent immigration countries in Europe, most countries do make it possible for foreigners to qualify for permanent residence and eventually for citizenship after a number of years of legal residence. Germany introduced a number of years ago a special admission programme to entice foreign professionals, including those from third countries[14] to work in the country. There are now more opportunities for foreign students to pursue tertiary level studies in Germany (in a few universities even in the English language) in what is seen as a move to attract foreign talents into the country. Foreign graduates from German universities can now stay in Germany for up to one year to find a job. In Denmark foreigners with a specific job offer with a yearly salary of at least EUR 50,300 can obtain a residence permit. In Ireland a "Green Card" programme was introduced in 2007 for highly skilled employees in most occupations with an annual salary above EUR 60,000. After two years of legal stay they can apply for permanent residence.

An emerging trend in policies to attract professionals is the increasing transparency of criteria and procedures for admission. Canada pioneered as far back as in 1968 the adoption of the points-based system of which there are now variants being followed by Australia and the United Kingdom. Their common feature is that admission is based on clearly stated criteria for each of which points have been assigned. In principle each candidate's admission depends on how well he or she scores on certain qualifications such as experience, education, proficiency in the language, health condition, having a close family member permanently residing in the country, etc. The United Kingdom boasts that interested foreign professionals can already get an idea of how they score by simply visiting the migration office website on the Internet and supplying the required information.

Australia has identified priority occupations for which there is high demand and assigns high points for applicants with the requisite skills. The same is true for outstanding talents, or business skills. Independent migrants or those not sponsored by an employer or relative in Australia must pass a points test which includes skills, age, and English language ability. One may also be admitted as so-called "Skilled-Australian Linked" if one passes a points test on skills, age and English ability and receives additional points for sponsorship by relatives in Australia.[15]. Australian employers may nominate (or "sponsor") personnel from overseas through the Employer Nomination Scheme (ENS), Regional Sponsored Migration Scheme (RSMS), and Labour Agreements. The government encourages successful business people of foreign nationality to settle permanently in Australia and develop new business opportunities, and also has a separate scheme for distinguished individuals with special or unique talents of benefit to Australia (Hugo Graeme 2005).

Immigration policies in the East Asian countries clearly dichotomize between skilled and unskilled. For most countries, the policy is to keep the skilled and "rotate" the unskilled foreign workers. In Hong Kong, professionals satisfying certain age, education, and skill requirements are allowed to enter even without a prior job offer under the "Admission of Talents scheme".[16] In both Japan and Korea, skilled migrant workers in specific categories are admitted and given multiple-entry visas, are entitled to extend their stay, move into new jobs, and more or less enjoy the same rights as local workers. In both Singapore and Malaysia, high skilled workers enter through a different visa than that of lower skilled workers, and are given more privileges, such as the right to bring dependents (depending on income) and the opportunity to become permanent residents. Foreign professionals who want to work or do business in Singapore and are able to command a monthly basic salary of more than S$2,500 are issued "Employment Passes". EP holders are not subject to the limitations imposed by the Employment of Foreign Workers Act, and hence are allowed to bring their families to Singapore and are eligible for consideration for permanent residency after a short stay. In early 2003 the plans to make Singapore a hub for medical services prompted the Singapore Medical Council to approve the direct hiring of foreign doctors by private hospitals and clinics. Previously these were required to be supervised for one year in public hospitals and clinics before they could register with the council and work in the private sector (Yap 2005).

Japan has traditionally adhered to a long-standing policy of not admitting unskilled foreign workers.[17] But the need to remain competitive in the global economy led a proactive programme to bring in even unskilled workers provided they could prove Japanese ancestry ("nikkeijin"). The decade of the 1990s saw hundreds of thousands of nikkeijin arriving from Brazil, Peru, and other South American countries to meet the need for blue-collar workers in manufacturing. Following the cue from other industrial countries, the Japanese Government also decided in 2004 to make it possible for foreigners who have graduated from Japanese universities to search for jobs. Students of graduate schools, universities, colleges, and vocational colleges in Japan with a valid "college student" status could from then on apply for a change in their status of residence to "engineer", "specialist in humanities/international service", or another status that enables them to work.[18] They would need to have the necessary qualifications and their academic background must satisfy the requirements of the status applied for.

In a similar vein, the Japanese Government adopted a programme to promote acceptance of foreign researchers and foreign information processing engineers. Adopted initially as an experiment and implemented in the Special Zones for Structural Reform until the end of fiscal year 2005, the programme has since been implemented nationwide. The Immigration Control and Refugee Recognition Act was correspondingly amended in 2006 to allow foreigners to be employed in designated research activities, but only for a temporary period since the maximum term of residence was only extended from three years to five years.

Policies of East Asian countries towards the less skilled are clearly aimed at precluding settlement or more permanent stay. The countries limit the stay of the less skilled to only a few years, deny them the right to bring their families with them, restrict their right to change employers, and exclude them from social security altogether, or to entitlement to old age benefits under social security. In Singapore IT and biotechnology researchers are encouraged to stay and enjoy the same rights as Singaporeans, but domestic helpers risk losing their work authorization if they become pregnant.

VII. CONCLUSIONS

Our examination of available evidence on the movements of the highly skilled in East Asia has led us to conclude that they still largely go outside the region, in particular, to North American destinations. While demographic trends suggest that there will be more pressures in the future for intraregional movements, their numbers in the rich countries of the region have so far remained unimpressive, and changes over the last decade do not point to any particular trend. The small share of foreigners in the skilled workforce of Japan (and probably also the Republic of Korea) appears to be due to reasons other than those that can be explained by level and rate of per capita income growth, structure of the economy, the age structure of the population, or tightness of the labour market. In much of the literature on the subject, this has frequently been attributed to historical and cultural factors (high value the Japanese continue to attach to maintaining a homogeneous society), but we are in no position to say if this is true. What our prediction model found is that Japan differs markedly in this respect from other economically advanced countries.

Japan and the Republic of Korea are faced with prospects of rapidly declining workforces. Whether or not this will lead to a choice of opening up their borders to more workers remains to be seen. Our comparison of the immigration policies of East Asian countries with those of the advanced countries in North America and Western Europe suggests that they are unlikely to win in the global competition for brains and talents. The latter are offering not only guarantees of equal treatment, but also easier access to labour market opportunities and the option of permanent settlement. Pressures will inevitably mount in East Asian countries to change immigration and social policies in the future to make their societies more attractive to the skilled and educated human resources that are so vital to being competitive in the global economy.

Notes

1. In this chapter we use the terms highly educated, tertiary educated, highly skilled and professionals interchangeably.
2. See <http://www.oecd.org/document/51/0,3343,en_2649_33931_40644339_1_1_1_1,00.html>.
3. India is also an important source of high skilled migrants to OECD countries, with almost a million tertiary educated migrants in the United States, the United Kingdom, and Canada.
4. Docquier and Marfouk (2006) incorporated data on 170 countries for 1990 into the OECD data for 190 countries for 2000. For an analysis of the OECD and Docquier data sets, see also Lowell (2007).
5. Excluding entertainers who are also in the category of professionals under Japan's immigration law.
6. Most are from Anglo-Saxon countries who teach English.
7. Filipinos leaving the country to settle in another country abroad are not included in these statistics.
8. Most of them were trained in their origin countries, but a significant number did acquire higher education in the countries of immigration on arrival. Educational institutions in the United States, Canada, Australia, and the United Kingdom have been referred to at times as immigration "gatekeepers".
9. Variable definitions:

Dependent Variables

fwrkr_sh	share of foreign workers to total number of workers
fprof_sh	share of foreign skilled workers to total number of skilled workers

Independent Variables

lnpcgdp_us	natural logarithm of per capita GDP (US$ 2000)
pcgdp_gr	average per capita GDP growth rate 2001–05
ind_sh	share of industry sector to total GDP
ind_gr	average annual growth rate of industry sector 2001–05
ser_sh	share of services sector to total GDP
ser_gr	average annual growth rate of services sector 2001–05

      pop_1564   share of population aged 15–64 to total population

      unemp   average unemployment rate 2001–05

10. Interestingly, the survey in India revealed that the ICT and pharmaceutical industries had the greatest difficulties filling up vacancies.

11. EIU surveyed 241 companies in the first survey, and 600 in the second.

12. See OECD (2006), as quoted in ILO (2008).

13. The exception is Singapore, which offers permanent residence status to certain categories of professionals deemed in short supply.

14. Those who are not nationals of other EU member states.

15. The shortage of skills in some regions led to the so-called "Regional Linked Admissions", which are not tested by points as long as one is sponsored by relatives in regional areas.

16. Hong Kong also had a special scheme for professionals from the mainland called the "Admission of Mainland Professionals".

17. The only exceptions are foreign nationals of Japanese descent or the so-called *Nikkeijin* who may stay permanently if they are second-generation Japanese even if unskilled, or after meeting certain requirements if they are third-generation Japanese.

18. Japan's Immigration Law allows the admission of foreign professionals under twenty-seven categories.

References

Docquier, Frederic, and Abdeslam Marfouk. *Measuring the International Mobility of Skilled Workers (1990–2000)*. Release 1.0 CADRE, University of Lille 2, 2006. At <http://www.ires.ucl.ac.be/CSSSP/home_pa_pers/docuier/oxlight.htm>.

Lowell, Lindsay. "Trends in International Migration Flows and stocks, 1975–2005". *OECD Social, Employment and Migration Working Papers*, No. 58. 2007.

Graeme, Hugo. *Australia Country Report*. Workshop on Migration and Labor Markets in Asia, jointly sponsored by the Japan Institute of Labor, OECD, and ILO. Tokyo, 2005.

Hui, Weng Tat. "Balancing Employment of Foreigners and Employment for Singaporeans". Paper prepared for presentation at the Institute of Policy Studies Conference on "Singapore Perspectives 2004: At the Dawn of a New Era", Singapore, 13 January 2004.

Hur, Jai-Joon, and Kyuyong Lee. "Demographic Change and International Labor Mobility in Korea". Paper presented at the PECC-ABAC Conference on "Demographic Change and International Labor Mobility in the Asia Pacific Region: Implications for Business and Cooperation". Seoul, 25–26 March 2008.

Iguchi, Y. *Possibilities and Limitations of Japanese Migration Policy in the Context of Economic Partnerships in East Asia*. UN Expert Group Meeting on International Migration and Development. Population Division, Department of Economic and Social Affairs, United Nations Secretariat. New York, 6–8 July 2005.

ILO. *Labour and Social Trends in ASEAN 2008: Driving Competitiveness and Prosperity with Decent Work*. Bangkok: ILO Regional Office for Asia and Pacific, 2008.

Kuroda, H. Speech before Asia Society Meeting. New York, September 2005. At <http://www.asiasociety.org/speeches/kuroda05.html>.

OECD. *PISA 2006: Science Competencies for Tomorrow's World: Vol. 1: Analysis*. Paris: OECD, 2006.

UNDESA. *Replacement Migration: Is It a Solution to Declining and Ageing Populations?* New York: Population Division, United Nations, 2001.

Yap, Mui-Teng. *Singapore Country Report*. Workshop on Migration and Labor Markets in Asia, jointly sponsored by the Japan Institute of Labor, OECD, and ILO. Tokyo, 2005.

7

Panel Discussion

Takashi Shiraishi (moderator)
Masahiko Hayashi
Peter J. Katzenstein
Vikram Nehru
Jiro Okamoto
Isamu Wakamatsu

Shiraishi: I am supposed to wrap up the speeches and presentations made so far, but I am not going to do this because so many points were raised that I simply cannot summarize or wrap up all these. Instead, I would rather go directly into the discussion given the fact that time is quite limited. I start the discussion by raising perhaps two or three questions.

Professor Katzenstein's lecture was very comprehensive and I suspect that many people here find it quite different from the kind of discussions you normally hear about East Asian regional integration. Normally, it is economists, rather than political scientists or area specialists, who talk about integration. The kind of language deployed in discussing regional integration is very often, or almost, always economistic, but here, it is not the case and I hope that this already shows a different way of looking at regional development.

A number of people raised the question of the importance of the current [global financial] crisis. I would like to ask Professor Katzenstein about the implication of the current crisis for the American imperium.

And another thing I noted, and found quite interesting, is the point Dr Surin Pitsuwan made in his eloquent speech and excellent presentation. Dr Okamoto argued that the kind of institution building over the last ten years or more in this region is offering us quite different perspectives. Dr Surin emphasized the centrality of ASEAN as well as incrementality. Dr Okamoto agreed with some of the points Dr Surin made, but stated that ASEAN is not exactly in the driver's seat. I would like to invite Dr Okamoto as well as others to respond to this point.

And finally, I invite some of the people to think about the ways in which the region or regional institutions which have been created over the last decade can be deployed to deal with the current crisis. I have in mind, of course, the Chiang Mai Initiative, and the questions of how feasible it is, what the role of the World Bank is, and of the Japanese Government and so on. Maybe Dr Nehru can at least comment on this.

I would like to invite all the panelists, starting with Professor Katzenstein, to respond to some of the questions and ask them to raise their own questions and comments, or tell us whatever came to their minds while they were listening to other people's lectures and presentations. Peter?

Katzenstein: Thank you very much. It was a very interesting set of discussions and I have five points, just things which occurred to me as I was listening. In the last point, I will address the issue of the financial crisis as I see it.

The first thing which struck me is the very different styles of analysis that we heard. This reminds me of the proverbial story of the blind men and the elephant. You ask the blind men to pin the tail on the elephant and some pin the tail on the head and some pin it on the trunk and some pin it onto the middle of the body. We had excellent detailed economic analysis, we had uplifting political speeches, we had statistical regression analysis and simulations and vocation economics, and we had a very probing political analysis by Dr Okamoto. So there is opposite thinking about the topic. There are many different avenues towards it and it is important to remind ourselves also that none of these by itself is likely to capture what is a very complex reality.

The second point which struck me was is that if one were to be travelling from another part of the world and did not know much about Asia, one would remember that there is a threat of war in the Taiwan Straits and a threat of war on the Korean Peninsula. There was war between China and Vietnam not so long ago and there was the Vietnam War and the Korean War. One might think that the major focus of thinking about regional integration would be how to assure the peace. That actually does not seem to be driving the discussion. This is remarkably different from Europe. In Europe after 1945, regional integration was driven by one objective only: how to defang and demilitarize Germany. And what emerged after forty or fifty years was the creation of what the Europeans call a security community, that is, a community of states in which there is a predictable expectation of peaceful change. This is the most important achievement of European integration. It is not more prosperity; it is peace. I found this very interesting and would certainly be interested in hearing the reaction of other panelists and the audience to this observation, why it is so, and whether my perception is correct.

My third observation is that there was a great deal of talk about the benefits of incrementalism, expertise, and functionalism. This was also very much the experience and the theorizing in the political, practical work in Europe. It was actually called "Functional Theory". A British scholar named David Mitrany wrote a book about it in the 1930s and it was modernized by Ernst Haas and became "Neo-functional Theory" in the 1950s. But functional and neo-functional theories always ran up against problems of high politics. Charles de Gaulle, for example, was not easily integrated into incremental politics and so my question is: how would one think about functionalism and incrementalism in a part of the world so much marked by, as Dr Surin pointed out, diversity? What are some of the issues that are challenges for that diversity, such as xenophobia, the environment? Most important, I think, is the politics of memory, because without memory, when states and peoples cannot agree on their past, I do not think they can agree on their future. I think memory politics is of enormous importance in East Asian region or community. And, of course, the thing on which we all, outside of East Asia, look towards East Asia, is: how will East Asia deal with the demographic crisis, which it will confront within this generation?

My fourth point is that there was, in the presentation of Dr Surin, an implicit assumption that "big is better". ASEAN started small, he said, but it grew, like an acorn grows into a large oak tree. It became ASEAN+3 and ASEAN+6 and behind it, there was the notion that an encompassing politics under one roof was better as East Asia confronted the current crisis, as the vulnerability was experienced as something collective. And he took great pride in this. But Dr Okamoto presented quite a different and, I thought, much more realistic picture, a much more European one actually, about how the politics of inclusion, which Dr Surin stressed, actually went hand-in-hand with the politics of exclusion. I had never thought of Australia being like Russia, but that is the picture I got. Is Russia part of Europe or not? Is Turkey part of Europe or not? That is a big debate in Europe. Is Australia part of ASEAN and East Asia?: big debate in Asia. The inclusionary move by the political leadership, which invokes a collective identity that does not exist and has to be created through politics (and the speech we heard was part of that politics), actually encounters very realistic opposition once you stop specifics. Creating an open regionalism, not as a market but as a political community, is something incredibly difficult. The Europeans have not succeeded in this. This is a great historic opportunity for East Asia to do better.

Finally, the financial crisis. I will defer in the economics of it to my colleagues, Dr Nehru and Mr Wakamatsu, but I do not see financial imbalances as a distant cause. I see it as a very proximate cause. This financial crisis is different in magnitude, but not different in structure from previous imbalances. The imperium I described has always, since the 1960s, imported capital. You can think of America as a large vacuum cleaner which absorbs other people's money and spends it. That is what empires do. America did it in the 1960s with European capital, did it in the 1970s with Saudi capital, did it in the 1980s and 1990s with Japanese capital. and is now trying to do it with Chinese capital. It has been an incredibly profitable operation for the Americans. You work and save and we spend it. That is the political deal and it seems to have created very counter-intuitively advantages for both sides. The Japanese pension funds, which lost US$2 to US$3 trillion because of the fluctuation of foreign exchange rates, the pensions which were not paid in Japan, but which we consumed in Wal-Mart, were part of a political deal.

Whether the political deal will extend to China remains to be seen. The political deal with Saudi Arabia was very, very clear. We traded in 1976 one promise (we will guarantee your national security with our troops) for another promise (you will denominate the price of oil in dollars). And that bargain has stuck for thirty years. It has not resolved the crisis in the Middle East, but that is the nature of the imperium. So the question is whether the growing financial imbalances since 2002 could have gone on without the crisis for another decade or two. And most economists I have asked about it said, no, it could not have.

What would happen now if, for example, Americans started saving more? The personal savings rate in America in the last two months has increased by four per cent. This is likely to free up capital, which in East Asia can be spent on infrastructure investment, on education, on the kinds of things which Dr Nehru was pointing out will lead to further economic advancement and this itself will change the nature of the imperium. Whether this is going to happen remains to be seen because the appreciation of the dollar in the time of crisis signals that political trust and confidence in the existing macrostructure of world politics still persist. Whether those are going to exist a year from now, or two years from now I do not venture to guess. Thank you.

Shiraishi: Thank you. Dr Nehru?

Nehru: Thank you very much. I also found the presentations excellent, but I must say I agree with you, Dr Shiraishi, that I really found Professor Katzenstein's lecture particularly interesting. It opened my eyes to a lot of issues, which I must admit I had not thought about. It is absolutely wonderful to get such a different perspective on exactly the same issues that we have been dealing with, as you say, for a long time and this area has been dominated by economics.

Let me address the three questions that you have raised. I will come to the United States and the financial crisis at the end. The first question you asked was: is ASEAN in the driver's seat? There is a very interesting analysis actually about the European Union. Barry

Eichengreen's recent article asked a very straightforward and simple question: to what extent has the European Union been responsible for the rapid growth of trade and incomes and convergence — or to what extent has this just been driven by market forces and would have happened anyway?[1] After quite considerable analysis and, of course, naturally a lot of assumptions, he came to the conclusion that, in fact, European per capita incomes would probably be only five per cent less had there not been a European Union. Indeed, a lot of the income convergence was driven by geographical proximity and the enormous capacity for trade across nations, by the movement of labour and movement of capital, for which the preconditions already existed prior to the formation of the European Union.

I guess you could perhaps extend that analysis to East Asia and argue that virtually all the integration that has taken place were a direct result of market forces. But now I think we are coming to a point where ASEAN can play a very important role. This brings me to the next point that you asked: What and how can regional institutions be deployed? Well, let me suggest three immediate areas where I think they can be deployed very effectively.

The first area is simply in the area of consultation. I do not think Dr Surin was being light-hearted when he said that during the East Asian crisis of 1998, there was very little communication across countries in East Asia. And this did lead to a considerable amount of confusion and movement of capital as investors were trying to figure out what was happening in different parts of the region. Let us take what happened in the United Kingdom and Ireland. When Ireland introduced a Deposit Guarantee Scheme, British banks found that deposits were being withdrawn from British banks and going into Irish banks — many of which had branches in the United Kingdom — and had to introduce Deposit Guarantee Schemes immediately. This then spread very rapidly across Europe. Here was an example of a country taking action without informing other countries in advance, which led to some temporary instability and which then had to rapidly be addressed and taken care of. There are many such examples where simply giving advance notice to other countries of policy actions that are likely to be taken might make a big difference to how other countries react to economic events.

The second is logistics. We had an excellent presentation about logistics issues and behind-the-border trade facilitation. Here ASEAN can play a very important role in establishing common standards. These are just basic, simple things like the track width of railways, the sort of container processing, bar-coding and so on. These are the sorts of things which facilitate customs management across borders through common arrangements. For example, if you have a container going from Vietnam all the way to Thailand, it has to pass through, say, Laos and Cambodia. What are the systems to make sure that that container is sealed and that system is managed, because it is that kind of system that allows for smooth trade and trade expansion? So I think ASEAN can play a very important role there.

The third area is the enormous number of free trade arrangements. There really is the question of whether the large number of free trade arrangements is indeed so advisable. Can ASEAN play a role in perhaps amalgamating, bringing together, all these FTAs so that you have simply one FTA within East Asia, pending, of course, any global outcome in the Doha round?

So I see lots of roles for regional organizations like ASEAN, ASEAN+3 or ASEAN+6. And incidentally on this point, bigger may be better in the sense that the more the countries that adhere to common standards, the more countries that adhere to common arrangements, the more beneficial for all the countries involved.

Lastly, on the implications of the financial crisis for the United States and for others, I think Professor Katzenstein made a very good point, and I will just extend it a little bit further.

I do believe that there is likely to be a structural break this time, that is to say, the crisis and the loss of wealth in the United States and in Europe to a very large extent is so great that there will need to be a change in savings behaviour in both those regions of the world. In order to get out of the debt which households have, corporations have, and now states have in the United States, as well as, of course, the Federal Government has, as if had to accumulate a large amount of debt, there has to be some point at which the country has to begin to save. I believe that that point has probably been reached, so there will be or there is likely to be reluctance on the part of other countries to continue to finance deficits of the magnitude that we have seen in the past several decades. But what does that mean?

I think the outcome of that is worrying in some sense because if aggregate savings in the world increases, where is the demand going to come from to pull the world out of recession? Where will the demand pull be for all the investments that have to be made? I think East Asia represents part of that answer, but is East Asia culturally ready to be a net importer of capital and not a net exporter of capital? This is the sort of thing which would make, say, a country like China very uncomfortable. Households are important savers and corporations there are very important savers, and the government has been an important saver. Will these habits change? Will economics overcome culture in this respect? So I think these are very important and fundamental questions which will have a bearing on how quickly the world economy will come out of this crisis. Thank you.

Shiraishi: Thank you. Now, I would like to invite Mr Hayashi to respond.

Hayashi: Thank you very much. First of all, I would like to say I am very sorry that Dr Abella was unable to come here because of what happened at the Thai airport. I believe the people here may not really know much about the ILO, so very briefly I would like to explain what we are doing in terms of migration and then I will try to answer the questions raised by Dr Shiraishi.

So, first of all, the ILO. We are working to substantiate the slogan, "Decent Work for All". We want to provide decent work to all people and we are carrying out activities towards that end. Decent work does not translate easily into Japanese, but we mean a very human way of working, work that is worth doing. Decent work is captured in four strategic objectives. This entails protecting the rights of workers, maintaining employment quality and quantity, and also social security, looking at the work conditions and the safety requirements of the work place. The fourth objective is promoting the Social Dialogue between the three parties, workers, employers, and the government. These are the four objectives of which we try to achieve our goal of decent work for all.

We are also tackling migration issues at the ILO. In his presentation, Dr Abella talked about the immigration of highly skilled workers. That was the focus. He did not really talk about what ILO does on a daily basis. Concerning migration issues, the ILO has five pillars for which we carry out our activities. Number one is directly linked to the decent work initiatives, in which we look at the rights of the migrant workers and make sure that their rights are protected; second, we look at the global migration of the workforce and monitor the situation; third, we look at whether or not countries have a cohesive policy towards migrant workers and support that; and fourth, we provide support for social dialogues. And number five is for the accepting countries to achieve the integration of migrant workers into the society of the accepting countries. So, basically these are the five pillars that we have in terms of migrant workers. This is the brief explanation about ILO itself.

But based on this, I would like to look at the multilateral framework that the governing body of the ILO came up with in March of 2006. This framework also cites the five pillars that I mentioned, and discusses what we want to do to strengthen these five pillars. It is a guideline, and is non-binding, but we do have this publication out.

Now, how should we consider migration or the movement of people? The sending country, the receiving country, and the workers that travel between the two countries — we need to have a win-win-win situation among the three. That is the idea. And in addition to that, these three parties and the workers who are already there also have to have a win-win situation. In other words, we need to establish a win-win-win-win situation. So what kind of acceptance policies does each country adopt? That is left up to each government, so the ILO will not mention anything about that.

But what will be the effect of the financial crisis? I believe I do not need to explain in detail that the financial crisis is affecting the real economy now and many people are out of work. As unemployment rises among countries, you will have many people unemployed with nowhere to work. Countries that export workers will want to send out many people, but the receiving countries will say, "stop, we do not need any more extra workers". This financial crisis is having a very negative effect on the flow of people. From the perspective of the ILO, the working conditions of the existing migrant workers may deteriorate. For example, people from East Asia who work in or have moved to the Middle East will be affected if the Middle East's real economy is affected; workers there may be laid off or they may see their wages cut. Thus, when we look at the flow of people in terms of the financial crisis, we see the crisis' potential for causing great damage. Workers' rights may be violated, so we need to keep an eye out on what happens. Thank you.

Shiraishi: Thank you. I now call on Mr Wakamatsu.

Wakamatsu: Yes. Thank you. I would like to respond to Professor Katzenstein on two points. One is on the style or characteristic of the economic integration, regional integration, and the other is on the U.S. financial crisis and the United States' financial role. I agree with Dr Okamoto that intraregional integration in Asia is characterized by functionalism and is very practical. I think that is because this regional integration is based on regional networks of companies.

On the other point regarding the financial crisis and the United States' role in the international market, I think it is very difficult for any countries to take the role of the United States as the absorber in the world economy, but so far the global imbalance is huge. So I think we need some kind of adjustment. Asia needs to stimulate more demand within the region to make world economy more stable. Thank you.

Shiraishi: Okay. Thank you. And now I would like to ask Dr Okamoto to respond to some of the questions.

Okamoto: Thank you very much. I would like to make three comments, which are actually linked together.

First of all, the sectoral or functional integration process that I have explained in my presentation, be it bilateral or multilateral, is a multilayered process and is based on the neo-functionalism that arose in the 1950s.

I mentioned that integration process in East Asia is like piling up pieces of [a] jigsaw puzzle, which are different in sizes and shapes. These layers of different pieces, the kind of functionalism I described, can be blocked by politics. FTAs and EPAs are prevailing in East Asia. The Chiang Mai Initiative and the collection of bilateral currency swaps are also emerging. But there is no challenging integration process yet in the East Asian region where the countries have to have a sharing of the sovereign power. If the Chiang Mai Initiative is to be made more robust by multilateralizing its structure, stronger surveillance functions should be put in place. There is a movement in recent years to create such a structure, but I am not so sure whether East Asian countries are quite ready to tackle such challenges.

The second comment is on the centrality of ASEAN in [the] integration process, or whether ASEAN is in the driver's seat. In some cases, ASEAN can keep sitting in the driver's seat, but in other cases, it cannot stay in the driver's seat. As I mentioned earlier, if East Asia is going to move ahead with strengthening the Chiang Mai Initiative structure, countries with huge foreign reserves, such as China and Japan, are expected to have [a] stronger voice. Another good example is FTAs in the region. There is an FTA called P4, or Trans-Pacific Strategic Economic Partnership. Brunei, Singapore, New Zealand, and Chile take part in this and the P4 is already in effect. The United States has expressed its will to join this scheme, and Australia and Peru have also declared its intention to take part in this. Some people argue that the expanded P4 would construct the basis for the FTAAP, the Free Trade Area of Asia and the Pacific. Can ASEAN play a central role in this process? I do not think that is the case. These are just some examples of how thing[s] may evolve in the future.

My last comment is on whether bigger is better. Basically I believe it is as Dr Nehru and Dr Surin have argued. But in reality, this is exactly where politics comes in. One of the main topics in my presentation is whether Australia belongs in East Asia or not. Thinking in terms of layered pieces of [a] jigsaw puzzle, Australia can join and has actually joined in some pieces, but not in others. It can be seen at least that "getting bigger" is not an automatic process.

Shiraishi: Here I have quite a lot of questions from the floor. Let me raise some of the questions for each of the panelist.

First of all, to Professor Katzenstein, there are two questions. One is: in your lecture you talked about the coming of the Obama administration on a hopeful note. Do you expect a new Obama Doctrine like Nixon Doctrine? What is the reason for your hope? And number two, do you expect more conflict among world regions such as East Asia, [the] European Union, Latin America, NAFTA, and so on? If you see the possibility of more conflict in coming years, how do you think those conflicts can be dealt with?

To Dr Abella, I hope Mr Hayashi can respond to this question. I think the person is asking about Japan. If you accept skilled workers from abroad into Japan, does that lead to a larger gap between skilled workers and non-skilled workers domestically?

And to Mr Wakamatsu, the question is about preferential tariffs in the ASEAN region. When a Japanese firm purchases a product from Thailand and sells it to Indonesia, is preferential tax applied to this case? I think probably you can generalize from your question in responding to these specific questions.

And to Dr Okamoto, when we talk about East Asia integration or the East Asia Summit, we include, of course, India, but always Pakistan, Bangladesh, and so on are left out. What are the conditions for the participation of these countries in the East Asia Summit process?

And finally, to Dr Nehru, how do you think about the gap in the process of integration, especially the gap between countries, and also the gap in each country or within each society?

These are the questions. I would like to invite again each of the panelists to discuss the questions for each panelist. If you want to respond to other panelist's remarks, please do so as well. Peter, please.

Katzenstein: Well, I would answer these two and then I will try to answer the question which I posed for which I did not hear an answer.

So the first question is about the character of the political leadership of President-elect Obama. Will there be an Obama Doctrine? I do not know and I do not want to make a prediction because this would be in the near future and I might be proven wrong. I think Obama embodies something which I have come to deeply admire about America, and which I think resonates quite deeply with how Japanese and other people in the Asia live their lives: pragmatism. Pragmatism is a deep philosophy; it is not a superficial philosophy. It is based on experiential learning, not on abstract learning.

I always try to tell my students that the best conversations I have had are not with professors, but with my plumber, who is a brilliant man, who learns on the job and figures out things, and I stay in there and watch him in admiration. It is a different way of learning and a different way of teaching. Obama strikes me as being like a plumber. He is a charismatic speech maker, but he respects facts and when the facts do not fit, he will change his mind. And he is a politician who can listen; he is not a preacher, he listens.

So my expectation is that if Obama had to pick a quote, he would pick a quote from John Maynard Keynes, who was accused by somebody in the 1930s of shifting around in the winds and never sticking to one message. Keynes answered: "When the facts change, I change my opinion. What, sir, do you do?" And that I think will be the flag under which Obama is sailing in a situation where practically all the facts, which he is going to encounter, are utterly novel and different.

Now the second question deals with the conflicts among regions and here I am reminded of something. Actually I am right now writing a book on civilizations, and regions are like civilizations. They are these macroconstructs and because the world is so confusing and we are so confused, we imbue these macroconstructs with some set of collective "actorhood". We impute that they have dispositional qualities, that they can act.

I do not think a region acts, I think people act. Regionalization and regional processes are sites in which people make choices. So the question imputes to its answer in the sense of which of these macroregions will start a war or conflict with the other region. It is not regions which start wars; it is political leaders like the Japanese leadership or the German leadership in the 1930s seeking to dominate the region which start wars. So, I expect there to be plenty of conflict.

I myself like conflict; I think without conflict, politics is boring, and I am a student of politics. But I do not like violent conflicts, that is, I think, violence against humans and property is on the whole unproductive, although I understand that in some situations it must be exercised. So conflict, yes, but not exercised by regions. We go to these constructs, East Asia or West Europe or Oceania, because they serve as a guide. They are like this walking stick for a blind man and I think we would be better served walking around the world not like blind man looking for that secret "actorhood", which does not exist, but opening our eyes and making our own choices. And making them in processes, political processes that balance off regional practices which make our lives better.

Let me answer then the third question, which I posed, which is: it is surprising that so much of the talk here is about prosperity and so little is about war. And I am thinking that it is actually a blessing in disguise, although an unintended one.

The Eichengreen Study, which Dr Nehru referred to, has the story
right. I think the prosperity effects of regional integration in Europe
are relatively modest over the last half century, but the political effect
was enormous, and in Europe, as here, it was mostly economists talking.
Well, the economists are a cheerful lot. I have never understood why
people say that economics is a dismal science. I think economics is
a cheerful science because economists move in the world of absolute
gains. They are utterly convinced that if one person gets better and
the other one does not get worse off, everybody is happy.

I am a political scientist and we do not believe this in political
science. We think it is a world of relative gains. If one of you gets
better off, I am worse off, and that is a dog-eat-dog world and the
theorist for that is Hobbes. Life is nasty, mean, brutish, and short. This
is not how the economists looked at the world. Life is wonderful. We
will all get rich and happy. Economists argue that regional integration
in Asia is an unintended consequence because it dissipates the doom
of the politicians and political scientists. But I think we will look
back twenty or thirty years from now and come to the conclusion
that while economists served that purpose, they did conceal the
big problems.

The big problems are not market integration and prosperity. The
big problems for the generation of my children and their children are
going to be the environment, and how they will support me when
I grow aged. Demography and the environment are the issues, and
for these, we need other kinds of social sciences around the table
and we have had some of them today, but I think in the end that is
going to be where Asia will have to grow into a leading role, not a
supporting role.

Becoming a leader in a financial crisis can be enormously taxing
because there is no time period for adjusting expectations. If you asked
somebody in New York in August 2008 whether they could imagine
a city without investment banking, they would have said I cannot
imagine it and you better go and see a doctor. And six weeks later,
there was not a private investment bank left in Manhattan.

Let us assume that the shock and expectations were to lead to a
collective collapse of trust and confidence in the imperial structure of
world politics in a very short time, say in a year or two, and suddenly
the East Asian states would be propelled by necessity to develop habits,

which they have not had time to adjust to, as Dr Nehru suggests. I think this would be a massive political crisis, international and domestic. So the crisis, if it comes, will lead to great political difficulties all over the world. If we are lucky to dodge this bullet and it is a gradual transition, I think there will be a gradual build-up of a crisis which will make economic integration and the gain of prosperity look small by comparison. Thank you.

Shiraishi: Okay, thank you. Dr Nehru.

Nehru: Well, I guess I have no choice now, but to be a cheerful counterpoint to what Professor Katzenstein has just said. The question that was posed to me was about the gap between countries and within countries. Let me focus purely on East Asia, and I am going to be cheerful because the gap, the inequality indices between countries, is closing because of the fact that countries which have lower per capita incomes on average are the countries which are growing faster. So, almost in a sense by definition, there is a closing of the gap within East Asia, but within [a] country inequality is rising, and rising rather rapidly.

The most dramatic instance of that is China, where there is such a rapid growth in the urban centres, particularly along the coast, that they are leaving the lagging regions, the ones in the interior, behind.

Now, part of that, you could argue, is the necessity or the implication of the rapid growth that has taken place. Economic concentration does lead to inequality. It has happened in the United States, it happened in Europe, it has happened in virtually every instance of successful development that we have seen. But I think here I do agree with Professor Katzenstein that if you have very large inequalities at the point where they actually threaten social stability, where people do begin to ask the question "why is somebody else getting better off, even if I am not worse off?", then I think it does lead to problems. Even though incomes are rising everywhere in China, they are rising so much faster in the urban areas, in the coastal areas, and this is posing a problem there. And it is a problem that is also emerging in many of the other Southeast Asian nations.

So, in aggregate, if you just take into account overall inequality in East Asia, if you do away with national boundaries, for example,

I think the answer is that, in fact, inequality in aggregate is rising in the region. Thank you.

Shiraishi: Mr Hayashi.

Hayashi: Well, the question to me was about skilled workers and the acceptance of skilled workers here in Japan. What do we imagine when we say "skilled worker"? That may change the question. But when we say skilled worker, we usually mean people or foreign workers who work in professional fields of expertise. Now, Dr Abella talked about skilled workers as tertiary educated people, a definition also used by OECD to refer to people with higher education, people who have graduated from junior colleges or have attained a higher level of education. Based on that, I would like to explain and answer the question.

First of all, let me explain the system we have here in Japan. The Japanese Government does have a policy about accepting foreign workers. Japan positively accepts professional or skilled workers, meaning that there are no barriers for these people to come in. Professionals — meaning people with a tertiary education, people who have college-level education and people who have specific technical knowledge or skills like being an athlete, an actor and a cook — are able to come into Japan to work.

How many foreign workers are here in Japan? It is still about one per cent or so of the whole labour force. We often hear that we have a lack of workers with high skills. I would like to ask the people from the business circles: are you having difficulty finding skilled labour, whether they be coming from Japan or elsewhere, or do you have sufficient workers? I believe that we do have the gates open, but not much is flowing in and probably [the] Japanese society is at the root of the problem. Social integration is not occurring in Japan and, as we heard from Dr Abella, tertiary educated people are all going to the United States and Canada instead.

So rather than saying that we will accept more skilled worker[s] given that these people are already free to come to Japan, we should ask what will make them want to come to Japan and will the Japanese companies really be willing to accept them? Will they be actively hiring these people? I think the will of the enterprises might be a determining factor because it is not permitted that foreign people with high skills come to Japan without [a] contract with a specific company, or a place to work.

Now, for the second question. Let us say that we do have a large inflow of skilled workers. Then what will happen to the income gap that we see in Japan? Right now, we do hear a lot about the income gap among workers in Japan, but mostly, this is a gap between regular workers and non-regular workers, including casual workers, part-time workers, and dispatched workers. So that is what creates the income gap in Japan. That is what many people say and I believe that it is essentially correct.

If more foreign workers with high skills can begin working in their company right away, without any additional training, and let us say that there are many foreign workers coming into Japan, taking up high-skilled jobs, then these people will be regular workers. If we have an influx of such workers, and if the number of jobs remains the same, it would mean that the skilled workers here in Japan may find difficulty getting these regular jobs and they may have to resort to taking the non-regular jobs with lower wages. If the number of jobs does not change, the Japanese workers may be disadvantaged, though, of course, I am not saying that the gap will widen. That is a possibility that we can see here.

Shiraishi: Mr Wakamatsu, please.

Wakamatsu: The question to me was whether Japanese companies in Thailand can utilize the AFTA preferential tariff arrangements, if they want to sell to Indonesia.

Well, every FTA has its rule of origin, which defines which country the product comes from. We have this 40-per cent value added rule within ASEAN. So if that rule is clear, a Japanese company or Thai company can sell to Indonesia. I believe Dr Nehru talked about the noodle bowl phenomenon. Many people point out that the rule of origin is different from FTA to FTA and that creates a very confusing, complex situation, so people cannot really rely on the different rules of FTAs.

In reality, it is not so complex that it hampers the business of companies. I will not go into detail here, but the value-added criteria and the changing tariff code criteria are the two major rules that are applied. In FTAs, either will be applied and that is not causing much confusion in reality. But you need to have the certificate of origin and the procedure to obtain this is quite troublesome, especially for cars and household electronics that utilize many different components. You need to gather the necessary documents and that could be really troublesome. That is why many companies are having trouble and that may be one problem of having so many FTAs. So you have to look at the benefits that are brought about by the many FTAs, as well as the troublesome aspects of having these FTAs. I think that is what we see at present.

Okamoto: I believe the question to me was about whether and how Bangladesh and Pakistan take part in the East Asian integration.

As I have mentioned in my presentation, if you look at Tables 1 and 2 in my slides, you can see that they are actually taking part in the integration process. Regarding the participation in the East Asia Summit, there are several conditions set in 2005 when the first East Asia Summit was convened. One of the conditions was that it must be a signatory of TAC, the Treaty of Amity and Cooperation in Southeast Asia. Australia's then Prime Minister John Howard was very much aware of its relationship with United States and he was initially hesitant about signing, but when the condition was finalized, Australia decided to sign this treaty. A country also must have substantial political and economic relationships with ASEAN and its members to take part in the East Asia Summit.

Shiraishi: Let me go around and ask several more questions. There are, it seems to me, three additional and frequently asked questions. One is mainly addressed to Mr Wakamatsu and Dr Nehru. Mr Wakamatsu pointed out the importance of logistics in regional integration and mentioned transnational the North-South and East-West corridors in [the] Greater Mekong Subregion. I can see Vietnam and Thailand benefiting a great deal from this development, but how about Laos and Cambodia? Are they serving merely as corridors that cars literally pass through, or is there any way for them to benefit from being part of the corridors?

To Mr Hayashi, the question is this: Dr Abella pointed out that Japan has been attracting far fewer tertiary educated professionals than it can expect to attract. Why so? What policy measures can you think of that can make Japan more attractive to educated professionals?

And finally, to Professor Katzenstein: When you point out that there is no fundamental transformation in the global regional order because of the rise of China, what do you mean by "fundamental"? Does it mean that the American imperium will remain and the kind of world of regions you describe in your book will remain?

Hayashi: Japan has not been able to attract talented people with higher education. I think that is probably true. What then should we do to attract more highly educated personnel? Well, I think you are also making the effort to attract talented people, and probably I am a layman so I am not very much qualified to answer this, but let me try, although what follows is just my personal observation.

Perhaps there are two or three policies or measures that we can adopt to attract people with higher education. Japanese society is said to be rather closed and Japan is giving the impression to people overseas that probably if they come to Japan, they will be in trouble and they will have hard times. In other words, the effort towards social inclusion is one of the things lacking in Japanese society.

Secondly, we have a language barrier. In some multinational corporations based in Japan, the Nissan model, for example, I heard they exchange views and opinions in English in official meetings, including executive meetings, and they write documents in English. There are some Japanese firms practising such things, but they are [the] minority. Even if the overseas people would like to come to Japan, they may feel rather hesitant because they think that they will not be able to understand the language in Japanese firms. So they feel more comfortable working in the U.S. companies or Canadian companies because there is no communication problems.

The third point concerns rewards or salaries and wages. The wage gap between the people with very high qualification[s] and the ordinary rank and file is not so large in Japan. This is not a problem or issue of good or bad, but if they go to the United States or North American companies, they will have bigger and better opportunities to earn more, given their higher education.

So I think there are three reasons why Japan is not able to attract people with higher education. This is somewhat related to how Japanese society should work and change. If we want to attract more people with higher education, probably we need to implement changes in these aspects. There is no panacea or a magic bullet for this, but if we really want to attract people with higher education, we need to change the corporate culture or the culture of the society at large.

Shiraishi: Our given time is sort of running out, so for the second question, I only ask Dr Nehru to respond.

Nehru: The question was how Cambodia and Laos may benefit as trans-shipment corridors. I think they can benefit in three ways.

First, trans-shipment fees. The services provided by Laos and Cambodia would not come necessarily for free. Secondly, with the infrastructure there, there is enormous potential for [the] supply of services for the traffic that flows across Laos and Cambodia, so there is a second source of income for them.

But third and probably most important, there is the simple point that supply creates its own demand. In these two countries, there is an enormous infrastructure deficit. With infrastructure in place, connecting these countries to the other countries, you have a potential for investment along those corridors, capitalizing on these new arteries that are being built. So I think these infrastructure corridors that are being considered in Southeast Asia are going to be critical, in fact, for the development of Laos and Cambodia. Thank you.

Shiraishi: Okay. Thank you. Now, Peter.

Katzenstein: I was afraid of that question. I think it is the right question and there is no easy answer, but let me try.

Fundamental or transformative would mean a different grammar for world politics. I argued that the imperium is marked by a coincidence of territorial military and non-territorial norm-setting powers. If we think about the first Bush Administration, between 2001 and 2004, it was trying to transform the world order. It was saying that the nature of American imperium will henceforth be redefined as the American empire. And it would come at enormous costs at home because, basically, the rule of law was systematically subverted in the interest of national security by the government, with the media being acquiescent in it. But it also had an enormous cost internationally because the doctrine of pre-emptive war was elevated to our national security doctrine.

The militarization of American society and the militarization of pre-emptive war in international politics would have transformed the nature of the imperium and the nature of world politics. It turned out that the world itself did have enough resources, as did American domestic society, to push back, and that transformative attempt was defeated.

Now, if you think about the rise of China in traditional terms of the rise of a mercantilist, nationalist, military superpower, then indeed I do not think we would have a transformative effect on world politics, but we would return to an older kind of politics. Call it the nineteenth century up to the mid-twentieth century style of politics. It would be familiar, it would be bloody, it would not be good.

The interpretation, which I gave in my talk on the concept of sinicization and the rise of China, was a different one. What strikes me about China is that its development model is dramatically different from that of Japan and Korea. In that sense, East Asia is not a community, but an experiment of different styles of economic development, for China has chosen a remarkably open economic development path compared with its East Asian neighbours.

And just as the trade ratio compared to GDP in China is so much higher than it is for Japan or the European Union or the United States, so is the social and cultural capital with which China can experiment, if one thinks about the Chinese diaspora as part of this China. This combination of territorial and non-territorial power of both attraction and repulsion leads to a kind of East Asian politics not marked only by a balance of power, but rather — because East Asian states actually understand this and have learnt it over centuries by a bandwagoning effect.

Balancing is a European style of politics. Bandwagoning, which means a different kind of balance of politics because you want to constrain the other by embracing it, is a different way of dealing with China. And add to that the concept — which I introduced in my lecture — of the balance of practices, which is this experientially-based learning, and a kind of Asian-style pragmatism, and I think this will be a winning combination, which can be accommodated in the structure of world politics which has emerged over the last half century.

Shiraishi: Thank you. On that note, we conclude this panel. I would like to thank all the panelists for an exciting discussion and also all these people who raised interesting questions. Thank you.

Note

1. Boltho, Andrea, and Barry Eichengreen. "The Economic Impact of European Integration". *CEPR Discussion Paper*, No. DP6820, May 2008.

Index

www.ingramcontent.com/pod-product-compliance
Lightning Source LLC
Chambersburg PA
CBHW050223270326
41914CB00003BA/545